NOTES

on the book of

LEVITICUS

by

C. H. MACKINTOSH

"All Scripture is given by inspiration of God."

LOIZEAUX BROTHERS
Neptune, New Jersey

FIRST EDITION 1880

TWENTY-SEVENTH PRINTING 1965

LOIZEAUX BROTHERS, Inc., PUBLISHERS

A Nonprofit Organization, Devoted to the Lord's Work
and to the Spread of His Truth

NEPTUNE, NEW JERSEY

PRINTED IN THE UNITED STATES OF AMERICA

PREFATORY NOTE

TO THE AMERICAN EDITION

A S several persons in America have, without any authority whatever from me, undertaken to publish my four* volumes of "Notes," I deem it my duty to inform the reader that I have given full permission to Messrs. LOIZEAUX BROTHERS to publish an edition of those books in such form as they shall consider most suitable.

C. H. MACKINTOSH.

6 West Park Terrace, Scarborough,
    May 1st, 1879.

----

* Now six.

PREFACE

IN the Person and work of the Lord Jesus Christ there is an infinite fullness, which meets every necessity of man, both as a sinner and as a worshiper. The infinite dignity of His Person gives eternal value to His work. In the book of Genesis we have seen "God's remedy for man's ruin" in the promised seed—the Ark of Salvation, and in the rich unfoldings of divine grace to fallen and sinful man. There we have the *Bud*, the full-blown glories and fragrance of which shall yet fill the heavens and the earth with joy and gladness.

In the book of Exodus we have seen "God's answer to man's question." There, man is not only outside of Eden, but he has fallen into the hands of a cruel and powerful enemy,—he is the bond-slave of the world. How is he to be delivered from Pharaoh's thraldom—from Egypt's furnace? How can he be redeemed, justified, and brought into the promised land? God only could answer such questions, and this He did in the blood of the slain Lamb. In the redemption-power of that blood, every question is settled. It meets Heaven's highest claims, and man's deepest necessities. Through its amazing efficacy, God is glorified, man is redeemed, saved, justified, and brought to God's holy habitation; while the enemy is completely overthrown, and his power destroyed.

And now, in our meditations on the book of Leviticus, we find most fully unfolded what we may call, "God's provision for man's need;" or, a Sacrifice, a Priest, and a Place of Worship. These are essentially necessary in drawing near unto God, as this book most abundantly proves. But every thing therewith connected was appointed by God, and established by His law. Nothing was left to be supplied by man's fertile imagination, or his prudential arrangement.—"So Aaron and his son's did *all things which the Lord commanded* by the hand of Moses." (Chap. viii. 36; ix. 6, 7.) Without the word of the Lord, neither priest nor people could take a single step in the right direction. *It is so still.* There is not a single ray of light in this dark world but that which is shed from holy Scripture.—"Thy Word is a lamp unto my feet, and a light unto my path." (Ps. cxix. 105.) It is truly happy when the children of God so honor His Word as to be guided by it in all things. We need *now*, as much as the Jew did *then*, divine direction and divine guidance for acceptable worship. "But the hour cometh, and now is, when the *true worshipers* shall worship the Father in spirit and in truth; for the Father seeketh such to worship Him." (John iv. 23, 24.) More than sincerity or devoutness of feeling is required in the children's worship: it must be in the unction of the Spirit, and according to the truth of God. But we have all (blessed be His name!) in the Person and work of our blessed Lord Jesus. He is both our Sacrifice and Priest, and our right of entrance into the holiest of all. O, to be kept near to His wounded side, and in the abiding sense that He is the ground, the material, and the sweet incense of all our worship!

Let us now briefly notice the three points already mentioned.

I. In the first place, we would observe that *sacrifice is the basis of worship.* Acceptable worship to God must be based on a sacrifice acceptable to Him. Man being in himself guilty and unclean, he needs a sacrifice to remove his guilt, cleanse him from his defilements, and fit him for the holy presence of God. "Without shedding of blood is no remission;" and without remission, and the *knowledge* of remission, there can be no happy worship,—no real, hearty praise, adoration, and thanksgiving. Going to what is called "a place of worship," and worshiping God, are widely different things. God is holy, and man must approach Him in His own way, and according to what He is. As Moses said unto Aaron on the solemn occasion of the sin of Nadab and Abihu, "This is it that the Lord spake, saying, '*I will be sanctified in them that come nigh Me*, and before all the people I will be glorified.'" The Lord alone could give directions as to how the people were to draw nigh unto Him: this is the great subject of the book of Leviticus. The "Notes" on the first seven and the sixteenth chapters will give the reader a very full and interesting view of the ordinance of sacrifice, and the character of Jewish worship.

It was on the ground of offered and accepted sacrifice that the children of Israel were constituted the worshiping people of God. It is on the same ground, namely, offered and accepted sacrifice, that believers in Jesus are constituted the worshiping people of God now. (Read carefully Lev. xvi; Heb. ix, x.) They have taken Israel's place, but after a much higher order, whether we look at the sacrifice, the priest, or the place of worship. The contrast between them is great, and strongly marked in Scripture, especially in the epistle to the Hebrews. The Jewish sacrifices never reached the *conscience* of the offerer, and the Jewish priest never could pronounce him "clean every whit." The gifts and sacrifices which were offered under the law, as the apostle tells us, "could not make him that did the service perfect, as pertaining to the conscience." The conscience, observe, always being the *reflection* of the sacrifice, it could not be perfect, seeing the sacrifice was not perfect; "for it is not possible that the blood of bulls and of goats should take away sins." Hence, Jewish worship was connected with inefficient sacrifices, a burdensome ritual, and an unpurged conscience, which gendered in the worshiper a spirit of bondage and fear.

But, now, mark the contrast to all this in the once-offered and accepted sacrifice of Christ. He "put away sin by the sacrifice of Himself." All is done. Having "by Himself purged our sins, He sat down on the right hand of the Majesty on high." When the worshiper comes before God on the ground of this Sacrifice, he finds that he has nothing to do save, as a priest, to show forth the praises of Him "who hath called us out of darkness into His marvelous light." Even Christ has nothing more to do as regards our justification and acceptance, "for by one offering He hath perfected forever them that are sanctified." The Jew, by his sacrifice, was merely *ceremonially* clean, and that only for a moment, as it were; but the Christian, through the sacrifice of Christ, is *really* so, and that forever. Oh, that sweet word, "FOREVER"! It is the common privilege of all believers to be perfected as worshipers before God, "through the offering of the body of Jesus Christ once for all." On this deeply important point the testimony of Scripture is most full and explicit. For the worshipers once purged should have *"no more conscience of sins."*—"The blood of Jesus Christ His Son cleanseth us from all sin."—"And their sins and iniquities will I remember no more." (1 John i. 7; Heb. x.) By the work of Christ *for us*, our sins were all put away; and now, by faith in God's word, we know that they are all forgiven and forgotten. Hence, we can draw near to God, and stand in His holy presence, in the happy assurance that there is neither sin nor stain upon us. Our Great High-Priest has pronounced us "clean every whit." (John xiii.) Believing this, the sense of guilt is taken away,— we have "NO MORE CONSCIENCE OF SINS."

This deeply precious truth, observe, does not mean that there is no more *consciousness* of sins. Far from it. Or that we may not get a bad conscience through failure; or that we need not be exercised "to have a conscience void of offense toward God and toward man." Not at all. It simply means that Christ, by the one, perfect, finished sacrifice of Himself, has forever put away all our sins— root and branch. And having been led to know and be-

lieve this, how can there be sins on the conscience?
Christ has put them all away. The precious blood of our
once-offered and accepted Sacrifice has cleansed us from
every spot and stain of sin. There may be the deepest
sense of indwelling sin, and of many sins and shortcomings in our every-day life, and the painful confession of
them all to God; still there is the full assurance that
Christ died for our sins, put them all away, and that not
one of them can ever be laid to our charge. This is indeed
a most wonderful truth; but it is the great, the needed
truth for a worshiper. How could we stand in God's
presence, where all is perfection, if we were not as clean
as He would have us to be? We must be clean enough
for the eye of Infinite Holiness. But, blessed be God, all
who believe in Jesus, and rest on His finished sacrifice, are
forgiven and justified; they have eternal life, righteousness, and peace. The first cry for mercy of the guilty
sinner is answered by the blood of the Sacrifice. It pene-
trates to the deepest depths of his need; it raises him to
the highest heights of heaven, and fits him to be there, a
happy worshiper, in the immediate presence of the throne
of God.—"For Christ also hath once suffered for sins, the
just for the unjust, that He might bring us to God."—
"For if the blood of bulls and of goats, and the ashes of
a heifer sprinkling the unclean, sanctifieth to the purifying
of the flesh; how much more shall the blood of Christ,
who through the Eternal Spirit offered Himself without
spot to God, purge your conscience from dead works to
serve the living God!" (1 Peter iii. 18; Heb. ix. 13, 14.)

II. In the second place, we have in the rich provisions
of God's grace, *the Lord Jesus Christ as our Great High-
Priest in the presence of God for us.* He ministers there
for us.—"We have such a High-Priest, who is set on the
right hand of the throne of the Majesty in the heavens; a
Minister of the sanctuary, and of the true tabernacle,
which the Lord pitched, and not man." (Heb. viii. 1, 2.)
His work of sacrifice having been fully completed, He sat

down. Aaron is represented as being always in a standing
position. His work was never finished. He stood "daily
ministering, and offering oftentimes the same sacrifices,
which can never take away sins; but this Man, after He
had offered one sacrifice for sins, forever sat down on the
right hand of God." Immediately after the law of the
Lord had been given as to sacrifice, the priesthood was
established. (See "Notes" on chapters viii, ix.) The
saints have both in Christ. He is our Sacrifice and our
Priest. He appeared once on the cross *for us:* He now
appears in heaven *for us:* ere long He will appear in glory
with us. To know what He accomplished on the cross,
and what He is now doing in the sanctuary above, will
nourish in our hearts the hope of His coming, and lead us
to long for His appearing in glory.

In the New Testament we only read of two orders of
priests, namely, Christ as the Great High-Priest in heaven,
and the common priesthood of all believers on the earth.
"Ye also, as lively stones, are built up a spiritual house,
a holy priesthood, to offer up spiritual sacrifices, acceptable to God by Jesus Christ." (1 Peter ii. 5.) And again,
"Unto Him that loved us, and washed us from our sins in
His own blood, and hath made us kings and priests unto
God and His Father." (Rev. i. 5. 6.) These passages
clearly prove the common standing of all believers as
priests unto God. There is no mention in the New Testament of any peculiar class or order of Christians who hold
the office of priests, as distinct from other Christians.
Christ is the *Great* High-Priest over the house of God, and
all His people are, in virtue of their connection with Him,
priests, and privileged to enter, as once-purged worshipers,
into the holiest of all. Even the apostles never took the
place of priests, as distinct from or superior to the humblest child of God. They might know their privileges
better than many, and enjoy them more. Their gifts and
callings as to the ministry of the Word were distinct and
special, but as worshipers, they stood on the same ground

as all others, and, together with them, worshiped God
through Jesus Christ, the Great High-Priest of all His
people.

In the priestly ministry of our blessed Lord, there are
many points of special interest; we only notice the two
following:—

1. As our Great High-Priest, He *represents* us in the
sanctuary above. And, oh, what a Representative!—God's
beloved Son, the glorified Man, whose name is above every
name!—"For Christ is not entered into the holy places
made with hands, which are the figures of the true; but
into heaven itself, now to appear in the presence of God
for us." (Heb. ix. 24.) Oh, what dignity! what nearness
to God is ours! Oh that our hearts appreciated it more!
When Aaron appeared before the Lord in his garments of
glory and beauty, he represented the children of Israel.
Their names were engraven in precious stones in the
beautiful breastplate. Blessed type of our real and everlasting place in the heart of Christ, who appears, not
annually, like Aaron of old, but *continually* in the presence
of God *for us*. The name of each believer is kept continually before the eye of God, in all the glory and beauty of
Christ, His well-beloved Son. He is our righteousness,
we possess His life, enjoy His peace, are filled with His
joy, and radiate His glory. Although without right, title,
or privilege in ourselves, we have all in Him. He is there
for us and *as us*. His name be forever praised.

"He stands in heaven their Great High-Priest,
And bears their names upon His breast."

It is by His continual intercession in heaven that saints on
earth are succored and sustained in their wilderness jour-
ney, and, at the same time, upheld as worshipers within
the vail, in all the sweet fragrance of His own divine
excellencies; and neither their ignorance nor their lack of
enjoyment of these things alters or affects their blessed,
glorious, and eternal reality, "seeing He ever liveth to
make intercession for them." (Heb. vii. 25.)

2. As our Great High-Priest, He presents to God the gifts and sacrifices of His worshiping people. Under the law, the worshiper brought his offering to the priest, and by him it was presented to the Lord, on His own altar. Every thing was arranged by the priest, according to the word of the Lord. How perfectly all this is done for the worshiper now by his High-Priest in heaven! Our prayers, praises, and thanksgiving, all pass through His hands before they reach the throne of God. What a wonderful mercy this is, when we think of our confused and mixed services! So much that is of the flesh mingles with that which is of the Spirit. But the blessed Lord knows how to divide and separate between them. That which is of the flesh must be rejected, and consumed as wood, hay, and stubble, while that which is of the Spirit is precious, preserved, and presented to God in the value and sweet savor of His own perfect sacrifice. "*By Him* therefore let us offer the sacrifice of praise to God continually, that is, the fruit of our lips giving thanks unto His name." (Heb. xiii. 15.) The kindness of the Philippians to Paul was "an odor of a sweet smell, a sacrifice acceptable, well-pleasing to God." Hence the importance of the exhortation, "Whatsoever ye do in word or deed, do all in the name of the Lord Jesus, giving thanks to God and the Father by Him." (Col. iii. 17.)

III. In the third place, we observe that *the Christian's only place of worship is inside the vail*, "whither the Forerunner is for us entered." Outside the camp is his place as a witness; inside the vail is his place as a worshiper. In both positions Christ is surely with him. "Let us go forth therefore unto Him without the camp, bearing His reproach." "Having therefore, brethren, *boldness to enter into the holiest* by the blood of Jesus." (Heb. xiii. 13; x. 19.) To know these two positions in communion with Christ Himself, through the teaching of the Spirit, is unspeakable blessedness. The Church has no divinely consecrated place of worship on earth. Our place is in heaven, in virtue of the sacrifice and of the priestly ministry of Christ there for us. Whatever may be the character of the building in which Christians are gathered together in the name of the Lord Jesus, their true and only sphere of worship is the heavenly sanctuary. Through faith in God's word, and by the power of His Holy Spirit, they worship Him in "the true tabernacle, which the Lord pitched, and not man."

Israel had "a worldly sanctuary," and accordingly the character of their worship was worldly; "the way into the holiest of all was not yet made manifest, while as the first tabernacle was yet standing." But the way has been opened up by the blood of Jesus. The same stroke that slew the Lamb rent the vail from top to bottom. The way into the holiest of all was then laid open, and Christ, with all His blood-washed ones, entered into the immediate presence of God, without a vail. There is no *outer*-court-worship now for the people, and *temple*-worship for the priest, as under the law. These distinctions are unknown in the Church of the living God. It is all priestly worship and temple worship now. All are equally near, all have equal liberty, all are equally acceptable, through the presence and intervention of the Great High-Priest of His people. The same precious blood that cleansed us from all sin, has brought us near to God as children, and as worshiping priests. And if we really know the wondrous efficacy and power of that blood in the heavenly places, we shall be at home and happy there in all the liberty and dignity of sonship, and in all the official nearness and standing of once-purged worshipers, in the most holy place.

Oh that our hearts may be kept in the sweet remembrance, knowledge, and power of the rich provisions of God's grace for all our need! Oh that we may never lose sight of the blood on the mercy-seat, the Minister of the sanctuary, and of our holy, heavenly, and eternal place of worship!

We must now leave the dear reader, earnestly commend-
ing to his most prayerful and diligent study this precious
book of Leviticus. The light which it sheds on the Person
and work of Christ—the ground and character of our
communion with God, is deeply blessed to the heart that
desires to live in the enjoyment of these eternal realities.
He will find the "Notes" most helpful in unfolding the
text, and in giving an interesting and practical view to
many of the ceremonies which we are prone to pass over
as uninteresting and uninstructive to us. See, for example, the eleventh chapter.

And now, may the Lord graciously own, use, and bless
this little volume, for the glory of His own name, and for
the comfort and blessing of many precious souls.

                                                A. M.

London, May, 1860.

PREFACE TO THE SECOND EDITION

THE rapid sale of a large edition of this volume evidences an amount of interest in the study of the book of Leviticus for which I unfeignedly bless the Lord. Too many, even of the people of God, seem to think that this section of inspiration contains nothing of any interest or value to them. They regard it as a detail of rites and ceremonies with which they have nothing to do—a record of by-gone institutions, affording no instruction or edification for them. That this is a great mistake, thousands are now discovering. Very many who for years looked upon the book of Leviticus as little more than a dry catalogue of Jewish ordinances, are now discovering in it an exhaustless mine of spiritual wealth, for which they cannot be too thankful. They have brought its marvelous pages under the light of the New Testament scriptures, and they can only wonder at that which is now unfolded to their gaze. That they may discover yet more of the precious treasure, is my earnest desire on their behalf.

I have carefully revised the following pages, and, I may say, I have left them very much as I found them. An expression here and there which seemed likely to be misunderstood, I have slightly touched. I have also added a brief note or two. These trifling matters excepted, the second edition is a reprint of the first, and, as such, it is again committed to the care of Him from whom all blessings flow. May He be graciously pleased to crown it still further with the stamp of His approval. His seal and sanction are all that any book requires to make it useful:

and truly, we may say, the book that has not these has nothing.

The Lord grant a more abundant blessing, and His name shall have all the praise.

C. H. M.

CONTENTS

NOTES

ON

THE BOOK OF LEVITICUS

CHAPTER I

ERE entering upon the details of the chapter before us, there are two things which demand our careful consideration; namely, first, Jehovah's position; and secondly, the order in which the offerings are presented.

"And the Lord called unto Moses, and spake unto him out of the tabernacle of the congregation." Such was the position from which Jehovah made the communications contained in this book. He had been speaking from Mount Sinai, and His position there gave marked character to the communication. From the fiery mount "went a fiery law;" but here, He speaks "out of the tabernacle of the congregation." This was an entirely different position. We have seen this tabernacle set up, at the close of the preceding book.—"And he reared up the court round about the tabernacle and the altar, and set up the hanging of the court gate. So Moses finished the work. Then a cloud covered the tent of the congregation, and the glory of the Lord filled the

tabernacle. . . . . For the cloud of the Lord **was**
upon the tabernacle by day, and fire was on it
by night, in the sight of all the house of Israel,
throughout all their journeys.'' (Exod. xl. 33–38.)

Now, the tabernacle was God's dwelling-place in
grace. He could take up His abode there, because
He was surrounded on all sides by that which vividly
set forth the ground of His relationship with the
people. Had He come into their midst in the full
display of the character revealed upon Mount Sinai,
it could only have been to ''consume them in a moment,'' as ''a stiff-necked people ;'' but He retired
within the vail—type of Christ's flesh (Heb. x. 20.),
and took His place on the mercy-seat, where the
blood of atonement, and not the ''stiff-neckedness''
of Israel, was that which met His view and satisfied
the claims of His nature. The blood which was
brought into the sanctuary by the high-priest was
the type of that precious blood which cleanses from
all sin ; and although Israel after the flesh saw nothing of this, it nevertheless justified God in abiding
amongst them—it ''sanctified to the purifying of
the flesh.'' (Heb. ix. 13.)

Thus much as to Jehovah's position in this book,
which must be taken into account in order to a
proper understanding of the communications made
therein. In them we shall find inflexible holiness
united with the purest grace. God is holy, no matter from whence He speaks. He was holy on Mount
Sinai, and holy above the mercy-seat ; but in the
former case, His holiness stood connected with ''a

devouring fire," in the latter, it was connected with patient grace. Now the connection of perfect holiness with perfect grace is that which characterizes the redemption which is in Christ Jesus, which redemption is, in various ways, shadowed forth in the book of Leviticus. God must be holy, even though it should be in the eternal condemnation of impenitent sinners; but the full display of His holiness in the salvation of sinners calls forth Heaven's loudest and loftiest note of praise.—"Glory to God in the highest, and on earth peace, good-will toward men." (Luke ii. 14.) This doxology could not have been sung in connection with "the fiery law." No doubt there was "glory to God in the highest," but there was no "peace on earth" nor "good pleasure in men," inasmuch as it was the declaration of what men ought to be ere God could take pleasure in them. But when "the Son" took His place as a man on the earth, the mind of Heaven could express its entire delight in Him as the One whose Person and work could combine, in the most perfect manner, divine glory with human blessedness.

And now, one word as to the order of the offerings, in the opening chapters of the book of Leviticus. The Lord begins with the burnt-offering, and ends with the trespass-offering. That is to say, He leaves off where we begin. This order is marked and most instructive. When first the arrow of conviction enters the soul, there are deep searchings of conscience in reference to sins actually committed. Memory casts back its enlightened eye over the page of one's past life, and sees it stained with numberless trespasses against God and man. At this point of the soul's history, it is not so much occupied with the question of the root from whence those trespasses have sprung, as with the stern and palpable fact that such and such things have actually been committed; and hence it needs to know that God has provided a Sacrifice through which "all trespasses" can be "frankly forgiven." This is presented to us in the trespass-offering.

But, as one advances in the divine life, he becomes conscious that those *sins* which he has committed are but branches from a root, streams from a fountain; and, moreover, that *sin* in his nature is that fountain—that root. This leads to far deeper exercise, which can only be met by a deeper insight into the work of the cross. In a word, the cross will need to be apprehended as that in which God Himself has "condemned *sin in the flesh.*" (Rom. viii. 3.) My reader will observe, it does not say, "*sins* in the *life*," but the root from whence these have sprung, namely, "*sin* in the *flesh*." This is a truth of immense importance. Christ not merely "died for our *sins*, according to the Scriptures," but He was "made *sin* for us." (2 Cor. v. 21.) This is the doctrine of the sin-offering.

Now, it is when the heart and conscience are set at rest, through the knowledge of Christ's work, that we can feed upon Himself as the ground of our peace and joy in the presence of God. The trespass-offering and the sin-offering must be known ere the peace-offering, joy-offering, or thanksgiving-offering can be appreciated. Hence, therefore, the order in which the peace-offering stands corresponds with the order of our spiritual apprehension of Christ.

The same perfect order is observable in reference to the meat-offering. When the soul is led to taste the sweetness of spiritual communion with Christ—to feed upon Him, in peace and thankfulness, in the divine presence, it is drawn out in earnest desire to know more of the wondrous mysteries of His Person; and this desire is most blessedly met in the meat-offering, which is the type of Christ's perfect manhood.

Then, in the burnt-offering, we are conducted to a point beyond which it is impossible to go, and that is, the work of the cross, as accomplished under the immediate eye of God, and as the expression of the unswerving devotion of the heart of Christ. All these things will come before us, in beauteous detail, as we pass along; we are here only looking at the order of the offerings, which is truly marvelous, whichever way we travel, whether *outward* from God to us, or *inward* from us to God. In either case, we begin with the cross and end with the cross. If we begin with the burnt-offering, we see Christ, on the cross, doing the will of God—making atonement according to the measure of His perfect surrender of Himself to God. If we begin with the trespass-offering, we see Christ, on the cross, bearing our sins, and putting them away according to the per-

fection of His atoning sacrifice; while in each and
all we behold the excellency, the beauty, and the
perfection of His divine and adorable Person.
Surely, all this is sufficient to awaken in our hearts
the deepest interest in the study of those precious
types which we shall now proceed to consider in
detail. And may God the Holy Ghost, who penned
the book of Leviticus, expound its contents in living
power to our hearts, that so, when we have reached
the close, we may have abundant cause to bless His
name for many thrilling and soul-stirring views of
the Person and work of our blessed Lord and Saviour
Jesus Christ, to whom be glory, now, henceforth,
and for evermore. Amen.

———

In the burnt-offering, with which our book opens,
we have a type of Christ "offering Himself without
spot to God." Hence the position which the Holy
Ghost assigns to it. If the Lord Jesus Christ came
forth to accomplish the glorious work of atonement,
His highest and most fondly cherished object in so
doing was the glory of God. "Lo, I come to do
Thy will, O God," was the grand motto in every
scene and circumstance of His life, and in none
more markedly than in the work of the cross. Let
the will of God be what it might, He came to do it.
Blessed be God, we know what our portion is in the
accomplishment of this "will;" for by it "we are
sanctified, through the offering of the body of Jesus
Christ once." (Heb. x. 10.) Still, the primary as-

pect of Christ's work was Godward. It was an ineffable delight to Him to accomplish the will of God on this earth. No one had ever done this before. Some had, through grace, done "that which was right in the sight of the Lord;" but no one had ever perfectly, invariably, from first to last, without hesitation, and without divergence, done the will of God. But this was exactly what the Lord Jesus did. He was "obedient unto death, even the death of the cross." (Phil. ii. 8.) "He steadfastly set His face to go to Jerusalem." And as He walked from the garden of Gethsemane to the cross of Calvary, the intense devotion of His heart told itself forth in these accents,—"The cup which My Father hath given Me, shall I not drink it?"

Now, in all this self-emptied devotedness to God there was truly a sweet savor. A perfect Man on the earth accomplishing the will of God, even in death, was an object of amazing interest to the mind of Heaven. Who could fathom the profound depths of that devoted heart which displayed itself, under the eye of God, on the cross? Surely, none but God; for in this, as in every thing else, it holds good that "no man knoweth the Son, but the Father," and no one can know aught about Him save as the Father reveals Him. The mind of man can, in some measure, grasp any subject of knowledge "under the sun,"—human science can be laid hold of by the human intellect; but no man knoweth the Son save as the Father reveals Him, by the power of the Holy Ghost, through the written Word. The

Holy Ghost delights to reveal the Son—to take of
the things of Jesus and show them unto us.   These
things we have, in all their fullness and beauty, in
the Word.   There can be no new revelation, inasmuch as the Spirit brought *"all* things" to the
apostles' memory, and led them into *"all* truth."
There can be nothing beyond "all truth;" and
hence, all pretension to a new revelation and the
development of new truth (meaning thereby truth
not contained in the sacred canon of inspiration) is
an effort on man's part to add to what God calls
"all truth."   No doubt the Spirit may unfold and
apply, with new and extraordinary power, truth
contained in the Word; but this is obviously a very
different thing from our traveling outside the range
of divine revelation for the purpose of finding principles, ideas, or dogmas which shall command the
conscience.   This latter can only be regarded in the
light of impious presumption.

   In the gospel narrative, we have Christ presented
to us in the varied phases of His character, His
Person, and His work.   To those precious docu-
ments the people of God in all ages have rejoiced to
betake themselves, and drink in their heavenly rev-
elations of the object of their love and confidence—
the One to whom they owed every thing, for time
and eternity.   But very few, comparatively, have
ever been led to regard the rites and ceremonies of
the Levitical economy as fraught with the most
minute instruction in reference to the same commanding theme.   The offerings of Leviticus, fo

example, have been too much regarded as so many antiquated records of Jewish customs, conveying no intelligible voice to our ears—no spiritual light to our understandings. However, it must be admitted that the apparently abstruse records of Leviticus, as well as the sublime strains of Isaiah, take their place amongst the "things which were written aforetime," and they are, therefore, "for our learning." True, we shall need to study those records, as indeed all Scripture, with a humble, self-emptied spirit; with reverent dependence upon the teaching of Him who graciously penned them for us; with sedulous attention to the general scope, bearing, and analogy of the entire body of divine revelation; with an effectual curb on the imagination, that it may not take unhallowed flights; but if thus, through grace, we enter upon the study of the types of Leviticus, we shall find in them a vein of the richest and finest ore.

We shall now proceed to examine the burnt-offering, which, as we have remarked, presents Christ offering Himself without spot to God.

"If his offering be a burnt sacrifice of the herd, let him offer a male, without blemish." The essential glory and dignity of Christ's Person form the basis of Christianity. He imparts that dignity and glory to every thing He does, and to every office He sustains. No office could possibly add glory to Him who is "God over all, blessed forever"—"God manifest in the flesh"—the glorious "Immanuel" —"God with us"—the Eternal Word—the Creator and Sustainer of the universe. What office could add to the dignity of such an One ? In point of fact, we know that all His offices are connected with His humanity; and in assuming that humanity, He stooped from the glory which He had with the Father before the world was. He thus stooped in order to glorify God perfectly in the very midst of a scene where all was hostile to Him. He came to be "eaten up" by a holy, unquenchable zeal for the glory of God, and the effectual carrying out of His eternal counsels.

The unblemished male of the first year was a type of the Lord Jesus Christ offering Himself for the perfect accomplishment of the will of God. There should be nothing expressive either of weakness or imperfection. "A male of the first year" was required. We shall see, when we come to examine the other offerings, that "a female" was in some cases permitted; but that was only expressive of the imperfection which attached to the worshiper's apprehension, and in no wise of any defect in the offering, inasmuch as it was "unblemished" in the one case as well as in the other. Here, however, it was an offering of the very highest order, because it was Christ offering Himself to God. Christ, in the burnt-offering, was exclusively for the eye and heart of God. This point should be distinctly apprehended. God alone could duly estimate the Person and work of Christ; He alone could fully appreciate the cross as the expression of Christ's perfect devotedness. The cross, as foreshadowed by the burnt-offering, had an element in it which only the divine mind could apprehend; it had depths so profound, that neither mortal nor angel could fathom them. There was a voice in it which was intended exclusively for, and went directly to, the ear of the Father. There were communications between the cross of Calvary and the throne of God which lay far beyond the highest range of created intelligence.

"He shall offer it of his own voluntary will at the door of the tabernacle of the congregation before the Lord." The use of the word "*voluntary*" here brings out with great clearness the grand idea in the burnt-offering. It leads us to contemplate the cross in an aspect which is not sufficiently apprehended. We are too apt to look upon the cross merely as the place where the great question of sin was gone into and settled between eternal Justice and the spotless Victim—as the place where our guilt was atoned for, and where Satan was gloriously vanquished. Eternal and universal praise to redeeming love! the cross was all this; but it was more than this,—it was the place where Christ's love to the Father was told out in language which only the Father could hear and understand. It is in the latter aspect that we have it typified in the burnt-offering, and therefore it is that the word "voluntary" occurs. Were it merely a question of the imputation of sin, and of enduring the wrath of God on account of sin, such an expression would not be in moral order. The blessed Lord Jesus could not, with strict propriety, be represented as *willing* to be "made sin"

—*willing* to endure the wrath of God and the hiding of His countenance; and in this one fact we learn, in the clearest manner, that the *burnt-offering does not foreshadow Christ on the cross bearing sin*, but Christ on the cross accomplishing the will of God. That Christ Himself contemplated the cross in these two aspects of it is evident from His own words. When He looked at the cross as the place of sin-bearing—when He anticipated the horrors with which, in this point of view, it stood invested, He exclaimed, "Father, if Thou be willing, remove this cup from Me." (Luke xxiii. 42.) He shrank from that which His work, as a sin-bearer, involved. His pure and holy mind shrank from the thought of contact with sin, and His loving heart shrank from the thought of losing, for a moment, the light of God's countenance.

But then, the cross had another aspect. It stood before the eye of Christ as a scene in which He could fully tell out all the deep secrets of His love to the Father—a place in which He could, "of His own voluntary will," take the cup which the Father had given Him, and drain it to the very dregs. True it is that the whole life of Christ emitted a fragrant odor, which ever ascended to the Father's throne—He did always those things which pleased the Father—He ever did the will of God; but the burnt-offering does not typify Him in His life—precious, beyond all thought, as was every act of that life,—but in His death, and in that, not as one "made a curse for us," but as one presenting to the heart of the Father an odor of incomparable fragrance.

This truth invests the cross with peculiar charms for the spiritual mind. It imparts to the sufferings of our blessed Lord an interest of the most intense character. The guilty sinner, no doubt, finds in the cross a divine answer to the deepest and most earnest cravings of heart and conscience: the true believer finds in the cross that which captivates every affection of his heart, and transfixes his whole moral being: the angels find in the cross a theme for ceaseless admiration. All this is true; but there is that in the cross which passes far beyond the loftiest conceptions of saints or angels, namely, the deep-toned devotion of the heart of the Son presented to and appreciated by the heart of the Father. This is the elevated aspect of the cross which is so strikingly shadowed forth in the burnt-offering.

And here let me remark that the distinctive beauty of the burnt-offering must be entirely sacrificed if we admit the idea that Christ was a sin-bearer all His life. There would then be no force, no value, no meaning in the word "voluntary." There could be no room for voluntary action in the case of one who was compelled, by the very necessity of his position, to yield up his life. If Christ were a sin-bearer in His life, then, assuredly, His death must have been a *necessary*, not a voluntary, act. Indeed, it may be safely asserted that there is not one of the offerings the beauty of which would not be marred, and its strict integrity sacrificed, by the theory of *a life* of sin-bearing. In the burnt-offering, this is especially the case, inasmuch as it is not, in it, a question of sin-bearing, or enduring the wrath of God, but entirely one of voluntary devotedness, manifested in the death of the cross. In the burnt-offering, we recognize a type of God the Son accomplishing, by God the Spirit, the will of God the Father. This He did "of His own voluntary will." "Therefore doth My Father love Me, because I lay down My life, that I might take it again." (John x. 17.) Here we have the burnt-offering aspect of the death of Christ. On the other hand, the prophet, contemplating Him as the sin-offering, says, "His life *is taken* from the earth" (Acts. viii. 33.) (which is the LXX. version of Isaiah liii. 8.). Again, Christ says, "No one [ου δεις] taketh it from Me, but I lay it down of Myself." Was He a sin-bearer when He said this? Observe, it is "No one,"—man, angel, devil, or else. It was His own voluntary act, to lay down His life that He might take it again. "I delight to do Thy will, O My God." Such was the language of the divine burnt-offering—of Him who found His unutterable joy in offering Himself without spot to God.

Now, it is of the last importance to apprehend with distinctness the primary object of the heart of Christ in the work of redemption. It tends to consolidate the believer's peace. The accomplishment of God's will, the establishment of God's counsels, and the display of God's glory, occupied the fullest, deepest, and largest place in that devoted heart

which viewed and estimated every thing in reference
to God. The Lord Jesus never once stopped to
inquire how any act or circumstance would affect
Himself. "He humbled Himself"—"He made
Himself of no reputation"—He surrendered all.
And hence, when He arrived at the close of His
career, He could look back upon it all, and say,
with His eyes lifted up to heaven, "I have glorified
Thee on the earth; I have finished the work which
Thou gavest Me to do." (John xvii. 4.) It is impossible to contemplate the work of Christ, in this
aspect of it, without having the heart filled with the
sweetest affections toward His Person. It does not
detract, in the smallest degree, from our sense of His
love to us, to know that He made God His primary
object in the work of the cross. Quite the opposite.
His love to us, and our salvation in Him, could only
be founded upon God's established glory. That glory
must form the solid basis of every thing. "As truly
as I live, all the earth shall be filled with the glory
of the Lord." (Numb. xiv. 21.) But we know that
God's eternal glory and the creature's eternal blessedness are, in the divine counsels, inseparably linked
together, so that if the former be secured, the latter
must needs be so likewise.

"And he shall put his hand upon the head of the
burnt-offering; and it shall be accepted for him, to
make atonement for him." The act of laying on
of hands was expressive of full identification. By
that significant act, the offerer and the offering became one; and this oneness, in the case of the

burnt-offering, secured for the offerer all the acceptableness of his offering. The application of this to
Christ and the believer sets forth a truth of the most
precious nature, and one largely developed in the
New Testament, namely, the believer's everlasting
identification with, and acceptance in, Christ. "As
He is, so are we in this world." "We are in Him
that is true." (1 John iv. 17 ; v. 20.) Nothing, in
any measure, short of this could avail. The man who
is not in Christ is in his sins. There is no middle
ground : you must be either in Christ or out of
Him.   There is no such thing as being *partly* in
Christ. If there is a single hair's breadth between
you and Christ, you are in an actual state of wrath
and condemnation ; but, on the other hand, if you
are in Him, then are you "as He is" before God,
and so accounted in the presence of infinite holiness.
Such is the plain teaching of the Word of God.
"Ye are complete in Him"—"accepted in the Beloved"—"members of His body, of His flesh, and
of His bones." "He that is joined unto the Lord
is one spirit." (1 Cor. vi. 17 ; Eph. i. 6 ; v. 30 ; Col.
ii. 10.) Now, it is not possible that the Head can
be in one degree of acceptance and the members in
another. No ; the head and the members are one.
God counts them one, and therefore they are one.
This truth is at once the ground of the loftiest confidence, and of the most profound humility.   It
imparts the fullest assurance of "boldness in the
day of judgment," inasmuch as it is not possible
that aught can be laid to the charge of Him with

whom we are united: it imparts the deep sense of
our own nothingness, inasmuch as our union with
Christ is founded upon the death of nature and the
utter abolition of all its claims and pretensions.

Since, therefore, the Head and the members are
viewed in the same position of infinite favor and
acceptance before God, it is perfectly evident that
all the members stand in one acceptance, in one
salvation, in one life, in one righteousness. There
are no degrees in justification. The babe in Christ
stands in the same justification as the saint of fifty
years' experience. The one is in Christ, and so is
the other; and this, as it is the only ground of life,
so it is the only ground of justification. There are
not two kinds of life, neither are there two kinds of
justification. No doubt there are various measures
of enjoyment of this justification—various degrees
in the knowledge of its fullness and extent—various
degrees in the ability to exhibit its power upon the
heart and life; and these things are frequently confounded with the justification itself, which, as being
divine, is necessarily eternal, absolute, unvarying,
entirely unaffected by the fluctuations of human
feeling and experience.

But, further, there is no such thing as progress in
justification. The believer is not more justified to-
day than he was yesterday; nor will he be more
justified to-morrow than he is to-day; yea, a soul
who is "in Christ Jesus" is as completely justified
as if he were before the throne. He is "*complete* in
Christ; he is "*as*" Christ. He is, on Christ's own

authority, "clean every whit." (John xiii. 10.)
What more could he be at this side of the glory?
He may [and if he walks in the Spirit, will] make
progress in the sense and enjoyment of this glorious
reality; but, as to the thing itself, the moment he,
by the power of the Holy Ghost, believed the
gospel, he passed from a positive state of unrighteousness and condemnation into a positive state of
righteousness and acceptance.   All this is based
upon the divine perfectness of Christ's work; just
as, in the case of the burnt-offering, the worshiper's
acceptance was based upon the acceptableness of
his offering.   It was not a question of what he was,
but simply of what the sacrifice was.—"*It* shall be
accepted *for him*, to make atonement for him."

   "And he shall kill the bullock before the Lord;
and the priests, Aaron's sons, shall bring the blood,
and sprinkle the blood round about upon the altar
that is by the door of the tabernacle of the congregation."   It is most needful, in studying the doctrine of the burnt-offering, to bear in mind that the
grand point set forth therein is not the meeting of
the sinner's need, but the presentation to God of
that which was infinitely acceptable to Him.   Christ
as foreshadowed by the burnt-offering is not for the
sinner's conscience, but for the heart of God.
Further, the cross in the burnt-offering is not the
exhibition of the exceeding hatefulness of sin, but
of Christ's unshaken and unshakable devotedness
to the Father; neither is it the scene of God's
outpoured wrath on Christ the sin-bearer, but of

the Father's unmingled complacency in Christ the
voluntary and most fragrant Sacrifice. Finally,
"atonement" as seen in the burnt-offering is not
merely commensurate with the claims of man's
conscience, but with the intense desire of the heart
of Christ to carry out the will and establish the
counsels of God—a desire which stopped not short
of surrendering up His spotless, precious life, as
"a voluntary offering" of "sweet savor" to God.

From the carrying out of this desire, no power of
earth or hell, men or devils, could shake Him.
When Peter ignorantly sought to dissuade Him, by
words of false tenderness, from encountering the
shame and degradation of the cross—"Pity Thyself,
Lord: this shall not be unto Thee"—what was the
reply? "Get thee behind Me, Satan: Thou art an
offense unto Me; for thou savorest not the things
that be of God, but those that be of men." (Matt.
xvi. 22, 23.) So, also, on another occasion, He
says to His disciples, "Hereafter I will not talk
much with you; for the prince of this world cometh,
and hath nothing in Me. But that the world may
know that *I love the Father*, and as the Father gave
Me commandment, even so I do." (John xiv. 30.)
These and numerous other kindred scriptures bring
out the burnt-offering phase of Christ's work, in
which, it is evident, the primary thought is His
"offering Himself without spot to God."

In full keeping with all that has been stated in
reference to the special point in the burnt-offering,
is the place which Aaron's sons get, and the func-

tions assigned them therein.   They "sprinkle the
blood;" they "put the fire upon the altar;" they
"lay the wood in order upon the fire;" they "lay
the parts, the head and the fat, in order upon the
wood that is on the fire which is upon the altar."
These are very prominent actions, and they form a
marked feature of the burnt-offering, as contrasted
with the sin-offering, in which Aaron's sons are not
mentioned at all.   "The sons of Aaron" represent
the Church, not as "one body," but as a priestly
house.   This is easily apprehended.   If Aaron was
a type of Christ, then Aaron's house was a type of
Christ's house, as we read, in Heb. iii, "But Christ
as a Son over His own house; whose house are we."
And again, "Behold I and the children whom God
hath given Me."   Now, it is the privilege of the
Church, as led and taught by the Holy Ghost, to
gaze upon and delight in that aspect of Christ which
is presented in this opening type of Leviticus.   "Our
fellowship is with the Father," who graciously calls
us to participate with Him in His thoughts about
Christ.   True, we can never rise to the height of
those thoughts, but we can have fellowship therein,
by the Holy Ghost, who dwells in us.   It is not
here a question of having the conscience tranquilized by the blood of Christ as the sin-bearer, but
of communion with God in the matter of Christ's
perfect surrender of Himself on the cross.

"*The priests*, Aaron's sons, shall bring the blood,
and sprinkle the blood round about upon the altar
that is by the door of the tabernacle of the con-

gregation." Here we have a type of the Church bringing the memorial of an accomplished sacrifice, and presenting it in the place of individual approach to God. But we must remember, it is the blood of the burnt-offering, and not of the sin-offering;— it is the Church, in the power of the Holy Ghost, entering into the stupendous thought of Christ's accomplished devotedness to God, and not a convicted sinner entering into the value of the blood of the sin-bearer. I need hardly say that the Church is composed of sinners, and convicted sinners, too; but "Aaron's sons" do not represent convicted sinners, but worshiping saints,—it is as *"priests"* they have to do with the burnt-offering. Many err as to this. They imagine that because one takes the place of a worshiper (being invited by the grace of God, and fitted by the blood of Christ so to do), he thereby refuses to acknowledge himself a poor worthless sinner. This is a great mistake. The believer is, in himself, "nothing at all;" but in Christ, he is a purged worshiper. He does not stand in the sanctuary as a guilty sinner, but as a worshiping priest, clothed in "garments of glory and beauty." To be occupied with my guilt in the presence of God is not humility as regards myself, but unbelief as regards the Sacrifice.

However, it must be very evident to my reader that the idea of sin-bearing—the imputation of sin —the wrath of God—does not appear in the burnt-offering. True, we read, "It shall be accepted for him, *to make atonement* for him;" but then, it is

"atonement," not according to the depths and enor-
mity of human guilt, but according to the perfection
of Christ's surrender of Himself to God, and the
intensity of God's delight in Christ. This gives us
the very loftiest idea of atonement. If I contemplate
Christ as the sin-offering, I see atonement made according to the claims of divine justice with respect
to sin; but when I see atonement in the burnt-
offering, it is according to the measure of Christ's
willingness and ability to accomplish the will of
God, and according to the measure of God's complacency in Christ and His work. What a perfect
atonement must that be which is the fruit of Christ's
devotion to God! Could there be any thing beyond
this? Assuredly not. The burnt-offering aspect of
atonement is that about which the priestly household
may well be occupied in the courts of the Lord's
house forever.

"And he shall flay the burnt-offering, and cut it
into his pieces." The ceremonial act of "flaying"
was peculiarly expressive. It was simply the re-
moving of the outward covering, in order that what
was *within* might be fully revealed. It was not
sufficient that the offering should be outwardly
"without blemish," "the hidden parts" should be
all disclosed, in order that every sinew and every
joint might be seen. It was only in the case of the
burnt-offering that this action was specially named.
This is quite in character, and tends to set forth the
depth of Christ's devotedness to the Father. It
was no mere surface-work with Him. The more

the secrets of His inner life were disclosed — the
more the depths of His being were explored, the
more clearly was it made manifest that pure devotion to the will of His Father, and earnest desire
for His glory, were the springs of action in the
great Antitype of the burnt-offering. He was,
most assuredly, a whole burnt-offering.

"And cut it into his pieces." This action presents a somewhat similar truth to that taught in the
"sweet incense *beaten small*." (Lev. xvi.) The
Holy Ghost delights to dwell upon the sweetness
and fragrance of the sacrifice of Christ, not only as
a whole, but also in all its minute details. Look
at the burnt-offering as a whole, and you see it
without blemish: look at it in all its parts, and you
see it to be the same. Such was Christ; and as
such He is shadowed forth in this important type.

"And the sons of Aaron the priest shall put fire
upon the altar, and lay the wood in order upon the
fire. And the priests, Aaron's sons, shall lay the
parts, the head, and the fat, in order upon the wood
that is on the fire which is upon the altar." This
was a high position for the priestly family. The
burnt-offering was wholly offered to God,—it was
all burnt upon the altar.* Man did not partake of

* It may be well, at this point, to inform the reader that the
Hebrew word which is rendered "burn" in the case of the burnt-
offering is wholly different from that which is used in the sin-
offering. I shall, because of the peculiar interest of the subject,
refer to a few of the passages in which each word occurs. The
word used in the burnt-offering signifies "incense," or to "burn
incense," and occurs in the following passages, in some one or
other of its various inflections: Lev. vi. 15—"And all the *frank-

it; but the sons of Aaron the priest (themselves
being likewise priests) are here seen standing round
the altar of God, to behold the flame of an acceptable sacrifice ascending to Him—an odor of sweet
smell. This was a high position—high communion
—a high order of priestly service—a striking type
of the Church having fellowship with God, in reference to the perfect accomplishment of His will in
the death of Christ. As convicted sinners, we gaze
on the cross of our Lord Jesus Christ, and behold
therein that which meets all our need. The cross,
in this aspect of it, gives perfect peace to the conscience. But then, as priests, as purged worshipers,
as members of the priestly family, we can look at
the cross in another light—even as the grand con-

---

incense, ... and shall *burn* it upon the altar;" Deut. xxxiii.
10—"They shall put *incense* before Thee, and whole *burnt*-sacrifice
upon Thine altar;" Exod. xxx. 1—"And thou shalt make an altar
to *burn incense* upon;" Ps. lxvi. 15—"With the *incense* of rams;"
Jer. xliv. 21—"The *incense* that ye *burned* in the cities of Judah;"
Cant. iii. 16—"Perfumed with myrrh and *frankincense.*" Passages
might be multiplied, but the above will suffice to show the use of
the word which occurs in the burnt-offering.

The Hebrew word which is rendered "burn" in connection with
the sin-offering, signifies to burn in general, and occurs in the
following passages: Gen. xl. 3—"Let us make brick, and *burn* them
thoroughly." Lev. x. 16—"And Moses diligently sought the goat
of the *sin*-offering, and, behold, it was *burnt.*" 2 Chron. xvi. 14—
"And they made a very great *burning* for him.

Thus, not only was the sin-offering burnt in a different place, but
a different word is adopted by the Holy Ghost to express the
burning of it. Now, we cannot imagine, for a moment, that this
distinction is a mere interchange of words, the use of which is
indifferent. I believe the wisdom of the Holy Ghost is as manifest
in the use of the two words as it is in any other point of difference
in the two offerings. The spiritual reader will attach the proper
value to the above most interesting distinction.

summation of Christ's holy purpose to carry out, even unto death, the will of the Father. As convicted sinners, we stand at the brazen altar, and find peace through the blood of atonement; but as priests, we stand there to behold and admire the completeness of that burnt-offering—the perfect surrender and presentation of the spotless One to God.

We should have a very defective apprehension of the mystery of the cross were we only to see in it that which meets man's need as a sinner. There were depths in that mystery which only the mind of God could fathom. It is therefore important to see that when the Holy Ghost would furnish us with foreshadowings of the cross, He gives us, in the very first place, one which sets it forth in its aspect Godward. This alone would be sufficient to teach us that there are heights and depths in the doctrine of the cross which man never could reach. He may approach to "that one well-spring of delight," and drink forever—he may satisfy the utmost longings of his spirit—he may explore it with all the powers of the renewed nature; but, after all, there is that in the cross which only God could know and appreciate. Hence it is that the burnt-offering gets the first place. It typifies Christ's death as viewed and valued by God alone. And surely, we may say, we could not have done without such a type as this; for not only does it give us the highest possible aspect of the death of Christ, but it also gives us a most precious thought in reference to God's peculiar interest in that death. The very fact of His insti-

tuting a type of Christ's death which was to be
exclusively for Himself, contains a volume of instruction for the spiritual mind.

But though neither man nor angel can ever fully
sound the amazing depths of the mystery of Christ's
death, we can, at least, see some features of it which
would needs make it precious, beyond all thought,
to the heart of God.   From the cross, He reaps His
richest harvest of glory.   In no other way could He
have been so glorified as by the death of Christ.
In Christ's voluntary surrender of Himself to death,
the divine glory shines out in its fullest brightness;
in it, too, the solid foundation of all the divine
counsels was laid.   This is a most comforting truth.
Creation never could have furnished such a basis.
Moreover, the cross furnishes a righteous channel
through which divine love can flow.   And, finally,
by the cross Satan is eternally confounded, and
"principalities and powers made a show of openly."
These are glorious fruits produced by the cross;
and, when we think of them, we can see just reason
why there should have been a type of the cross
exclusively for God Himself, and also a reason why
that type should occupy the leading place—should
stand at the very top of the list.   Again let me
say, there would have been a grievous blank among
the types had the burnt-offering been lacking, and
there would be a grievous blank in the page of
inspiration had the record of that type been with-
held.

"But his inwards and his legs shall he wash in

water; and the priest shall burn all on the altar, to be a burnt-sacrifice, an offering made by fire, of a sweet savor unto the Lord." This action rendered the sacrifice typically what Christ was essentially— pure—both inwardly and outwardly pure. There was the most perfect correspondence between Christ's inward motives and His outward conduct. The latter was the index of the former. All tended to the one point, namely, the glory of God. The members of His body perfectly obeyed and carried out the counsels of His devoted heart—that heart which only beat for God, and for His glory, in the salvation of men. Well, therefore, might the priest "burn *all* on the altar." It was all typically pure, and all designed only as food for the altar of God. Of some sacrifices the priest partook; of some, the offerer; but the burnt-offering was "all" consumed on the altar. It was exclusively for God. The priests might arrange the wood and the fire, and see the flame ascend (and a high and holy privilege it was so to do); but they did not eat of the sacrifice: God alone was the object of Christ in the burnt-offering aspect of His death. We cannot be too simple in our apprehension of this. From the moment that the unblemished male was voluntarily presented at the door of the tabernacle of the congregation, until it was reduced to ashes by the action of the fire, we discern in it Christ offering Himself, by the Eternal Spirit, without spot to God.

This makes the burnt-offering unspeakably precious to the soul. It gives us the most exalted view

of Christ's work. In that work, God had His own
peculiar joy—a joy into which no created intelligence
could enter. This must never be lost sight of. It
is unfolded in the burnt-offering, and confirmed by
"the law of the burnt-offering," to which we shall
just refer.

"And the Lord spake unto Moses, saying, 'Command Aaron and his sons, saying, This is the law
of the burnt-offering: It is the burnt-offering, because of the burning upon the altar all night unto the
morning, and the fire of the altar shall be burning
in it. And the priest shall put on his linen garment,
and his linen breeches shall he put upon his flesh,
and take up the ashes which the fire hath consumed
with the burnt-offering on the altar, and he shall
put them beside the altar. And he shall put off his
garments, and put on other garments, and carry
forth the ashes without the camp unto a clean place.
And the fire upon the altar shall be burning in it; it
shall not be put out: and the priest shall burn wood
on it every morning, and lay the burnt-offering in
order upon it; and he shall burn thereon the fat of
the peace-offerings. The fire shall ever be burning
upon the altar; it shall never go out.'" (Lev. vi.
8–13.) The fire on the altar consumed the burnt-
offering and the fat of the peace-offering. It was
the apt expression of divine holiness, which found
in Christ and His perfect sacrifice a proper material on which to feed. That fire was never to go
out. There was to be the perpetual maintenance of
that which set forth the action of divine holiness.

Through the dark and silent watches of the night, the fire blazed on the altar of God.

"And the priest shall put on his linen garment," etc. Here, the priest takes, in type, the place of Christ, whose personal righteousness is set forth by the white linen garment. He having given Himself up to the death of the cross in order to accomplish the will of God, has entered, in His own eternal righteousness, into heaven, bearing with Him the memorials of His finished work. The ashes declared the completion of the sacrifice, and God's acceptance thereof. Those ashes placed beside the altar indicated that the fire had consumed the sacrifice —that it was not only a completed, but also an accepted, sacrifice. The ashes of the burnt-offering declared the acceptance of the sacrifice: the ashes of the sin-offering declared the judgment of the sin.

Many of the points on which we have been dwelling will, with the divine blessing, come before us with increasing clearness, fullness, precision, and power as we proceed with the offerings. Each offering is, as it were, thrown into relief by being viewed in contrast with all the rest. All the offerings taken together give us a full view of Christ. They are like so many mirrors, arranged in such a manner as to reflect in various ways the figure of that true and only-perfect Sacrifice. No one type could fully present Him. We needed to have Him reflected in life and in death—as a Man and as a Victim, Godward and usward; and we have Him thus in the offerings of Leviticus. God has graciously met our need; and may He give us an enlarged capacity to enter into and enjoy His provision.

———————

CHAPTER II.

WE now come to consider the meat-offering, which presents, in a very distinct manner, "the Man Christ Jesus." As the burnt-offering typifies Christ in *death*, the meat-offering typifies Him in *life*. In neither the one nor the other is there a question of sin-bearing. In the burnt-offering, we see atonement, but no sin-bearing*—no imputation of sin —no outpoured wrath on account of sin. How can we know this? Because it was all consumed on the altar. Had there been aught of sin-bearing, it would have been consumed outside the camp. (Comp. Lev. iv. 11, 12, with Heb. xiii. 11.)

But in the meat-offering, there was not even a question of bloodshedding. We simply find in it a beauteous type of Christ as He lived and walked and served down here on this earth. This one fact is, of itself, sufficient to draw the spiritual mind to the close and prayerful consideration of this offering. The pure and perfect manhood of our blessed Lord is a theme which must command the attention of every true Christian. It is to be feared that great looseness of thought prevails in reference to this

———————

* That is to say, sin-bearing is not prominent. Of course, where there is atonement, sin must be in question.

holy mystery. The expressions which one some-times hears and reads are sufficient to prove that the fundamental doctrine of incarnation is not laid hold of as the Word presents it. Such expressions may very probably proceed from misapprehension as to the real nature of His relations, and as to the true character of His sufferings ; but, from what cause soever they arise, they should be judged in the light of holy Scripture, and rejected. Doubtless, many who make use of those expressions would recoil, with just horror and indignation, from the real doctrine contained in them were it put before them in its broad and true characters ; and, for this reason, one should be sorry to attribute unsoundness as to fun-damental truth, where it may merely be inaccuracy of statement.

There is, however, one consideration which should weigh heavily in the estimation of every Christian, and that is, the vital nature of the doctrine of Christ's humanity. It lies at the very foundation of Christianity ; and, for this reason, Satan has diligently sought, from the beginning, to lead people astray in reference to it. Almost all the leading errors which have found their way into the professing church disclose the satanic purpose to undermine the truth as to the Person of Christ. And even when earnest, godly men have sought to combat those errors, they have, in many cases, plunged into errors on the opposite side. Hence, therefore, the need of close adherence to the veritable words which the Holy Ghost has made use of in unfolding this

profound and most sacred mystery. Indeed, I believe that, in every case, subjection to the authority
of holy Scripture, and the energy of the divine life
in the soul, will prove effectual safeguards against
every complexion of error. It does not require
high theological attainments to enable a soul to
keep clear of error with respect to the doctrine of
Christ. If only the word of Christ be dwelling
richly, and "the Spirit of Christ" be in energy, in
the soul, there will be no room for Satan to thrust
in his dark and horrible suggestions. If the heart
be delighting in the Christ which Scripture unfolds,
it will assuredly shrink from the false Christs which
Satan would introduce. If we are feeding upon
God's reality, we shall unhesitatingly reject Satan's
counterfeit. This is the best possible way in which
to escape the entanglements of error, in every shape
and character. "The sheep *hear His voice*, and
. . . . follow Him; for they *know His voice*. And
a stranger will they not follow, but will flee from
him; for *they know not the voice of strangers*." (John
x. 3–5.) It is not, by any means, needful to be
acquainted with the voice of a stranger in order to
turn away from it: all we require is to know the
voice of "the good Shepherd." This will secure us
against the ensnaring influence of every strange
sound. While, therefore, I feel called upon to warn
the reader against strange sounds in reference to the
divine mystery of Christ's humanity, I do not deem
it needful to discuss such sounds, but would rather
seek, through grace, to arm him against them by

unfolding the doctrine of Scripture on the subject.

There are few things in which we exhibit more failure than in maintaining vigorous communion with the perfect manhood of the Lord Jesus Christ. Hence it is that we suffer so much from vacancy, barrenness, restlessness, and wandering. Did we but enter with a more artless faith into the truth that there is a real Man at the right hand of the Majesty in the heavens—One whose sympathy is perfect, whose love is fathomless, whose power is omnipotent, whose wisdom is infinite, whose resources are exhaustless, whose riches are unsearchable, whose ear is open to our every breathing, whose hand is open to our every need, whose heart is full of unspeakable love and tenderness towards us—how much more happy and elevated we should be, and how much more independent of creature streams, through what channel soever they may flow! There is nothing the heart can crave which we have not in Jesus. Does it long for genuine sympathy? Where can it find it, save in Him who could mingle His tears with those of the bereaved sisters of Bethany? Does it desire the enjoyment of sincere affection? It can only find it in that heart which told forth its love in drops of blood. Does it seek the protection of real power? It has but to look to Him who made the world. Does it feel the need of unerring wisdom to guide? Let it betake itself to Him who is wisdom personified, and "who of God is made unto us wisdom." In one word, we have all in Christ. The divine mind and the divine affections

have found a perfect object in "the Man Christ
Jesus;" and surely, if there is that in the Person of
Christ which can perfectly satisfy God, there is that
which ought to satisfy us, and which will satisfy us
in proportion as, by the grace of the Holy Ghost,
we walk in communion with God.

The Lord Jesus Christ was the only perfect Man
that ever trod this earth.   He was all perfect—perfect in thought, perfect in word, perfect in action.
In Him every moral quality met in divine and
therefore perfect proportion.   No one feature pre-
ponderated.   In Him were exquisitely blended a
majesty which overawed, and a gentleness which
gave perfect ease in His presence.   The scribes and
the Pharisees met His withering rebuke, while the
poor Samaritan and "the woman that was a sinner"
found themselves unaccountably, yet irresistibly, at-
tracted to Him.   No one feature displaced another,
for all was in fair and comely proportion.   This may
be traced in every scene of His perfect life.   He
could say, in reference to five thousand hungry
people, "Give ye them to eat;" and when they
were filled, He could say, "Gather up the fragments
that remain, that nothing be lost."   The benevolence
and the economy are both perfect, and neither interferes with the other: each shines in its own proper
sphere.   He could not send unsatisfied hunger
away; neither could He suffer a single fragment of
God's creatures to be wasted.   He would meet, with
a full and liberal hand, the need of the human family,
and when that was done, He would carefully treas-

ure up every atom. The self-same hand that was widely open to every form of human need was firmly closed against all prodigality. There was nothing niggardly nor yet extravagant in the character of the perfect—the heavenly Man.

What a lesson for us! How often, with us, does benevolence resolve itself into an unwarrantable profusion! and, on the other hand, how often is our economy marred by the exhibition of a miserly spirit! At times, too, our niggard hearts refuse to open themselves to the full extent of the need which presents itself before us; while, at other times, we squander, through a wanton extravagance, that which might satisfy many a needy fellow-creature. Oh, my reader, let us carefully study the divine picture set before us in the life of "the Man Christ Jesus." How refreshing and strengthening to "the inward man" to be occupied with Him who was perfect in all His ways, and who "in all things must have the pre-eminence"!

See Him in the garden of Gethsemane. There, He kneels in the profound depths of a humility which none but Himself could exhibit; but yet before the traitor's band He exhibits a self-posses-sion and majesty which cause them to go backward and fall to the ground. His deportment before God is prostration; before His judges and accusers, un-bending dignity. All is perfect. The self-emptiness and the self-possession, the prostration and the dignity, are all divine.

So, also, when we contemplate the beauteous

combination of His divine and human relations, the same perfectness is observable. He could say, "How was it that ye sought Me? Wist ye not that I must be about My Father's business?" And, at the same time, He could go down to Nazareth, and there set an example of perfect subjection to parental authority. (See Luke ii. 49–51.) He could say to His mother, "Woman, what have I to do with thee?" And yet, when passing through the unutterable agony of the cross, He could tenderly commit that mother to the care of the beloved disciple. In the former case, He separated Himself, in the spirit of perfect Nazariteship, to accomplish His Father's will; while in the latter, He gave expression to the tender feelings of the perfect human heart. The devotion of the Nazarite and the affection of the Man were both perfect. Neither was permitted to interfere with the other: each shone with undimmed lustre in its proper sphere.

Now, the shadow of this perfect Man passes before us in the "fine flour" which formed the basis of the meat-offering. There was not so much as a single coarse grain. There was nothing uneven— nothing unequal—nothing rough to the touch. No matter what pressure came from without, there was always an even surface. He was never ruffled by any circumstance or set of circumstances. He never had to retrace a step or recall a word. Come what might, He always met it in that perfect evenness which is so strikingly typified by the "fine flour."

In all these things, it is needless to say, He stands in marked contrast with His most honored and devoted servants. For example, Moses, though "the meekest man in all the earth," yet "spoke unadvisedly with his lips." In Peter, we find a zeal and an energy which at times proved too much for the occasion; and, again, a cowardice which shrank from the place of testimony and reproach. There was the assertion of a devotedness which, when the time for action arrived, was not forthcoming. John, who breathed so much of the atmosphere of the immediate presence of Christ, exhibited, at times, a sectarian and an intolerant spirit. In Paul, the most devoted of servants, we observe considerable unevenness. He uttered words to the high-priest which he had to recall: he sent a letter to the Corinthians of which at first he repented and afterwards repented not. In all, we find some flaw, save in Him who is "the fairest among ten thousand, and altogether lovely."

In the examination of the meat-offering, it will give clearness and simplicity to our thoughts to consider, first, the materials of which it was composed; secondly, the various forms in which it was presented; and, thirdly, the persons who partook of it.

As to the materials, the "fine flour" may be regarded as the basis of the offering; and in it we have a type of Christ's humanity, wherein every perfection met. Every virtue was there, and ready for effectual action in due season. The Holy Ghost delights to unfold the glories of Christ's Person, to

set Him forth in all His peerless excellence, to place
Him before us in contrast with all beside. He con-
trasts Him with Adam, even in his very best and
highest state; as we read, "The first man is of the
earth, earthy: the second Man is the Lord from
heaven." (1 Cor. xv. 47.) The first Adam, even
in his unfallen condition, was "of the earth;" but
the second Man was "the Lord from heaven."

The "oil," in the meat-offering, is a type of the
Holy Ghost. But inasmuch as the oil is applied in
a twofold way, so we have the Holy Ghost presented
in a double aspect, in *connection* with the *incarnation*
of the Son. The fine flour was "*mingled*" with oil,
and there was oil "*poured*" upon it. Such was the
type; and in the Antitype, we see the blessed Lord
Jesus Christ first "*conceived*," and then "*anointed*,"
by the Holy Ghost. (Comp. Matt. i. 18–23 with chap.
iii. 16.) This is divine! The accuracy, which is
here so apparent, draws forth the soul's admiration.
It is one and the same Spirit which records the ingredients of the type, and gives us the facts in the
Antitype. The One who has detailed for us, with
such amazing precision, the types and shadows of
the book of Leviticus, has also given us the glorious
subject thereof in the gospel narratives. The same
Spirit breathes through the pages of the Old and
those of the New Testament, and enables us to see
how exactly the one corresponds with the other.

The conception of Christ's humanity by the Holy
Ghost, in the womb of the virgin, unfolds one of
the most profound mysteries which can possibly

engage the attention of the renewed mind. It is most fully set forth in Luke's gospel; and this is entirely characteristic, inasmuch as, throughout that gospel, it would seem to be the special object of the Holy Ghost to unfold, in His own divinely touching manner, "the Man Christ Jesus." In Matthew, we have "the Son of Abraham—the Son of David;" in Mark, we have the divine Servant—the heavenly Workman; in John, we have "the Son of God"— the Eternal Word—the Life—the Light, by whom all things were made; but the great theme of the Holy Ghost in Luke is "the Son of Man."

When the angel Gabriel had announced to Mary the dignity which was about to be conferred upon her, in connection with the great work of incarnation, she, not in a spirit of scepticism, but of honest ignorance, inquired, "How shall this be, seeing I know not a man?" It manifestly seemed to her that the birth of this glorious Person who was about to appear should be according to the ordinary principles of generation; and this her thought is made the occasion, in the exceeding goodness of God, of developing much valuable light in reference to the cardinal truth of incarnation. The angel's reply to the virgin's question is unspeakably interesting, and cannot be too closely considered. "And the angel answered and said unto her, 'The Holy Ghost shall come upon thee, and the power of the Highest shall overshadow thee; *therefore* also that *holy Thing* which shall be born of thee shall be called the Son of God." (Luke i. 35.)

From this magnificent passage, we learn that the human body into which the Eternal Son entered was formed by "the power of the Highest." "A body hast *Thou* prepared Me." (Comp. Ps. xl. 6 with Heb. x. 5.) It was a real human body—real "flesh and blood." There is no possible foundation here on which gnosticism or mysticism can base its vapid and worthless theories,—no warrant for the cold abstractions of the former, or the misty fancies of the latter. All is deep, solid, and divine reality: the very thing which our hearts needed—the very thing which God has given. The early promise had declared that "the seed of the woman shall bruise the serpent's head," and none but a real man could accomplish this prediction—one whose nature was as real as it was pure and incorruptible. "Thou shalt conceive in thy womb," said the angelic messenger, "and bring forth a Son." * And then, lest there should be any room for an error in reference to the mode of this conception, he adds such words as prove, unanswerably, that the "flesh and blood" of which the Eternal Son "took part," while absolutely real, was absolutely incapable of receiving, of retaining, or of communicating a single taint. The humanity of the Lord Jesus was emphatically "*that holy Thing.*" And inasmuch as it was wholly without taint, it was wholly without a seed of mortality.

---

* "But when the fullness of the time was come, God sent forth His Son, made of a woman, made under the law." (γενομενον εκ γυναικος, γενομενον υπο νομον.) This is a most important passage, inasmuch as it sets forth our blessed Lord as Son of God and Son of Man.—"God sent forth *His* Son, made *of a woman.*" Precious testimony!

We cannot think of mortality, save in connection with sin; and Christ's humanity had naught to do with sin, either personally or relatively. Sin was imputed to Him on the cross, where He was "made sin for us." But the meat-offering is not the type of Christ as a sin-bearer. It foreshadows Him in His perfect life here below—a life in which He suffered, no doubt, but not as a sin-bearer—not as a substitute—not at the hand of God. Let this be distinctly noted. Neither in the burnt-offering nor in the meat-offering have we Christ as a sin-bearer. In the latter, we see Him *living;* and in the former, we see Him *dying;* but in neither is there a question of the imputation of sin, nor of enduring the wrath of God on account of sin. In short, to present Christ as the sinner's substitute any where else save on the cross, is to rob His life of all its divine beauty and excellency, and to displace the cross altogether. Moreover, it would involve the types of Leviticus in hopeless confusion.

I would, at this point, solemnly admonish my reader, that he cannot be too jealous in reference to the vital truth of the Person and the relations of the Lord Jesus Christ. If there be error as to this, there is no security as to any thing. God cannot give the sanction of His presence to aught that has not this truth for its foundation. The Person of Christ is the living—the divine centre round which the Holy Ghost carries on all His operations. Let slip the truth as to Him, and you are like a vessel broken from its moorings, and carried, without rudder or compass, over the wild watery waste, and in imminent danger of being dashed to fragments upon the rocks of Arianism, Infidelity, or Atheism. Question the eternal Sonship of Christ, question His deity, question His unspotted humanity, and you have opened the floodgate for a desolating tide of deadly error to rush in. Let no one imagine, for a moment, that this is a mere matter to be discussed by learned theologians—a curious question—a recondite mystery—a point about which we may lawfully differ. No; it is a vital, fundamental truth, to be held in the power of the Holy Ghost, and maintained at the expense of all beside—yea, to be confessed under all circumstances, whatever may be the consequences.

What we want, is, simply to receive into our hearts, by the grace of the Holy Spirit, the Father's revelation of the Son, and then our souls shall be effectually preserved from the snares of the enemy, let them take what shape they may. He may speciously cover the trap of Arianism or Socinianism with the grass and leaves of a most plausible and attractive system of interpretation; but directly the devoted heart discovers what this system attempts to make of the blessed One to whom it owes every thing, and where it attempts to put Him, it finds but little difficulty in sending it back to where it manifestly came from. We can well afford to do without human theories; but we can never do without Christ—the Christ of God—the Christ of God's affections—the Christ of God's counsels—the Christ of God's word.

The Lord Jesus Christ, God's eternal Son—a distinct Person in the glorious Trinity—God manifest in the flesh—God over all, blessed forever, assumed a body which was inherently and divinely pure, holy, and without the possibility of taint—absolutely free from every seed or principle of sin and mortality. Such was the humanity of Christ, that He could at any moment, so far as He was personally concerned, have returned to heaven, from whence He had come and to which He belonged. I speak not here of the eternal counsels of redeeming love, or of the unswerving love of the heart of Jesus —His love to God—His love to God's elect, or of the work that was needful to ratify God's everlasting covenant with the seed of Abraham and with the whole creation. Christ's own words teach us that "it behoved Him to suffer, and to rise from the dead the third day." (Luke xxiv. 46.) It was necessary that He should suffer, in order to the full manifestation and perfect accomplishment of the great mystery of redemption. It was His gracious purpose to "bring many sons unto glory." He would not "abide alone," and therefore He, as the "corn of wheat," should "fall into the ground and die." The more fully we enter into the *truth* of His Person, the more fully do we apprehend the *grace* of His work.

When the apostle speaks of Christ's being "made perfect through suffering," it is as "the Captain of our salvation" that he contemplates Him, and not as the Eternal Son, who, as regards His own abstract Person and nature, was divinely perfect, and could not possibly have aught added to Him. So, also, when He Himself says, "Behold, I cast out devils, and I do cures to-day and to-morrow, and the third day I shall be perfected" (Luke xiii. 32.), He refers to His being perfected, in the power of resurrection, as the Accomplisher of the entire work of redemption. So far as He was personally concerned, He could say, even on His way forth from the garden of Gethsemane, "Thinkest thou that I cannot now pray to My Father, and He shall presently give Me more than twelve legions of angels? But how then shall the Scriptures be fulfilled, that thus it must be?" (Matt. xxvi. 53, 54.)

It is well that the soul be clear as to this—well to have a divine sense of the harmony which exists between those scriptures which present Christ in the essential dignity of His Person and the divine purity of His nature, and those which present Him in His relation with His people and as accomplishing the great work of redemption. At times we find both these things combined in the same passage, as in Heb. v. 8, 9,—"Though *He were a Son*, yet learned He obedience by the things which He suffered; and being made perfect, He became the author of eternal salvation to all them that obey Him." We must, however, bear in mind that not one of those relations into which Christ voluntarily entered—whether as the expression of divine love to a lost world, or the Servant of the divine counsels —not one of these could possibly interfere with the essential purity, excellency, and glory of His Person.

"The Holy Ghost came upon" the virgin, and "the power of the Highest overshadowed her;" and "therefore that holy Thing which was born of her was called the Son of God." Most magnificent unfolding, this, of the deep secret of Christ's pure and perfect humanity—-the great Antitype of the "*fine flour mingled with oil*"!

And here let me observe, that between humanity as seen in the Lord Jesus Christ and humanity as seen in us there could be no union. That which is pure could never coalesce with that which is impure. That which is incorruptible could never unite with that which is corruptible. The spiritual and the carnal—the heavenly and the earthly—could never combine. Hence, therefore, it follows that incarnation was not, as some have attempted to teach, Christ's taking our fallen nature into union with Himself. If He could have done this, there would have been no need of the death of the cross. He needed not, in that case, to feel "straitened" until the baptism was accomplished—the corn of wheat did not need to "fall into the ground and die." This is a point of grave moment. Let the spiritual mind ponder it deeply. Christ could not possibly take sinful humanity into union with Himself. Hear what the angel saith to Joseph, in the first chapter of Matthew's gospel,—"Joseph, thou son of David, fear not to take unto thee Mary thy wife; for *that which is conceived in her is of the Holy Ghost*." See how Joseph's natural sensibilities, as well as Mary's pious ignorance, are made the occasion of a fuller unfolding of the holy mystery of Christ's humanity; and also of guarding that humanity against all the blasphemous attacks of the enemy.

How, then, is it that believers are united to Christ? Is it in incarnation, or resurrection? In resurrection, assuredly. How is this proved? "Except a corn of wheat fall into the ground and die, it abideth *alone*." (John xii. 24.) At this side of death, there could be no union between Christ and His people. It is in the power of a new life that believers are united to Christ. They were dead *in sin*, and He, in perfect grace, came down and (though Himself pure and sinless) was "made sin," "died *unto sin*," put it away, rose triumphant over it and all pertaining to it, and, in resurrection, became the Head of a new race. Adam was the head of the old creation, which fell with him. Christ, by dying, put Himself under the full weight of His people's condition, and having perfectly met all that was against them, rose victorious over all, and carried them with Him into the new creation, of which He is the glorious Head and Centre. Hence, we read, "He that is joined unto the Lord is one spirit." (1 Cor. vi. 17.) "But God, who is rich in mercy, for His great love wherewith He loved us, even when were *dead in sins*, hath quickened us *together with Christ*, (by grace ye are saved;) and hath raised us up together, and made us sit together in heavenly places in Christ Jesus." (Eph. ii. 4–6.) "For we are members of His body, of His flesh, and of His bones." (Eph. v. 30.) "And you, being *dead in your sins* and the uncircumcision of your flesh, *hath He quickened together with Him*, having forgiven you all trespasses." (Col. ii. 13.)

Passages might be multiplied, but the above are amply sufficient to prove that it was not in incarnation, but in death, that Christ took a position in which His people could be "quickened together with Him." Does this seem unimportant to the reader? Let him examine it in the light of Scripture. Let him weigh all the consequences. Let him view it in its bearing upon Christ's Person, upon His life, upon His death, upon our condition by nature in the old creation, and our place through mercy in the new. Let him consider it thus, and I feel persuaded he will no longer regard it as a light matter. Of one thing, at least, he may rest assured, that the writer of these pages would not pen a single line to prove this point did he not consider it to be fraught with the most momentous results. The whole of divine revelation so hangs together—is so adjusted by the hand of the Holy Ghost—is so consistent in all its parts, that if one truth be disturbed, the entire arch is injured. This consideration should suffice to produce, in the mind of every Christian, a holy caution, lest, by some rude touch, he mar the beauteous superstructure. Every stone must be left in its divinely appointed place; and, unquestionably, the truth as to Christ's Person is the key-stone of the arch.

Having thus endeavored to unfold the truth typified by the "fine flour *mingled* with oil," we may

remark another point of much interest in the ex
pression, "He shall *pour* oil upon it." In this we
have a type of the anointing of the Lord Jesus
Christ by the Holy Ghost. The body of the Lord
Jesus was not merely formed mysteriously by the
Holy Ghost, but that pure and holy vessel was
also anointed for service by the same power. "And
it came to pass when all the people were baptized,
and Jesus also being baptized, and praying, the
heaven was opened, and the Holy Ghost descended
in a bodily shape as a dove upon Him, and there
was a voice from heaven, saying, 'Thou art My
beloved Son; in Thee I am well pleased." (Luke
iii. 21, 22.)

The anointing of the Lord Jesus by the Holy Ghost
previous to His entrance upon His public ministry
is of immense practical importance to every one who
really desires to be a true and an effectual servant
of God. Though conceived, as to His manhood, by
the Holy Ghost; though, in His own proper Person,
"God manifest in the flesh;" though embodying
in Himself all the fullness of the Godhead; yet, be
it well observed, when coming forth as man to do
the will of God on the earth, whatever that will
might be—whether preaching the gospel, teaching
in the synagogues, healing the sick, cleansing the
leper, casting out devils, feeding the hungry, or
raising the dead—He did all by the Holy Ghost.
That holy and heavenly vessel in which God the Son
was pleased to appear in this world was formed,
filled, anointed, and led by the Holy Ghost.

What a deep and holy lesson for us! A most needful and salutary lesson! How prone are we to run unsent! How prone to act in the mere energy of the flesh! How much of that which looks like ministry is only the restless and unhallowed activity of a nature which has never been measured and judged in the divine presence! Truly, we need to contemplate more closely our divine "meat-offering" —to understand more fully the meaning of the "fine flour anointed with oil." We need to meditate more deeply upon Christ Himself, who, though possessing, in His own Person, divine power, nevertheless, did all His work, wrought all His miracles, and, finally, "offered Himself, without spot to God, by the eternal Spirit." He could say, "I by the Spirit of God cast out devils."

Nothing is of any value save that which is wrought by the power of the Holy Ghost. A man may write; but if his pen be not guided and used by the Holy Ghost, his lines will produce no permanent results. A man may speak; but if his lips be not anointed by the Holy Ghost, his word will not take permanent root. This is a solemn consideration, and if properly weighed, would lead to much watchfulness over ourselves, and much earnest dependence upon the Holy Ghost. What we need is thorough self-emptiness, so that there may be room left for the Spirit to act by us. It is impossible that a man full of himself can be the vessel of the Holy Ghost. Such an one must first be emptied of himself, and then the Spirit can use him. When we contemplate the Person and ministry of the Lord Jesus, we see how that in every scene and circumstance He acted by the direct power of the Holy Ghost. Having taken His place as man down here, He showed that man should not only live by the Word, but act by the Spirit of God. Even though, as man, His will was perfect—His thoughts, His words, His acts, all perfect—yet He would not act save by the direct authority of the Word, and by the direct power of the Holy Ghost. Oh that in this, as in every thing else, we could more closely, more faithfully, follow in His steps! Then, indeed, would our ministry be more effective, our testimony more fruitful, our whole course more entirely to the glory of God.

The next ingredient in the meat-offering demanding our consideration is "the frankincense." As has been remarked, the "fine flour" was the basis of the offering. The "oil" and "frankincense" were the two leading adjuncts; and, truly, the connection between these two latter is most instructive. The "oil" typifies the *power* of Christ's ministry; the "frankincense" typifies the *object* thereof. The former teaches us that He did every thing by the Spirit of God; the latter, that He did every thing to the glory of God. The frankincense presents that in the life of Christ which was exclusively for God. This is evident from the second verse—"And he shall bring it [the meat-offering] to Aaron's sons, the priests: and he shall take thereout his handful of flour thereof, and of the oil thereof, with *all the frankincense* thereof; and the priest shall burn the memorial of it upon the altar, to be an offering made by fire, of a sweet savor unto the Lord." Thus was it in the true meat-offering—the Man Christ Jesus. There was that in His blessed life which was exclusively for God. Every thought, every word, every look, every act of His emitted a fragrance which went up immediately to God. And as, in the type, it was the "fire of the altar" that drew forth the sweet odor of the frankincense; so, in the Antitype, the more He was "tried," in all the scenes and circumstances of His blessed life, the more fully was it manifested that, in His manhood, there was nothing that could not ascend as an odor of a sweet smell to the throne of God. If in the burnt-offering we behold Christ "offering Himself without spot to God," in th meat-offering we behold Him presenting all the intrinsic excellence and perfect actings of His human nature to God. A perfect, a self-emptied, an obedient Man on the earth doing the will of God, acting by the authority of the Word, and by the power of the Spirit, had a sweet odor which could only be for divine acceptance. The fact that "all the frankincense" was consumed on the altar, fixes its import in the simplest manner.

It now only remains for us to consider an ingredient which was an inseparable adjunct of the meat-offering, namely, "*salt*."—"And every oblation of thy meat-offering shalt thou season with salt; neither shalt thou suffer the salt of the covenant of thy God to be lacking from thy meat-offering: with all thine offerings thou shalt offer salt." The expression, "Salt of the covenant," sets forth the enduring character of that covenant. God Himself has so ordained it, in all things, that naught can ever alter it—no influence can ever corrupt it. In a spiritual and practical point of view, it is impossible to overestimate the value of such an ingredient. "Let your conversation be always with grace, seasoned with *salt*." The whole conversation of the Perfect Man exhibited the power of this principle. His words were not merely words of grace, but words of pungent power—words divinely adapted to preserve from all taint and corrupting influence. He never uttered a word which was not redolent with "frankincense," and "seasoned with salt." The former was most acceptable to God; the latter, most profitable for man.

Sometimes, alas! man's corrupt heart and vitiated taste could not tolerate the pungency of the divinely-salted meat-offering. Witness, for example, the scene in the synagogue of Nazareth. (Luke iv. 16–29.) The people could "bear Him witness, and wonder at the *gracious* words which proceeded out of His mouth;" but when He proceeded to season those words with *salt*, which was so needful in order to preserve them from the corrupting influence of their national pride, they would fain have cast Him over the brow of the hill whereon their city was built.

So, also, in Luke xiv, when His words of "grace" had drawn "great multitudes" after Him, He instantly throws in the "salt," by setting forth, in words of holy faithfulness, the sure results of following Him. "Come, for all things are now ready,"—here was the "grace;" but then, "Whosoever forsaketh not all that he hath, cannot be My disciple,"—here was the "salt." Grace is attractive; but "salt is good." Gracious discourse may be popular; but salted discourse never will. The pure gospel of the grace of God may, at certain times, and under certain circumstances, be run after by "the multitude" for awhile; but when the "salt" of a fervid and faithful application is introduced, it will soon thin the benches of all save such as are brought under the power of the Word.

Having thus considered the ingredients which composed the meat-offering, we shall now refer to those which were excluded from it.

The first of these was "leaven." "No meat-offering, which ye shall bring unto the Lord, shall be made with leaven." This ingredient is used throughout the inspired volume, without so much as a single exception, as the symbol of *evil*. In chap. xxiii. of our book, which will be noticed in due course, we find leaven admitted in the two loaves which were offered on the day of Pentecost; but from the meat-offering leaven was most sedulously excluded. There was to be nothing sour—nothing that would puff up—nothing expressive of evil in that which typified "the Man Christ Jesus." In Him, there could be nothing savoring of nature's sourness, nothing turgid—nothing inflated: all was pure, solid, and genuine. His word might, at times, cut to the quick; but it was never sour. His style never rose above the occasion. His deportment ever exhibited the deep reality of one walking in the immediate presence of God.

In those who bear the name of Jesus, we know, too well, alas! how leaven shows itself in all its properties and effects. There has been but one untainted sheaf of human fruit—but one perfectly unleavened meat-offering; and, blessed be God, that one is ours—ours to feed upon in the sanctuary of the divine presence, in fellowship with God No exercise can be more truly edifying and refreshing for the renewed mind than to dwell upon the unleavened perfectness of Christ's humanity—to contemplate the life and ministry of One who was absolutely and essentially unleavened. In all His springs of thought, affection, desire, and imagination, there was not so much as a particle of leaven. He was the sinless, spotless, perfect Man. And the more we are enabled, by the power of the Spirit, to enter into all this, the deeper will be our experience of the grace which led this perfect One to place Himself under the full consequences of His people's sins, as He did when He hung upon the cross. This thought, however, belongs entirely to the sin-offering aspect of our blessed Lord. In the meat-offering, sin is not in question. It is not the type of a sin-bearer, but of a real, perfect, unblemished Man, conceived and anointed by the Holy Ghost, possessing an unleavened nature, and living an unleavened life down here, emitting ever Godward the fragrance of His own personal excellency.

and maintaining amongst men a deportment characterized by "grace seasoned with salt."

But there was another ingredient, as positively excluded from the meat-offering as "leaven," and that was "honey."—"For ye shall burn no leaven, *nor any honey*, in any offering of the Lord made by fire." (Ver. 11.) Now, as "leaven" is the expression of that which is positively and palpably *evil* in nature, we may regard "honey" as the significant symbol of that which is apparently *sweet* and attractive. Both are disallowed of God, both were carefully excluded from the meat-offering, both were unfit for the altar. Men may undertake, like Saul, to distinguish between what is "vile and refuse" and what is not; but the judgment of God ranks the delicate Agag with the vilest of the sons of Amalek. No doubt, there are some good moral qualities in man, which must be taken for what they are worth. "Hast thou found *honey*, eat so much as is convenient;" but, be it remembered, it found no place in the meat-offering, nor in its Antitype. There was the fullness of the Holy Ghost, there was the fragrant odor of the frankincense, there was the preservative virtue of "the salt of the covenant,"— all these things accompanied the "fine flour" in the Person of the true "Meat-offering," but "no honey."

What a lesson for the heart is here! yea, what a volume of wholesome instruction! The blessed Lord Jesus knew how to give nature and its relationships their proper place: He knew how much

"honey" was "convenient." He could say to His mother, "Wist ye not that I must be about My Father's business?" and yet He could say, again, to the beloved disciple, "Behold thy mother." In other words, nature's claims were never allowed to interfere with the presentation to God of all the energies of Christ's perfect manhood. Mary, and others too, might have thought that her human relation to the blessed One gave her some peculiar claim or influence, on merely natural grounds. "There came, then, His brethren ["after the flesh"] and His mother, and standing without, sent unto Him, calling Him. And the multitude sat about Him; and they said unto Him, 'Behold, Thy mother and Thy brethren without seek for Thee.'" What was the reply of the true Meat-offering? Did He at once abandon His work, in order to respond to nature's call? By no means. Had He done so, it would have been to mingle "honey" with the meat-offering, which could not be. The honey was faithfully excluded on this as on every occasion when God's claims were to be attended to, and instead thereof, the power of the Spirit, the odor of the "frankincense," and the virtues of the "salt" were blessedly exhibited. "And he answered them, saying, 'Who is My mother, or My brethren?' And He looked round about on them which sat about Him, and said, 'Behold My mother and My brethren! For whosoever shall do the will of God, the same is My brother, and My sister, and mother.'"*
(Mark iii. 31-35.) (* Note, next page.)

There are few things which the servant of Christ finds more difficult than to adjust, with spiritual accuracy, the claims of natural relationship, so as not to suffer them to interfere with the claims of the Master. In the case of our blessed Lord, as we know, the adjustment was divine. In our case, it often happens that divinely recognized duties are openly neglected for what we imagine to be the service of Christ,—the doctrine of God is constantly sacrificed to the apparent work of the gospel. Now, it is well to remember that true devotedness always

---

* How important to see, in the above beautiful passage, that doing God's will brings the soul into a relationship with Christ of which His brethren according to the flesh knew nothing, on merely natural grounds! It was as true with respect to those brethren as any one else that "except a man be born again, he cannot see the kingdom of God." Mary would not have been saved by the mere fact of her being the mother of Jesus. She needed personal faith in Christ as much as any other member of Adam's fallen family: she needed to pass, by being born again, out of the old creation into the new. It was by treasuring up Christ's words in her heart that this blessed woman was saved. No doubt she was "highly favored" in being chosen as a vessel to such a holy office; but then, as a lost sinner, she needed to "rejoice in God her Saviour," like any one else. She stands on the same platform, is washed in the same blood, clothed in the same righteousness, and will sing the same song as all the rest of God's redeemed.

This simple fact will give additional force and clearness to a point already stated, namely, that incarnation was not Christ's taking our nature into union with Himself. This truth should be carefully pondered. It is fully brought out in 2 Cor. v.—"For the love of Christ constraineth us; because we thus judge, that if one died for all, then were all dead: and that He died for all, that they which live should not henceforth live unto themselves, but unto Him which died for them, and rose again. Wherefore henceforth know we no man after the flesh; yea, *though we have known Christ after the flesh, yet now henceforth know we Him no more.* Therefore if any man be *in Christ*, he is a new creation: old things are passed away; behold, all things are become new." (Ver. 14-17.)

starts from a point within which all godly claims
are fully secured. If I hold a situation which demands my services from ten till four every day, I
have no right to go out to visit or preach during
those hours. If I am in business, I am bound to
maintain the integrity of that business in a godly
manner. I have no right to run hither and thither
preaching while my business at home lies "in sixes
and sevens," bringing great reproach on the holy
doctrine of God. A man may say, I feel myself
called to preach the gospel, and I find my situation,
or my business, a clog. Well, *if you are divinely
called and fitted* for the work of the gospel, and that
you cannot combine the two things, then resign
your situation, or wind up your business, in a godly
manner, and go forth in the name of the Lord.
But, clearly, so long as I hold a situation, or carry
on a business, my work in the gospel must begin
from a point within which the godly claims of such
business or situation are fully responded to. This
is devotedness: aught else is confusion, however
well intended. Blessed be God, we have a perfect
example before us in the life of the Lord Jesus, and
ample guidance for the new man in the Word of
God; so that we need not make any mistakes in the
varied relationships which we may be called, in the
providence of God, to fill, or as to the various claims
which God's moral government has set up in connection with such relationships.

II. The second point in our theme is the mode
in which the meat-offering was prepared. This was,

as we read, by the action of fire,—it was "baken in an oven"—"baken in a pan," or "baken in a frying-pan." The process of baking suggests the idea of suffering. But inasmuch as the meat-offering is called "a sweet savor" (a term which is never applied to the sin-offering or trespass-offering), it is evident that there is no thought of suffering for sin —no thought of suffering the wrath of God on account of sin—no thought of suffering at the hand of Infinite Justice, as the sinner's substitute. The two ideas of "sweet savor" and suffering for sin are wholly incompatible according to the Levitical economy. It would completely destroy the type of the meat-offering were we to introduce into it the idea of suffering for sin.

In contemplating the *life* of the Lord Jesus, which, as we have already remarked, is the special subject foreshadowed in the meat-offering, we may notice three distinct kinds of suffering, namely, suffering for righteousness, suffering by the power of sympathy, and suffering in anticipation.

As the righteous Servant of God, He suffered in the midst of a scene in which all was contrary to Him; but this was the very opposite of suffering for sin. It is of the utmost importance to distinguish between these two kinds of suffering. The confounding of them must lead to serious error. Suffering as a righteous One standing amongst men on God's behalf is one thing, and suffering instead of man under the hand of God is quite another. The Lord Jesus suffered for righteousness during

His *life*: He suffered for sin in His *death*. During His life, man and Satan did their utmost; and even at the cross they put forth all their powers; but when all that they could do was done—when they had traveled, in their deadly enmity, to the utmost limit of human and diabolical opposition, there lay, far beyond, a region of impenetrable gloom and horror into which the Sin-bearer had to travel, in the accomplishment of His work. During His life, He ever walked in the unclouded light of the divine countenance; but on the cursed tree, the dark shadow of sin intervened and shut out that light, and drew forth that mysterious cry, "My God, My God, why hast Thou forsaken Me?" This was a moment which stands absolutely alone in the annals of eternity. From time to time during the life of Christ down here, heaven had opened to give forth the expression of divine complacency in Him; but on the cross, God forsook Him, because He was making His soul an offering for sin. If Christ had been a sin-bearer all His life, then what was the difference between the cross and any other period? Why was He not forsaken of God during His entire course? What was the difference between Christ on the cross, and Christ on the holy mount of transfiguration? Was He forsaken of God on the mount? was He a sin-bearer there? These are very simple questions, which should be answered by those who maintain the idea of a life of sin-bearing.

The plain fact is this: there was nothing either in Christ's humanity or in the nature of His associations which could possibly connect Him with sin, or wrath, or death. He was "made sin" on the cross; and there He endured the wrath of God, and there He gave up His life, as an all-sufficient atonement for sin; but nothing of this finds a place in the meat-offering. True, we have the process of baking —the action of fire; but this is not the wrath of God. The meat-offering was not a sin-offering, but a "sweet savor" offering. Thus, its import is definitely fixed; and, moreover, the intelligent interpretation of it must ever guard, with holy jealousy, the precious truth of Christ's spotless humanity, and the true nature of His associations. To make Him, by the necessity of His birth, a sin-bearer, or to place Him thereby under the curse of the law and the wrath of God, is to contradict the entire truth of God as to incarnation— truth announced by the angel, and repeated again and again by the inspired apostle. Moreover, it destroys the entire character and object of Christ's life, and robs the cross of its distinctive glory. It lowers the sense of what sin is, and of what atonement is. In one word, it removes the key-stone of the arch of revelation, and lays all in hopeless ruin and confusion around us.

But, again, the Lord Jesus suffered by the power of sympathy; and this character of suffering unfolds to us the deep secrets of His tender heart. Human sorrow and human misery ever touched a chord in that bosom of love. It was impossible that a perfect human heart could avoid feeling, according to its own divine sensibilities, the miseries which sin had entailed upon the human family. Though personally free both from the cause and the effect—though belonging to heaven, and living a perfect heavenly life on the earth, yet did He descend, by the power of an intense sympathy, into the deepest depths of human sorrow; yea, He felt the sorrow more keenly, by far, than those who were the direct subjects thereof, inasmuch as His humanity was perfect. And, further, He was able to contemplate both the sorrow and its cause according to their just measure and character in the presence of God. He felt as none else could feel. His feelings, His affections, His sensibilities, His whole moral and mental constitution, were perfect; and hence none can tell what such an One must have suffered in passing through such a world as this. He beheld the human family struggling beneath the ponderous weight of guilt and wretchedness; He beheld the whole creation groaning under the yoke; the cry of the prisoner fell upon His ear; the tear of the widow met His view; bereavement and poverty touched His sensitive heart; sickness and death made Him "groan in the spirit;" His sympathetic sufferings were beyond all human conception.

I shall quote a passage for my reader, illustrative of that character of suffering to which we are now referring.—"When the even was come, they brought unto Him many that were possessed with devils; and He cast out the spirits with His word, and healed all that were sick; that it might be fulfilled

which was spoken by Esaias the prophet, saying,
'*Himself took our infirmities. and bare our sick-nesses.*'" (Matt. viii. 16, 17.) This was entirely
sympathetic—the power of fellow-feeling, which
in Him was perfect. He had no sicknesses or
infirmities of His own. Those things which are
sometimes spoken of as "sinless infirmities," were,
in His case, but the evidences of a veritable, a real,
a perfect manhood. But by sympathy—by perfect
fellow-feeling, "He *took* our infirmities, and *bare*
our sicknesses." None but a perfect man could
have done this. We may feel for and with each
other, but only Jesus could make human infirmity
and sickness His own.

Now, had He been bearing all these things by the
necessity of His birth, or of His relations with Israel
and the human family, we should have lost all the
beauty and preciousness of His voluntary sympathy.
There could be no room for voluntary action when
absolute necessity was laid upon Him. But, on the
other hand, when we see His entire freedom, both
personally and relatively, from human misery and
that which produced it, we can enter into that perfect grace and compassion which led Him to "take
our infirmities, and bear our sicknesses," in the
power of true sympathy. There is, therefore, a
very manifest difference between Christ's suffering
as a voluntary sympathizer with human misery, and
His sufferings as the sinner's substitute. The former
are apparent throughout His entire *life;* the latter
are confined to His *death.*

Finally, we have to consider Christ's sufferings by anticipation. We find the dark shadow of the cross casting itself athwart His path, and producing a very keen order of suffering, which, however, must be as clearly distinguished from His atoning suffering as either His suffering for righteousness or His suffering by sympathy. Let us take a passage in proof—"And He came out, and went, as He was wont, to the mount of Olives; and His disciples also followed Him. And when He was at the place, He said unto them, 'Pray that ye enter not into temptation.' And He was withdrawn from them about a stone's cast, and kneeled down, and prayed, saying, 'Father, if Thou be willing, remove this cup from Me: nevertheless not My will, but Thine, be done.' And there appeared an angel unto Him from heaven, strengthening Him. And being in an agony, He prayed more earnestly: and His sweat was as it were great drops of blood falling down to the ground." (Luke xxii. 39–44.) Again, we read, "And He took with Him Peter and the two sons of Zebedee, and began to be sorrowful and very heavy. Then saith He unto them, 'My soul is exceeding sorrowful, even unto death: tarry ye here, and watch with Me.' . . . . He went away again the second time, and prayed, saying, 'O My Father, if this cup may not pass from Me, except I drink it, Thy will be done.'" (Matt. xxvi. 37–42.)

From these verses, it is evident there was a something in prospect which the blessed Lord had never encountered before,—there was a "cup" being

filled out for Him of which He had not yet drunk.
If He had been a sin-bearer all His life, then why
this intense "agony" at the thought of coming in
contact with sin and enduring the wrath of God
on account of sin? What was the difference between Christ in Gethsemane and Christ at Calvary
if He were a sin-bearer all His life? There was a
material difference; but it is because He was not a
sin-bearer all His life. What is the difference? In
Gethsemane, He was *anticipating* the cross; at
Calvary, He was actually *enduring* it. In Gethsemane, "there appeared an angel unto Him from
heaven, strengthening Him;" at Calvary, He was
forsaken of all. There was no angelic ministry
there. In Gethsemane, He addresses God as
"*Father*," thus enjoying the full communion of
that ineffable relationship; but at Calvary, He
cries, "My *God*, My *God*, why hast Thou forsaken
Me?" Here the Sin-bearer looks up and beholds
the throne of Eternal Justice enveloped in dark
clouds, and the countenance of Inflexible Holiness
averted from Him, because He was being "made
sin for us."

The reader will, I trust, find no difficulty in
examining this subject for himself. He will be
able to trace, in detail, the three characters of the
life-sufferings of our blessed Lord, and to distinguish between them and His *death*-sufferings—His
sufferings for sin. He will see how that when man
and Satan had done their utmost, there yet remained
a character of suffering which was perfectly unique,

namely, suffering at the hand of God on account of sin—suffering as the sinner's substitute. Until He came to the cross, He could ever look up and bask in the clear light of His Father's countenance; in the darkest hour, He found a sure resource above. His path down here was a rough one. How could it be otherwise, in a world where all was directly contrary to His pure and holy nature? He had to "endure the contradiction of sinners against Himself;" He had to endure "the reproach of them that reproached God." What had He not to endure? He was misunderstood, misinterpreted, abused, maligned, accused of being mad, and of having a devil. He was betrayed, denied, deserted, mocked, buffeted, spit upon, crowned with thorns, cast out, condemned, and nailed between two malefactors. All these things He endured at the hand of man, together with all the unutterable terrors which Satan brought to bear upon His spirit; but, let it be once more emphatically repeated, when man and Satan had exhausted their power and enmity, our blessed Lord and Saviour had to endure a something compared with which all the rest was as nothing, and that was the hiding of God's countenance—the three hours of darkness and awful gloom, during which He suffered what none but God could know.

Now, when Scripture speaks of our having fellowship with Christ's sufferings, it refers simply to His sufferings for righteousness—His sufferings at the hand of man. Christ suffered for sin that we might not have to suffer for it,—He endured the wrath of

God that we might not have to endure it (this is the ground of our peace); but as regards suffering from man, we shall always find that the more faithfully we follow in the footsteps of Christ, the more we shall suffer in this respect; but this is a matter of gift, a matter of privilege, a favor, a dignity. (See Phil. i. 29, 30.) To walk in the footsteps of Christ—to enjoy companionship with Him—to be thrown into a place of sympathy with Him, are privileges of the very highest order. Would that we all entered more fully into them! But, alas! we are too well content to do without them—too well satisfied, like Peter, to "follow afar off"—to keep aloof from a despised and suffering Christ. All this is, undoubtedly, our heavy loss. Had we only more fellowship with His sufferings, the crown would glisten far more brightly in our soul's vision. When we shrink from fellowship with Christ's sufferings, we rob ourselves of the deep joy of His present companionship, and also of the moral power of the hope of His future glory.

III. Having considered the ingredients which composed the meat-offering, and the various forms in which it was presented, it only remains for us to refer to the persons who partook of it. These were the head and members of the priestly house. "And that which is left of the meat-offering shall be Aaron's and his sons': it is a thing most holy of the offerings of the Lord made by fire." (Ver. 10.) As in the burnt-offering we observed the sons of Aaron introduced as types of all true believers, not as convicted sinners, but as worshiping priests; so in the meat-offering we find them feeding upon the remnant of that which had been laid, as it were, on the table of the God of Israel. This was a high and holy privilege. None but priests could enjoy it. This is set forth with great distinctness in "the law of the meat-offering," which I shall here quote at length.—"And this is the law of the meat-offering: The sons of Aaron shall offer it before the Lord, before the altar. And he shall take of it his handful, of the flour of the meat-offering, and of the oil thereof, and *all the frankincense* which is upon the meat-offering, and shall burn it upon the altar for a sweet savor, even the memorial of it, unto the Lord. And the remainder thereof shall Aaron and his sons eat: *with unleavened bread* shall it be eaten *in the holy place;* in the court of the tabernacle of the congregation they shall eat it. It shall not be baken with leaven. I have given it unto them for their portion of My offerings made by fire; it is most holy, as is the sin-offering, and as the trespass-offering. *All the males* among the children of Aaron shall eat of it. It shall be a statute forever in your generations concerning the offerings of the Lord made by fire: *every one that toucheth them shall be holy.*" (Lev. vi. 14–18.)

Here, then, we are furnished with a beauteous figure of the Church feeding "in the holy place," in the power of practical holiness, upon the perfections of "the Man Christ Jesus." This is our portion, through the grace of God; but, we must remember, it is to be eaten "with unleavened bread." We cannot feed upon Christ if we are indulging in any thing evil. "Every one that toucheth them shall be holy." Moreover, it must be "in the holy place." Our position, our practice, our persons, our associations, must be holy ere we can feed upon the meat-offering. Finally, it is "all the males among the children of Aaron shall eat of it." That is to say, real priestly energy, according to the divine idea of it, is required in order to enjoy this holy portion. Aaron's "*sons*" set forth the idea of *energy* in priestly action: his "*daughters*," *feebleness* therein. (Compare Numb. xviii. 8–13.) There were some things which the sons could eat which the daughters could not. Our hearts should earnestly desire the highest measure of priestly energy, so that we may discharge the highest priestly functions, and partake of the highest order of priestly food.

In conclusion, let me add, that inasmuch as we are made, through grace, "partakers of the divine nature," we can, if living in the energy of that nature, walk in the footsteps of Him who is foreshadowed in the meat-offering. If only we are self-emptied, our every act may emit a sweet odor to God. The smallest as well as the greatest services may, by the power of the Holy Ghost, present the fragrance of Christ. The paying of a visit, the writing of a letter, the public ministry of the Word, giving a cup of cold water to a disciple, giving a penny to a pauper, yea, the commonplace acts of eating and drinking—all may emit the sweet perfume of the name and grace of Jesus.

So, also, if only nature be kept in the place of death, there may be in us the exhibition of that which is not corruptible, even a conversation seasoned with the "salt" of abiding communion with God.   But in all these things we fail and come short; we grieve the Holy Spirit of God in our ways. We are prone to self-seeking or men-pleasing in our very best services, and we fail to "season" our conversation.   Hence our constant deficiency in the "oil," the "frankincense," and the "salt;" while, at the same time, there is the tendency to suffer the "leaven" or the "honey" of nature to make its appearance. There has been but one perfect "meat-offering;" and, blessed be God, we are accepted in Him. We are the "sons" of the true Aaron; our place is in the sanctuary, where we can feed upon the holy portion. Happy place! Happy portion! May we enjoy them more than ever we have done! May our retirement of heart from all but Christ be more profound! May our gaze at Him be so intense that we shall have no heart for the attractions of the scene around us, nor yet for the ten thousand petty circumstances in our path which would fret the heart and perplex the mind ! May we rejoice in Christ in the sunshine and in the darkness; when the gentle breezes of summer play around us, and when the storms of winter rage fiercely abroad ; when passing over the surface of a placid lake, or tossed on the bosom of a stormy ocean. Thank God, "we have found Him" who is to be our satisfying portion forever! We shall spend eternity dwelling upon the divine perfections of the Lord Jesus. Our eyes shall never be averted from Him when once we have seen Him as He is.

May the Spirit of God work mightily in us, to strengthen us "in the inner man"! May He enable us to feed upon that perfect Meat-offering, the memorial of which has been fed upon by God Himself! This is our holy and happy privilege. May we realize it yet more fully!

CHAPTER III.

THE more closely we contemplate the offerings, the more fully do we see how that no one offering furnishes a complete view of Christ. It is only by putting all together that any thing like a just idea can be formed. Each offering, as might be expected, has features peculiar to itself. The peace-offering differs from the burnt-offering in many points, and a clear understanding of the points in which any one type differs from the others will be found to help much in the apprehension of its special import.

Thus, in comparing the peace-offering with the burnt-offering, we find that the threefold action of "flaying," "cutting it into its pieces," and "washing the inwards and legs" is entirely omitted: and this is quite in character. In the burnt-offering, as we have seen, we find Christ offering Himself to and accepted by God; and hence the completeness of His self-surrender, and also the searching process to which He submitted Himself, had to be typified. In the peace-offering, the leading thought is the communion of the worshiper. It is not Christ as enjoyed exclusively by God, but as enjoyed by the worshiper in communion with God; therefore it is that the whole line of action is less intense. No heart, be its love ever so elevated, could possibly rise to the height of Christ's devotedness to God, or of God's acceptance of Christ. None but God Himself could duly note the pulsations of that heart which throbbed in the bosom of Jesus; and therefore a type was needed to set forth that one feature of Christ's death, namely, His perfect devotedness therein to God. This type we have in the burnt-offering, in which alone we observe the threefold action above referred to.

So also in reference to the character of the sacrifice. In the burnt-offering, it should be ''a male without blemish;'' whereas in the peace-offering, it might be ''a male or female,'' though equally ''without blemish.'' The nature of Christ, whether we view Him as enjoyed exclusively by God, or by the worshiper in fellowship with God, must ever be one and the same; there can be no alteration in that. The only reason why ''a female'' was permitted in the peace-offering, was because it was a question of the worshiper's capacity to enjoy that

blessed One, who, in Himself, is "the same yesterday, to-day, and forever." (Heb. xiii.)

Again, in the burnt-offering, we read, "The priest
shall burn *all;*" whereas in the peace-offering, *a
part* only was burnt, that is, "the fat, the kidneys,
and the caul." This makes it exceedingly simple.
The most excellent portion of the sacrifice was laid
on God's altar. The inward parts—the hidden
energies—the tender sensibilities of the blessed
Jesus, were devoted to God, as the only One who
could perfectly enjoy them. Aaron and his sons
fed upon "the wave breast" and "the heave shoulder." * (See, carefully, Lev. vii. 28–36.) All the
members of the priestly family, in communion with
their head, had their proper portion of the peace-
offering; and now, all true believers constituted, by
grace, priests unto God, can feed upon the *affections*
and the *strength* of the true Peace-offering,—can
enjoy the happy assurance of having His loving
heart and powerful shoulder to comfort and sustain
them continually.† "This is the portion of the
anointing of Aaron, and of the anointing of his
sons, out of the offerings of the Lord made by fire,
in the day when he presented them to minister unto
the Lord in the priest's office; which the Lord commanded to be given them of the children of Israel,

---

*The "breast" and the "shoulder" are emblematical of love
and power—strength and affection.

† There is much force and beauty in verse 31—"The breast shall
be Aaron's and his sons'." It is the privilege of all true believers
to feed upon the affections of Christ—the changeless love of that
heart which beats with a deathless and changeless love for them.

in the day that He anointed them by a statute forever throughout their generations.'' (Chap. vii. 35, 36.)

All these are important points of difference between the burnt-offering and the peace-offering, and when taken together, they set the two offerings with great clearness before the mind. There is something more in the peace-offering than the abstract devotedness of Christ to the will of God. The worshiper is introduced; and that not merely as a spectator, but as a participator—not merely to gaze, but to feed. This gives very marked character to this offering. When I look at the Lord Jesus in the burnt-offering, I see Him as One whose heart was devoted to the one object of glorifying God and accomplishing His will; but when I see Him in the peace-offering, I find One who has a place in His loving heart and on His powerful shoulder for a worthless, helpless sinner. In the burnt-offering, the breast and shoulder, legs and inwards, head and fat, were all burnt on the altar—all went up as a sweet savor to God; but in the peace-offering, the very portion that suits me is left for me. Nor am I left to feed in solitude on that which meets my individual need. By no means. I feed in communion—in communion with God, and in communion with my fellow-priests. I feed in the full and happy intelligence that the self-same sacrifice which feeds my soul has already refreshed the heart of God; and, moreover, that the same portion which feeds me feeds all my fellow-worshipers. Communion is the order here,—communion with God—the communion of saints. There was no such thing as isolation in the peace-offering. God had His portion, and so had the priestly family.

Thus it is in connection with the Antitype of the peace-offering. The very same Jesus who is the object of Heaven's delight, is the spring of joy, of strength, and of comfort to every believing heart; and not only to every heart in particular, but also to the whole church of God in fellowship. God, in His exceeding grace, has given His people the very same object that He has Himself. "Truly our fellowship is with the Father, and with His Son Jesus Christ." (1 John i.) True, our thoughts of Jesus can never rise to the height of God's thoughts. Our estimation of such an object must ever fall far short of His; and hence, in the type, the house of Aaron could not partake of the fat. But though we can never rise to the standard of the divine estimation of Christ's Person and sacrifice, it is nevertheless the same object we are occupied with, and therefore the house of Aaron had "the wave breast and the heave shoulder." All this is replete with comfort and joy to the heart. The Lord Jesus Christ, the One "who was dead, but is alive for evermore," is now the exclusive object before the eye and thoughts of God; and, in perfect grace, He has given unto us a portion in the same blessed and all-glorious Person. Christ is our object too— the object of our hearts and the theme of our song. "Having made peace by the blood of His cross," He ascended into heaven, and sent down the Holy

Ghost, that "other Comforter," by whose powerful
ministrations we feed upon "the breast and shoulder" of our divine "Peace-offering." He is indeed
our peace ; and it is our exceeding joy to know that
such is God's delight in the establishment of our
peace, that the sweet odor of our Peace-offering has
refreshed His heart. This imparts a peculiar charm
to this type. Christ as the Burnt-offering commands
the admiration of the heart; Christ as the Peace-
offering establishes the peace of the conscience, and
meets the deep and manifold necessities of the soul.
The sons of Aaron might stand around the altar of
burnt-offering ; they might behold the flame of that
offering ascending to the God of Israel ; they might
see the sacrifice reduced to ashes ; they might, in
view of all this, bow their heads and worship ; but
they carried naught away for themselves. Not so
in the peace-offering. In it, they not only beheld
that which was capable of emitting a sweet odor to
God, but also of yielding a most substantial portion
for themselves, on which they could feed in happy
and holy fellowship.

And, assuredly, it heightens the enjoyment of
every true priest to know that God (to use the
language of our type) has had His portion ere he
gets the breast and the shoulder. The thought of
this gives tone and energy, unction and elevation, to
the worship and communion ; it unfolds the amazing
grace of Him who has given us the same object, the
same theme, the same joy with Himself. Nothing
lower—nothing less than this could satisfy Him.

The Father will have the prodigal feeding upon the fatted calf, in fellowship with Himself. He will not assign him a lower place than at His own table, nor any other portion than that on which He feeds Himself. The language of the peace-offering is, "It is meet that *we* should make merry and be glad,"— "Let *us* eat and be merry." Such is the precious grace of God! No doubt we have reason to be glad, as being the partakers of such grace; but when we can hear the blessed God saying, "Let *us* eat and be merry," it should call forth from our hearts a continual stream of praise and thanksgiving. God's joy in the salvation of sinners, and His joy in the communion of saints, may well elicit the admiration of men and angels throughout eternity.

Having thus compared the peace-offering with the burnt-offering, we may now briefly glance at it in connection with the meat-offering. The leading point of difference here is, that in the peace-offering there was blood-shedding, and in the meat-offering there was not. They were both "sweet savor" offerings; and, as we learn from chap. vii. 12, the two offerings were very intimately associated. Now, both the connection and the contrast are full of meaning and instruction.

It is only in communion with God that the soul can delight itself in contemplating the perfect humanity of the Lord Jesus Christ. God the Holy Ghost must *impart*, as He must also *direct*, by the Word, the vision by which we can gaze on "the Man Christ Jesus." He might have been revealed

"in the likeness of sinful flesh,"—He might have
lived and labored on this earth,—He might have
shone amid the darkness of this world in all the
heavenly lustre and beauty which belonged to His
Person, — He might have passed rapidly, like a
brilliant luminary, across this world's horizon,—
and all the while have been beyond the range of
the sinner's vision.

Man could not enter into the deep joy of communion with all this, simply because there would be
no basis laid down on which this communion might
rest.   In the peace-offering, this necessary basis is
fully and clearly established.—"He shall lay his
hand upon the head of his offering, and kill it at
the door of the tabernacle of the congregation: and
Aaron's sons, the priests, shall sprinkle the blood
upon the altar round about." (Chap. iii. 2.)   Here,
we have that which the meat-offering does not supply, namely, a solid foundation for the worshiper's
communion with all the fullness, the preciousness,
and the beauty of Christ, so far as he, by the gracious energy of the Holy Ghost, is enabled to enter
thereinto.   Standing on the platform which "the
precious blood of Christ" provides, we can range,
with tranquilized hearts and worshiping spirits,
throughout all the wondrous scenes of the manhood
of the Lord Jesus Christ.   Had we naught save the
meat-offering aspect of Christ, we should lack the
title by which, and the ground on which, we can
contemplate and enjoy Him therein.   If there were
no blood-shedding, there could be no title—no

standing-place for the sinner. But Leviticus vii. 12 links the meat-offering with the peace-offering, and, by so doing, teaches us, that, when our souls have found peace, we can delight in the One who has "made peace," and who is "our peace."

But let it be distinctly understood that while in the peace-offering we have the shedding and sprinkling of blood, yet sin-bearing is not the thought. When we view Christ in the peace-offering, He does not stand before us as the bearer of our sins, as in the sin and trespass offerings, but (having borne them) as the ground of our peaceful and happy fellowship with God. If sin-bearing were in question, it could not be said, "It is an offering made by fire, of a sweet savor unto the Lord." (Chap. iii. 5, comp. with chap. iv. 10–12.) Still, though sin-bearing is not the thought, there is full provision for one who knows himself to be a sinner, else he could not have any portion therein. To have fellowship with God, we must be "in the light;" and how can we be there? Only on the ground of that precious statement—"The blood of Jesus Christ His Son cleanseth us from *all* sin." (1 John i.) The more we abide in the light, the deeper will be our sense of every thing which is contrary to that light; and the deeper, also, our sense of the value of that blood which entitles us to be there. The more closely we walk with God, the more we shall know of "the unsearchable riches of Christ."

It is most needful to be established in the truth that we are in the presence of God only as the partakers of divine life, and as standing in divine righteousness. The father could only have the prodigal at his table clothed in "the best robe," and in all the integrity of that relationship in which he viewed him. Had the prodigal been left in his rags, or placed "as a hired servant" in the house, we never should have heard those glorious words, "Let us eat and be merry: for this *my son* was dead, and is alive again; he was lost, and is found." Thus it is with all true believers. Their old nature is not recognized as existing before God. He counts it dead, and so should they. It is dead to God, dead to faith. It must be kept in the place of death. It is not by improving our old nature that we get into the divine presence, but as the possessors of a new nature. It was not by repairing the rags of his former condition that the prodigal got a place at the father's table, but by being clothed in a robe which he had never seen or thought of before. He did not bring this robe with him from the "far country," neither did he provide it as he came along; but the father had it for him in the house. The prodigal did not make it, or help to make it; but the father provided it for him, and rejoiced to see it on him. Thus it was they sat down together, to feed in happy fellowship upon "the fatted calf."

I shall now preceed to quote at length "the law of the sacrifice of peace-offering," in which we shall find some additional points of much interest—points which belong peculiarly to itself.—"And this is the law of the sacrifice of peace-offerings, which he shall offer unto the Lord: If he offer it for a thanksgiving, then he shall offer with the sacrifice of thanksgiving unleavened cakes mingled with oil, and unleavened wafers anointed with oil, and cakes mingled with oil, of fine flour, fried. Besides the cakes, he shall offer for his offering leavened bread with the sacrifice of thanksgiving of his peace-offerings. And of it he shall offer one out of the whole oblation for a heave-offering unto the Lord, and it shall be the priest's that sprinkleth the blood of the peace-offerings. And the flesh of the sacrifice of his peace-offerings for thanksgiving shall be eaten the same day that it is offered; he shall not leave any of it until the morning. But if the sacrifice of his offering be a vow, or a voluntary offering, it shall be eaten the same day that he offereth his sacrifice; and on the morrow also the remainder of it shall be eaten; but the remainder of the flesh of the sacrifice on the third day shall be burnt with fire. And if any of the flesh of the sacrifice of his peace-offerings be eaten at all on the third day, it shall not be accepted, neither shall it be imputed unto him that offereth it: it shall be an abomination, and the soul that eateth of it shall bear his iniquity. And the flesh that toucheth any unclean thing shall not be eaten; it shall be burnt with fire: and as for the flesh, all that be clean shall eat thereof. But the soul that eateth of the flesh of the sacrifice of peace-offerings, that pertain unto the Lord, having his uncleanness upon him, even that soul shall be cut off from his people. Moreover the soul that shall touch any unclean thing, as the uncleanness of man, or any unclean beast, or any abominable unclean thing, and eat of the flesh of the sacrifice of peace-offerings, which pertain unto the Lord, even that soul shall be cut off from his people." (Lev. vii. 11–21.)

It is of the utmost importance that we accurately distinguish between sin *in the flesh* and sin *on the conscience.* If we confound these two, our souls must necessarily be unhinged, and our worship marred. An attentive consideration of 1 John i. 8–10 will throw much light upon this subject, the understanding of which is so essential to a due appreciation of the entire doctrine of the peace-offering, and more especially of that point therein at which we have now arrived. There is no one who will be so conscious of indwelling sin as the man who walks in the light. "If we say that we have *no sin*, we deceive ourselves, and the truth is not in us." In the verse immediately preceding, we read, "The blood of Jesus Christ His Son cleanseth us from *all sin.*" Here, the distinction between sin *in* us and sin *on* us is fully brought out and established. To say that there is sin on the believer, in the presence of God, is to call in question the purging efficacy of the blood of Jesus, and to deny the truth of the divine record. If the blood of Jesus can perfectly purge, then the believer's conscience is perfectly purged. The Word of God thus puts the matter; and we must ever remember that it is from God Himself we are to learn what the true condition of the believer is in His sight. We are more disposed to be occupied in telling God what we are in ourselves, than to allow Him to tell us what we are in Christ. In other words, we are more taken up with our own self-consciousness than with God's revelation of Himself. God speaks to us on the ground of what He is in Himself, and of what He has accomplished in Christ. Such is the nature and character of His revelation, of which faith takes hold, and thus fills the soul with perfect peace. God's revelation is one thing; my consciousness is quite another.

But the same Word which tells us we have no sin *on* us, tells us, with equal force and clearness, that we have sin *in* us. "If we say that we have no sin, we deceive ourselves, and the truth is not in us." Every one who has "truth" in him, will know that he has "*sin*" in him likewise; for truth reveals every thing as it is. What, then, are we to do? It is our privilege so to walk in the power of the new nature, that the "*sin*" which dwells in us may not manifest itself in the form of "*sins.*" The Christian's position is one of victory and liberty. He is not only delivered from the guilt of sin, but also from sin as a ruling principle in his life. "Knowing this, that our old man is crucified with Him, that the body of sin might be destroyed, that henceforth we should not serve sin. For he that is dead is freed from sin. . . . . Let not sin therefore *reign* in your mortal body, that ye should *obey it* in the lusts thereof. . . . . . For sin shall not have dominion over you; for ye are not under the law,

but under grace.'' (Rom. vi. 6–14.)   Sin is there
in all its native vileness; but the believer is "dead
to it.''   How?   He died in Christ.   By nature,
he was dead *in* sin: by grace, he is dead *to* it.
What claim can any thing or any one have upon a
dead man?   None whatever.   Christ "died unto
sin once,'' and the believer died in Him.   "Now
if we be dead with Christ, we believe that we shall
also live with Him: knowing that Christ being raised
from the dead dieth no more; death hath no more
dominion over Him.   For in that He died, He died
unto sin once; but in that He liveth, He liveth unto
God.''   What is the result of this in reference to
believers?   "*Likewise* reckon ye also yourselves to
be *dead indeed unto sin*, but alive unto God through
Jesus Christ our Lord.''   Such is the believer's
unalterable position before God! so that it is his
holy privilege to enjoy freedom from sin as a *ruler*
over him, though it be a *dweller* in him.

But then, "if any man sin,'' what is to be done?
The inspired apostle furnishes a full and most blessed
answer,—"If we confess our sins, He is faithful and
just to forgive us our sins, and to cleanse us from
all unrighteousness.'' (1 John i. 9.)   Confession is
the mode in which the conscience is to be kept free.
The apostle does not say, If we pray for pardon,
He is gracious and merciful to forgive us.   No doubt
it is ever happy for a child to breathe the sense of
need into his father's ear—to tell him of feebleness,
to confess folly, infirmity, and failure.   All this is
most true; and, moreover, it is equally true that

our Father is most gracious and merciful to meet His children in all their weakness and ignorance; but, while all this is true, the Holy Ghost declares, by the apostle, that "if we *confess*," God is "*faithful* and *just* to forgive." Confession, therefore, is the divine mode. A Christian, having erred, in thought, word, or deed, might pray for pardon for days and months together, and not have any assurance, from 1 John i. 9, that he was forgiven; whereas the moment he truly confesses his sin before God, it is a simple matter of faith to know that he is perfectly forgiven and perfectly cleansed.

There is an immense moral difference between praying for forgiveness and confessing our sins, whether we look at it in reference to the character of God, the sacrifice of Christ, or the condition of the soul. It is quite possible that a person's prayer may involve the confession of his sin, whatever it may happen to be, and thus come to the same thing; but then it is always well to keep close to Scripture in what we think and say and do. It must be evident that when the Holy Ghost speaks of *confession*, He does not mean *praying;* and it is equally evident that He knows there are moral elements in, and practical results flowing out of, confession, which do not belong to prayer. In point of fact, one has often found that a habit of importuning God for the forgiveness of sins displayed ignorance as to the way in which God has revealed Himself in the Person and work of Christ, as to the relation in which the sacrifice of Christ has set the believer, and as to

the divine mode of getting the conscience relieved
from the burden and purified from the soil of sin.

God has been perfectly satisfied as to all the believer's sins in the cross of Christ. On that cross,
a full atonement was presented for every jot and
tittle of sin in the believer's nature and on his
conscience. Hence, therefore, God does not need
any further propitiation. He does not need aught
to draw His heart toward the believer. We do not
require to supplicate Him to be "faithful and just,"
when His faithfulness and justice have been so gloriously displayed, vindicated, and answered in the
death of Christ. Our sins can never come into
God's presence, inasmuch as Christ, who bore them
all and put them away, is there instead. But if we
sin, conscience will feel it—must feel it,—yea, the
Holy Ghost will make us feel it. He cannot allow
so much as a single light thought to pass unjudged.
What then? Has our sin made its way into the
presence of God? Has it found its place in the
unsullied light of the inner sanctuary? God forbid! The "Advocate" is there—"Jesus Christ the
righteous," to maintain, in unbroken integrity, the
relationship in which we stand. But though sin
cannot affect God's thoughts in reference to us, it
can and does affect our thoughts in reference to
Him;* though it cannot make its way into His

---

*The reader will bear in mind that the subject treated of in the
text leaves wholly untouched the important and most practical
truth taught in John xiv. 21-23, namely, the peculiar love of the
Father for an obedient child, and the special communion of such
a child with the Father and the Son. May this truth be written on
all our hearts, by the pen of God the Holy Ghost!

presence, it can make its way into ours, in a most distressing and humiliating manner; though it cannot hide the Advocate from God's view, it can hide Him from ours. It gathers, like a thick, dark cloud, on our spiritual horizon, so that our souls cannot bask in the blessed beams of our Father's countenance. It cannot affect our relationship with God, but it can very seriously affect our enjoyment thereof. What, therefore, are we to do? The Word answers, "If we confess our sins, He is faithful and just to forgive us our sins, and to cleanse us from all unrighteousness." By confession, we get our conscience cleared, the sweet sense of relationship restored, the dark cloud dispersed, the chilling, withering influence removed, our thoughts of God set straight. Such is the divine method; and we may truly say that the heart that knows what it is to have ever been in the place of confession, will feel the divine power of the apostle's words—"My little children, these things write I unto you, THAT YE SIN NOT." (1 John ii. 1.)

Then, again, there is a style of praying for forgiveness which involves a losing sight of the perfect ground of forgiveness which has been laid in the sacrifice of the cross. If God forgives sins, He must be "faithful and just" in so doing; but it is quite clear that our prayers, be they ever so sincere and earnest, could not form the basis of God's faithfulness and justice in forgiving us our sins. Naught save the work of the cross could do this. There, the faithfulness and justice of God have had their fullest establishment, and that, too, in immediate reference to our actual sins, as well as to the root thereof in our nature. God has already judged our sins in the Person of our Substitute "on the tree;" and, in the act of confession, we judge ourselves. This is essential to divine forgiveness and restoration. The very smallest unconfessed, unjudged sin on the conscience will entirely mar our communion with God. Sin *in* us need not do this; but if we suffer sin to remain *on* us, we cannot have fellowship with God. He has put away our sins in such a manner as that He can have us in His presence; and so long as we abide in His presence, sin does not trouble us; but if we get out of His presence, and commit sin, even in thought, our communion must, of necessity, be suspended, until, by confession, we have got rid of the sin. All this, I need hardly add, is founded exclusively upon the perfect sacrifice and righteous advocacy of the Lord Jesus Christ.

Finally, as to the difference between prayer and confession, as respects the condition of the heart before God, and its moral sense of the hatefulness of sin, it cannot possibly be over-estimated. It is a much easier thing to ask, in a general way, for the forgiveness of our sins than to confess those sins. Confession involves *self-judgment;* asking for forgiveness may not, and, in itself, does not. This alone would be sufficient to point out the difference. Self-judgment is one of the most valuable and healthful exercises of the Christian life, and therefore any thing which produces it must be highly esteemed by every earnest Christian.

The difference between asking for pardon and confessing the sin is continually exemplified in dealing with children. If a child has done any thing wrong, he finds much less difficulty in asking his father to forgive him than in openly and unreservedly confessing the wrong. In asking for forgiveness, the child may have in his mind a number of things which tend to lessen the sense of the evil, —he may be secretly thinking that he was not so much to blame after all, though, to be sure, it is only proper to ask his father to forgive him; whereas, in confessing the wrong, there is just the one thing, and that is, self-judgment. Further, in asking for forgiveness, the child may be influenced mainly by a desire to escape the consequences of his wrong; whereas, a judicious parent will seek to produce a just sense of its moral evil, which can only exist in connection with the full confession of the fault—in connection with self-judgment.

Thus it is, in reference to God's dealings with His children when they do wrong. He must have the whole thing brought out and thoroughly judged. He will make us not only dread the consequences of sin (which are unutterable), but hate the thing itself, because of its hatefulness in His sight. Were it possible for us, when we commit sin, to be forgiven merely for the asking, our sense of sin and our shrinking from it would not be nearly so intense, and, as a consequence, our estimate of the fellowship with which we are blessed would not be nearly so high. The moral effect of all this upon the general tone of our spiritual constitution, and also upon our whole character and practical career, must be obvious to every experienced Christian.*

This entire train of thought is intimately connected with, and fully borne out by, two leading principles laid down in "the law of the peace-offering."

In verse 13 of the seventh of Leviticus we read, "He shall offer for his offering *leavened* bread;" and yet at verse 20 we read, "But the soul that eateth of the flesh of the sacrifice of peace-offerings, that pertain unto the Lord, having his uncleanness *upon* him, even that soul shall be cut off from his people." Here, we have the two things clearly set before us, namely, sin *in* us and sin *on* us. "Leaven" was permitted, because there was sin in the worshiper's nature: "uncleanness" was forbidden, because there should be no sin on the worshiper's conscience. If sin be in question, communion must be out of the question. God has

---

*The case of Simon Magus, in Acts viii, may present a difficulty to the reader. But of him, it is sufficient to say that one "in the gall of bitterness and in the bond of iniquity" could never be set forth as a model for God's dear children. His case in no wise interferes with the doctrine of 1 John i. 9. He was not in the relationship of a child, and, as a consequence, not a subject of the advocacy. I would further add, that the subject of the Lord's prayer is by no means involved in what is stated above. I wish to confine myself to the immediate passage under consideration. We must ever avoid laying down iron rules. A soul may cry to God under any circumstances, and ask for what it needs: He is ever ready to hear and answer.

met and provided for the sin, which He knows to be in us, by the blood of atonement; and hence, of the leavened bread in the peace-offering, we read, "Of it he shall offer one out of the whole oblation for a heave offering unto the Lord, and it shall be *the priest's that sprinkleth the blood of the peace-offerings.*" (Ver. 14.) In other words, the "leaven" in the worshiper's nature was perfectly met by the "blood" of the sacrifice. The priest who gets the leavened bread must be the sprinkler of the blood. God has put our sin out of His sight forever. Though it be in us, it is not the object on which His eye rests. He sees only the blood, and therefore He can go on with us, and allow us the most unhindered fellowship with Him. But if we allow the "*sin*" which is in us to develop itself in the shape of "*sins,*" there must be confession, forgiveness, and cleansing ere we can again eat of the flesh of the Peace-offering. The cutting off of the worshiper because of ceremonial uncleanness, answers to the suspension of the believer's communion now because of unconfessed sin. To attempt to have fellowship with God in our sins would involve the blasphemous insinuation that He could walk in companionship with sin. "If we say that we have fellowship with Him, and walk in darkness, we lie, and do not the truth." (1 John i. 6.)

In the light of the foregoing line of truth, we may easily see how much we err when we imagine it to be a mark of spirituality to be occupied with our sins. Could sin or sins ever be the ground or

material of our communion with God? Assuredly
not. We have just seen that, so long as sin is the
object before us, communion must be interrupted.
Fellowship can only be "in the light;" and, undoubtedly, there is no sin in the light. There is
naught to be seen there save the blood which has put
our sins away and brought us nigh, and the Advocate which keeps us nigh. Sin has been forever
obliterated from that platform on which God and
the worshiper stand in hallowed fellowship. What
was it which constituted the material of communion
between the father and the prodigal? Was it the
rags of the latter? Was it the husks of "the far
country"? By no means. It was not any thing that
the prodigal brought with him: it was the rich provision of the father's love—"the fatted calf." Thus
it is with God and every true worshiper. They feed
together, in holy and elevated communion, upon
Him whose precious blood has brought them into
everlasting association, in that light to which no
sin can ever approach.

Nor need we, for an instant, suppose that true
humility is either evidenced or promoted by looking
at or dwelling upon our sins. An unhallowed and
melancholy mopishness may thus be superinduced;
but the deepest humility springs from a totally different source. Whether was the prodigal a humbler
man "when he came to himself" in the far country,
or when he came to the father's bosom and the
father's house? Is it not evident that the grace
which elevates us to the loftiest heights of fellowship

with God is that alone which leads us into the most profound depths of a genuine humility? Unquestionably. The humility which springs from the removal of our sins must ever be deeper than that which springs from the discovery of them. The former connects us with God: the latter has to do with self. The way to be truly humble is to walk with God in the intelligence and power of the relationship in which He has set us. He has made us His children; and if only we walk as such, we shall be humble.

Ere leaving this part of our subject, I would offer a remark as to the Lord's Supper, which, as being a prominent act of the Church's communion, may, with strict propriety, be looked at in connection with the doctrine of the peace-offering. The intelligent celebration of the Lord's Supper must ever depend upon the recognition of its purely eucharistic or thanksgiving character. It is very especially a feast of thanksgiving—thanksgiving for an accomplished redemption. "The cup of blessing which we bless, is it not the communion of the blood of Christ? The bread which we break, is it not the communion of the body of Christ?" (1 Cor. x. 16.) Hence, a soul bowed down under the heavy burden of sin cannot, with spiritual intelligence, eat the Lord's Supper, inasmuch as that feast is expressive of the complete removal of sin by the death of Christ.—"Ye do show the Lord's death till He come." (1 Cor. xi.) In the death of Christ, faith sees the end of every thing that pertained to

our old-creation standing; and seeing that the
Lord's Supper "shows forth" that death, it is to
be viewed as the memento of the glorious fact that
the believer's burden of sin was borne by One who
put it away forever. It declares that the chain of
our sins, which once tied and bound us, has been
eternally snapped by the death of Christ, and can
never tie and bind us again. We gather round the
Lord's table in all the joy of conquerors. We look
back to the cross, where the battle was fought and
won; and we look forward to the glory, where we
shall enter into the full and eternal results of the
victory.

True, we have "leaven" *in* us; but we have no
"uncleanness" *on* us. We are not to gaze upon our
sins, but upon Him who bore them on the cross and
put them away forever. We are not to "deceive
ourselves" by the vain notion "that we have no
sin" in us; nor are we to deny the truth of God's
Word, and the efficacy of Christ's blood, by refusing
to rejoice in the precious truth that we have no
sin on us, for "the blood of Jesus Christ His Son
cleanseth us from all sin." It is truly deplorable
to observe the heavy cloud that gathers round the
Supper of the Lord, in the judgment of so many
professing Christians. It tends, as much as any
thing else, to reveal the immense amount of misapprehension which obtains in reference to the very
elementary truths of the gospel. In fact, we know
that when the Lord's Supper is resorted to on any
ground save that of known salvation—enjoyed for-

giveness—conscious deliverance, the soul becomes wrapped up in thicker and darker mists than ever. That which is only a memorial of Christ is used to displace Him,—that which celebrates an accomplished redemption is used as a stepping-stone thereto. It is thus that the ordinances are abused, and souls plunged in darkness, confusion, and error.

How different from this is the beautiful ordinance of the peace-offering! In this latter, looked at in its typical import, we see that the moment the blood was shed, God and the worshiper could feed in happy, peaceful fellowship. Nothing more was needed. Peace was established by the blood, and on that ground the communion proceeded. A single question as to the establishment of peace must be the death-blow to communion. If we are to be occupied with the vain attempt to make peace with God, we must be total strangers to either communion or worship. If the blood of the peace-offering has not been shed, it is impossible that we can feed upon "the wave breast" or "the heave shoulder." But if, on the other hand, the blood has been shed, then peace is made already. God Himself has made it, and this is enough for faith; and therefore, by faith, we have fellowship with God, in the intelligence and joy of accomplished redemption. We taste the freshness of God's own joy in that which He has wrought. We feed upon Christ in all the fullness and blessedness of God's presence.

This latter point is connected with and based upon another leading truth laid down in "the law of the

peace-offering."—"And the flesh of the sacrifice of
his peace-offerings for thanksgiving shall be eaten
the same day that it is offered: he shall not leave
any of it until the morning." That is to say, the
communion of the worshiper must never be separated from the sacrifice on which that communion is
founded. So long as one has spiritual energy to
maintain the connection, the worship and communion are also maintained, in freshness and acceptableness; but no longer. *We must keep close to the
Sacrifice*, in the spirit of our minds, the affections of
our hearts, and the experience of our souls. This
will impart power and permanency to our worship.
We may commence some act or expression of worship with our hearts in immediate occupation with
Christ, and ere we reach the close we may become
occupied with what we are doing or saying, or with
the persons who are listening to us, and, in this way,
fall into what may be termed "iniquity in our holy
things." This is deeply solemn, and should make
us very watchful. We may begin our worship in
the Spirit and end in the flesh. Our care should
ever be, not to suffer ourselves to proceed for a
single moment beyond the energy of the Spirit, at
the time; for the Spirit will always keep us occupied
directly with Christ. If the Holy Ghost produces
"five words" of worship or thanksgiving, let us
utter the five and have done. If we proceed further, we are eating the flesh of our sacrifice beyond
the time; and, so far from its being "accepted," it
is really "an abomination." Let us remember this,

and be watchful. It need not alarm us. God would have us led by the Spirit, and so filled with Christ in all our worship. He can only accept of that which is divine, and therefore He would have us presenting that only which is divine.

"But if the sacrifice of his offering be a vow or a voluntary-offering, it shall be eaten the same day that he offereth his sacrifice: and *on the morrow also the remainder of it shall be eaten.*" (Chap. vii. 16.) When the soul goes forth to God in a voluntary act of worship, such worship will be the result of a larger measure of spiritual energy than where it merely springs from some special mercy experienced at the time. If one had been visited with some marked favor from the Lord's own hand, the soul at once ascends in thanksgiving. In this case, the worship is awakened by and connected with that favor or mercy, whatever it may happen to be, and there it ends; but where the heart is led forth by the Holy Ghost in some voluntary or deliberate expression of praise, it will be of a more enduring character. But spiritual worship will always connect itself with the precious sacrifice of Christ.

"The remainder of the flesh of the sacrifice, on the third day, shall be burnt with fire. And if any of the flesh of the sacrifice of his peace-offerings be eaten at all on the third day, it shall not be accepted, neither shall it be imputed unto him that offereth it: it shall be an abomination, and the soul that eateth of it shall bear his iniquity." Nothing is of any value, in the judgment of God, which is not

immediately connected with Christ. There may be
a great deal of what looks like worship, which is,
after all, the mere excitement and outgoing of natural feeling; there may be much apparent devotion,
which is merely fleshly pietism. Nature may be
acted upon, in a religious way, by a variety of
things, such as pomp, ceremony, and parade, tones
and attitudes, robes and vestments, an eloquent lit-
urgy, all the varied attractions of a splendid ritual-
ism, while there may be a total absence of spiritual
worship. Yea, it not unfrequently happens that the
very same tastes and tendencies which are called
forth and gratified by the splendid appliances of
so-called religious worship, would find most suited
aliment at the opera or in the concert-room.

All this has to be watched against by those who
desire to remember that "God is a spirit, and they
that worship Him must worship Him in spirit and
in truth." (John iv.) Religion, so called, is, at
this moment, decking herself with her most powerful charms. Casting off the grossness of the middle
ages, she is calling to her aid all the resources of
refined taste, and of a cultivated and enlightened
age. Sculpture, music, and painting are pouring
their rich treasures into her lap, in order that she
may therewith prepare a powerful opiate to lull the
thoughtless multitude into a slumber, which shall
only be broken in upon by the unutterable horrors
of death, judgment, and the lake of fire. She, too,
can say, "I have *peace-offerings* with me; this day
have I paid my *vows.* . . . . I have decked my

bed with coverings of tapestry, with carved works, with fine linen of Egypt. I have perfumed my bed with myrrh, aloes, and cinnamon." (Prov. vii.) Thus does corrupt religion allure, by her powerful influence, those who will not hearken to Wisdom's heavenly voice.

Reader, beware of all this. See that your worship stands inseparably connected with the work of the cross. See that Christ is the ground, Christ the material, and the Holy Ghost the power of your worship. Take care that your outward act of worship does not stretch itself beyond the inward power. It demands much watchfulness to keep clear of this evil. Its incipient workings are most difficult to be detected and counteracted. We may commence a hymn in the true spirit of worship, and, through lack of spiritual power, we may, ere we reach the close, fall into the evil which answers to the ceremonial act of eating the flesh of the peace-offering on the third day. Our only security is in keeping close to Jesus. If we lift up our hearts in "thanksgiving" for some special mercy, let us do so in the power of the name and sacrifice of Christ. If our souls go forth in "voluntary" worship, let it be in the energy of the Holy Ghost. In this way shall our worship exhibit that freshness, that fragrance, that depth of tone, that moral elevation, which must result from having the Father as the object, the Son as the ground, and the Holy Ghost as the power of our worship.*

---

*The statement in the text affords no warrant for the idea that

Thus may it be, O Lord, with all Thy worshiping people, until we find ourselves—body, soul, and spirit—in the security of Thine own eternal presence, beyond the reach of all the unhallowed influences of false worship and corrupt religion, and also beyond the reach of the various hindrances which arise from these bodies of sin and death which we carry about with us!

Note.—It is interesting to observe that although the peace-offering itself stands third in order, yet "the law" thereof is given us last of all. This circumstance is not without its import. There is none of the offerings in which the communion of the worshiper is so fully unfolded as in the peace-offering. In the burnt-offering, it is Christ offering

---

our Lord Jesus Christ is not, equally with the Father, the object of worship. We utterly abhor and reject such a blasphemy.

Let the reader turn to John v. 23—"That all men should honor the Son, even as they honor the Father. He that honoreth not the Son honoreth not the Father which hath sent Him." How can any one, in the face of such a passage as this, attempt to teach that it is wrong to present worship to the Lord Jesus? Woe be to the man who so teaches! He is plainly at issue with God.

Again, look at Rev. v. 12—"Worthy is the Lamb that was slain to receive power, and riches, and wisdom, and strength, and honor, and glory, and blessing." What mean these words if our Lord Jesus Christ is not to be addressed in prayer or worship?

Was the martyr, Stephen, wrong when he said, "Lord Jesus, receive my spirit"? Was Paul mistaken when he besought the Lord to remove the thorn?

But it is needless to multiply passages: the teaching of the inspired volume, from cover to cover, establishes, beyond all question, the rightness of presenting prayer and worship to our Lord Jesus Christ; and therefore all who teach otherwise are in direct opposition to the Word of God.

Himself to God. In the meat-offering, we have Christ's perfect humanity. Then, passing on to the sin-offering, we learn that *sin*, in its root, is fully met. In the trespass-offering, there is a full answer to the actual *sins*, in the life. But in none is the doctrine of the communion of the worshiper unfolded. This latter belongs to "the peace-offering;" and hence, I believe, the position which the law of that offering occupies. It comes in at the close of all, thereby teaching us that, when it becomes a question of the soul's feeding upon Christ, it must be a full Christ,—looked at in every possible phase of His life, His character, His Person, His work, His offices; and, furthermore, that, when we shall have done forever with sin and sins, we shall delight in Christ, and feed upon Him, throughout the everlasting ages. It would, I believe, be a serious defect in our study of the offerings were we to pass over a circumstance so worthy of notice as the above. If "the law of the peace-offering" were given in the order in which the offering itself occurs, it would come in immediately after the law of the meat-offering; but instead of that, "the law of the sin-offering" and "the law of the trespass-offering" are given, and then "the law of the peace-offering" closes the entire.

HAVING considered the "sweet savor" offerings, we now approach the "sacrifices for sin." These were divided into two classes, namely, sin-offerings and trespass-offerings. Of the former, there were three grades; first, the offering for "the priest that is anointed," and for "the whole congregation." These two were the same in their rites and ceremonies. (Compare ver. 3–12 with ver. 13–21.) It was the same in result, whether it were the representative of the assembly or the assembly itself that sinned. In either case there were three things involved,—God's dwelling-place in the assembly, the worship of the assembly, and individual conscience. Now, inasmuch as all three depended upon the blood, we find, in the first grade of sin-offering, there were three things done with the blood. It was sprinkled "seven times before the Lord, *before the vail of the sanctuary.*" This secured Jehovah's relationship with the people, and His dwelling in their midst. Again, we read, "The priest shall put some of the blood upon the horns of the altar of sweet incense before the Lord, which is in the tabernacle of the congregation." This secured the worship of the assembly. By putting the blood upon "the golden altar," the true basis of worship was preserved; so that the flame of the incense and the fragrance thereof might continually ascend. Finally, "He shall pour all the blood of the bullock at the bottom of the altar of the burnt-offering, which is at the door of the tabernacle of the congregation." Here, we have the claims of individual conscience fully answered; for the brazen altar was the place of individual approach,—it was the place where God met the sinner.

In the two remaining grades—for "a ruler" or "one of the common people," it was merely a question of individual conscience, and therefore there was only one thing done with the blood,—it was all poured "at the bottom of the altar of burnt-offering." (Comp. ver. 7 with ver. 25, 30.) There is divine precision in all this, which demands the close attention of my reader, if only he desires to enter into the marvelous detail of this type.*

---

*There is this difference between the offering for "a ruler" and for "one of the common people:" in the former, it was "a *male* without blemish;" in the latter, "a *female* without blemish." The sin of a ruler would necessarily exert a wider influence than that of a common person, and therefore a more powerful application of the value of the blood was needed. In chapter v. 13, we find cases demanding a still lower application of the sin-offering—cases of swearing, and of touching any uncleanness, in which "the tenth part of an ephah of fine flour" was admitted as a sin-offering. (See chap. v. 11-13.) What a contrast between the view of atonement presented by a ruler's bullock and a poor man's handful of flour! And yet, in the latter, just as truly as in the former, we read, "It shall be forgiven him."

The reader will observe that chapter v. 1-13 forms a part of chapter iv. Both are comprehended under one head, and present the doctrine of the sin-offering in all its applications, from the bullock to the handful of flour. Each class of offering is introduced by the words, "And the Lord spake unto Moses." Thus, for example, the sweet savor offerings (chap. i.-iii.) are introduced by the words, "The Lord called unto Moses." These words are not repeated until chapter iv. 1, where they introduce the sin-offering. They occur again at chapter v. 14, where they introduce the trespass-offering for wrongs done "in the holy things of the

The effect of individual sin could not extend beyond individual conscience. The sin of "a ruler," or of "one of the common people," could not, in its influence, reach "the altar of incense" —the place of priestly worship; neither could it reach to "the vail of the sanctuary"—the sacred boundary of God's dwelling-place in the midst of His people. It is well to ponder this. We must never raise a question of personal sin or failure in the place of priestly worship or in the assembly; it must be settled in the place of personal approach. Many err as to this. They come into the assembly, or into the ostensible place of priestly worship, with their conscience defiled, and thus drag down the whole assembly and mar its worship. This should be closely looked into, and carefully guarded against. We need to walk more watchfully, in order that our conscience may ever be in the light. And when we fail, (as, alas! we do in many things,) let us have to do with God in secret about our failure, in order that true worship and the true position of the assembly may always be kept with fullness and clearness before the soul.

Having said thus much as to the three grades of sin-offering, we shall proceed to examine, in detail, the principles unfolded in the first of these. In so

Lord;" and again at chapter vi. 1, where they introduce the trespass-offering for wrongs done to one's neighbor.

This classification is beautifully simple, and will help the reader to understand the different classes of offering. As to the different grades in each class, whether "a bullock," "a ram," "a female," "a bird," or "a handful of flour," they would seem to be so many varied applications of the same grand truth.

doing, we shall be able to form, in some measure, a just conception of the principles of all. Before, however, entering upon the direct comparison already proposed, I would call my reader's attention to a very prominent point set forth in the second verse of this fourth chapter; it is contained in the expression, "If a soul shall sin through *ignorance*." This presents a truth of the deepest blessedness, in connection with the atonement of the Lord Jesus Christ. In contemplating that atonement, we see infinitely more than the mere satisfaction of the claims of conscience, even though that conscience had reached the highest point of refined sensibility. It is our privilege to see therein that which has fully satisfied all the claims of divine holiness, divine justice, and divine majesty. The holiness of God's dwelling-place, and the ground of His association with His people, could never be regulated by the standard of man's conscience, no matter how high the standard might be. There are many things which man's conscience would pass over—many things which might escape man's cognizance—many things which his heart might deem all right, which God could not tolerate; and which, as a consequence, would interfere with man's approach to, his worship of, and his relationship with God. Wherefore, if the atonement of Christ merely made provision for such sins as come within the compass of man's apprehension, we should find ourselves very far short of the true ground of peace. We need to understand that sin has been atoned for, according to God's measurement there-of—that the claims of His throne have been per-fectly answered—that sin, as seen in the light of His inflexible holiness, has been divinely judged. This is what gives settled peace to the soul. A full atonement has been made for the believer's sins of ignorance, as well as for his known sins. The sac-rifice of Christ lays the foundation of his relation-ship and fellowship with God, according to the divine estimate of the claims thereof.

A clear sense of this is of unspeakable value. Unless this feature of the atonement be laid hold of, there cannot be settled peace; nor will there be any just moral sense of the extent and fullness of the work of Christ, or of the true nature of the relationship founded thereon. God knew what was needed in order that man might be in His presence without a single misgiving, and He has made ample provision for it in the cross. Fellowship between God and man were utterly impossible if sin had not been disposed of according to God's thoughts about it; for, albeit man's conscience were satisfied, the question would ever be suggesting itself, Has God been satisfied? If this question could not be answered in the affirmative, fellowship could never subsist.* The thought would be continually intrud-

*I would desire it to be particularly remembered that the point before us in the text is simply atonement. The Christian reader is fully aware, I doubt not, that the possession of "the divine nature" is essential to fellowship with God. I not only need a *title* to ap-proach God, but a *nature* to enjoy Him. The soul that "believes in the name of the only begotten Son of God" has both the one and the other. (See John i. 12, 13; iii. 36; v. 24; xx. 31; 1 John v. 11-13.)

ing itself upon the heart, that things were manifesting themselves in the details of life which divine
holiness could not tolerate. True, we might be
doing such things "through ignorance," but this
could not alter the matter before God, inasmuch as
all is known to Him. Hence, there would be continual apprehension, doubt, and misgiving. All
these things are divinely met by the fact that sin
has been atoned for, not according to our "ignorance," but according to God's knowledge. The
assurance of this gives great rest to the heart and
conscience. All God's claims have been answered
by His own work. He Himself has made the provision; and therefore the more refined the believer's
conscience becomes, under the combined action of
the Word and Spirit of God—the more he grows in
a divinely-adjusted sense of all that morally befits
the sanctuary—the more keenly alive he becomes
to every thing which is unsuited to the divine presence, the fuller, clearer, deeper, and more vigorous
will be his apprehension of the infinite value of that
Sin-offering which has not only traveled beyond the
utmost bounds of human conscience, but also met,
in absolute perfection, all the requirements of divine
holiness.

Nothing can more forcibly express man's incompetency to deal with sin than the fact of there being
such a thing as a "sin of ignorance." How could
he deal with that which he knows not? How could
he dispose of that which has never even come within the range of his conscience? Impossible. Man's

ignorance of sin proves his total inability to put it away. If he does not know of it, what can he do about it? Nothing. He is as powerless as he is ignorant. Nor is this all. The fact of a "sin of ignorance" demonstrates most clearly the uncertainty which must attend upon every settlement of the question of sin, in which no higher claims have been responded to than those put forth by the most refined human conscience. There can never be settled peace upon this ground. There will always be the painful apprehension that there is something wrong underneath. If the heart be not led into settled repose by the Scripture testimony that the inflexible claims of divine Justice have been answered, there must, of necessity, be a sensation of uneasiness, and every such sensation presents a barrier to our worship, our communion, and our testimony. If I am uneasy in reference to the settlement of the question of sin, I cannot worship, I cannot enjoy communion either with God or His people, nor can I be an intelligent or effective witness for Christ. The heart must be at rest before God as to the perfect remission of sin ere we can "worship Him in spirit and in truth." If there be guilt on the conscience, there must be terror in the heart; and, assuredly, a heart filled with terror cannot be a happy or a worshiping heart. It is only from a heart filled with that sweet and sacred repose which the blood of Christ imparts, that true and acceptable worship can ascend to the Father. The same principle holds good with respect to our fellowship with the people of God and our service and testimony amongst men,—all must rest upon the foundation of settled peace, and this peace rests upon the foundation of a perfectly purged conscience, and this purged conscience rests upon the foundation of the perfect remission of all our sins, whether they be sins of knowledge or sins of ignorance.

We shall now proceed to compare the sin-offering with the burnt-offering, in doing which we shall find two very different aspects of Christ. But although the aspects are different, it is one and the same Christ; and hence the sacrifice in each case was "without blemish." This is easily understood. It matters not in what aspect we contemplate the Lord Jesus Christ, He must ever be seen as the same pure, spotless, holy, perfect One. True, He did, in His abounding grace, stoop to be the Sin-bearer of His people; but it was a perfect, spotless Christ who did so; and it would be nothing short of diabolical wickedness to take occasion from the depth of His humiliation to tarnish the personal glory of the humbled One. The intrinsic excellence, the unsullied purity, and the divine glory of our blessed Lord appear in the sin-offering as fully as in the burnt-offering. It matters not in what relationship He stands, what office He fills, what work He performs, what position He occupies, His personal glories shine out in all their divine effulgence.

This truth of one and the same Christ, whether in the burnt-offering or in the sin-offering, is seen not only in the fact that in each case the offering was "without blemish," but also in "the law of the sin-offering," where we read, "This is the law of the sin-offering: In the place where the burnt-offering is killed shall the sin-offering be killed before the Lord: it is most holy." (Lev. vi. 25.) Both types point to one and the same great Antitype, though they present Him in such contrasted aspects of His work. In the burnt-offering, Christ is seen meeting the divine affections; in the sin-offering, He is seen meeting the depths of human need. That presents Him to us as the Accomplisher of the will of God; this, as the Bearer of the sin of man. In the former, we are taught the preciousness of the Sacrifice; in the latter, the hatefulness of sin. Thus much as to the two offerings, in the main. The most minute examination of the details will only tend to establish the mind in the truth of this general statement.

In the first place, when considering the burnt-offering, we observed that it was a voluntary offering.—"He shall offer it of his own voluntary will." * Now, the word "voluntary" does not occur in the sin-offering. This is precisely what we might expect. It is in full keeping with the specific object of the Holy Ghost, in the burnt-offering, to set it forth as

---

* Some may find difficulty in the fact that the word "voluntary" has reference to the worshiper and not to the sacrifice; but this can in no wise affect the doctrine put forward in the text, which is founded upon the fact that a special word used in the burnt-offering is omitted in the sin-offering. The contrast holds good whether we think of the offerer or the offering.

a free-will offering. It was Christ's meat and drink
to do the will of God, whatever that will might be.
He never thought of inquiring what ingredients
were in the cup which the Father was putting into
His hand. It was quite sufficient for Him that the
Father had mingled it. Thus it was with the Lord
Jesus as foreshadowed by the burnt-offering. But
in the sin-offering, we have quite a different line of
truth unfolded. This type introduces Christ to our
thoughts, not as the "voluntary" Accomplisher of
the will of God, but as the Bearer of that terrible
thing called "sin," and the Endurer of all its appalling consequences, of which the most appalling
to Him was the hiding of God's countenance.
Hence, the word "voluntary" would not harmonize
with the object of the Spirit in the sin-offering.
It would be as completely out of place in that type
as it is divinely in place in the burnt-offering. Its
presence and its absence are alike divine; and both
alike exhibit the perfect, the divine precision of the
types of Leviticus.

Now, the point of contrast which we have been
considering, explains, or rather harmonizes, two
expressions used by our Lord. He says, on one
occasion, "The cup which My Father hath given
Me, shall I not drink it?" And again, "Father,
if it be possible, let this cup pass from Me." The
former of these expressions was the full carrying
out of the words with which He entered upon His
course, namely, "Lo, I come to do Thy will, O
God;" and, moreover, it is the utterance of Christ

as the Burnt-offering. The latter, on the other
hand, is the utterance of Christ when contemplating the place which He was about to occupy as
the Sin-offering. What that place was, and what
was involved to Him in taking it, we shall see as we
proceed ; but it is interesting and instructive to find
the entire doctrine of the two offerings involved, as
it were, in the fact that a single word introduced in
the one is omitted in the other. If in the burnt-
offering we find the perfect readiness of heart with
which Christ offered Himself for the accomplishment
of the will of God, then in the sin-offering we find
how perfectly He entered into all the consequences
of man's sin, and how He traveled into the most
remote distance of man's position as regards God.
He delighted to do the will of God ; He shrank from
losing, for a moment, the light of His blessed countenance. No one offering could have foreshadowed
Him in both these phases. We needed a type to
present Him to us as One delighting to do the will
of God, and we needed a type to present Him to us
as One whose holy nature shrank from the consequences of imputed sin. Blessed be God, we have
both. The burnt-offering furnishes the one ; the
sin-offering, the other. Wherefore, the more fully
we enter into the devotion of Christ's heart to God,
the more fully we shall apprehend His abhorrence
of sin ; and *vice versa*. Each throws the other into
relief; and the use of the word "voluntary" in the
one and not in the other, fixes the leading import
of each.

But it may be said, Was it not the will of God that Christ should offer Himself as an atonement for sin? and if so, how could there be aught of shrinking from the accomplishment of that will? Assuredly, it was "the determinate counsel" of God that Christ should suffer, and, moreover, it was Christ's joy to do the will of God; but how are we to understand the expression, "If it be possible, let this cup pass from Me"? Is it not the utterance of Christ? And is there no express type of the Utterer thereof? Unquestionably. There would be a serious blank among the types of the Mosaic economy were there not one to reflect the Lord Jesus in the exact attitude in which the above expression presents Him. But the burnt-offering does not thus reflect Him. There is not a single circumstance connected with that offering which would correspond with such language. The sin-offering alone furnishes the fitting type of the Lord Jesus as the One who poured forth those accents of intense agony; for in it alone do we find the circumstances which evoked such accents from the depths of His spotless soul. The awful shadow of the cross, with its shame, its curse, and its exclusion from the light of God's countenance, was passing across His spirit, and He could not even contemplate it without an "If it be possible, let this cup pass from Me." But no sooner had He uttered these words than His profound subjection manifests itself in "Thy will be done." What a bitter "cup" it must have been to elicit from a perfectly subject heart the words,

"Let it pass from Me"! What perfect subjection there must have been, when, in the presence of so bitter a cup, the heart could breath forth, "Thy will be done"!

We shall now consider the typical act of "laying on of hands." This act was common both to the burnt-offering and the sin-offering; but in the case of the former, it identified the offerer with an unblemished offering; in the case of the latter, it involved the transfer of the sin of the offerer to the head of the offering. Thus it was in the type; and when we look at the Antitype, we learn a truth of the most comforting and edifying nature—a truth which, were it more clearly understood and fully experienced, would impart a far more settled peace than is ordinarily possessed.

What, then, is the doctrine set forth in the laying on of hands? It is this: Christ was "made sin for us, that we might be made the righteousness of God in Him." (2 Cor. v.) He took our position with all its consequences, in order that we might get His position with all its consequences. He was treated as sin upon the cross, that we might be treated as righteousness in the presence of Infinite Holiness. He was cast out of God's presence because He had sin on Him by imputation, that we might be received into God's house and into His bosom because we have a perfect righteousness by imputation. He had to endure the hiding of God's countenance, that we might bask in the light of that countenance. He had to pass through three hours' darkness, that we might walk in everlasting light. He was forsaken of God for a time, that we might enjoy His presence forever. All that was due to us as ruined sinners was laid upon Him, in order that all that was due to Him as the Accomplisher of redemption might be ours. There was every thing against Him when He hung upon the cursed tree, in order that there might be nothing against us. He was identified with us in the reality of death and judgment, in order that we might be identified with Him in the reality of life and righteousness. He drank the cup of wrath—the cup of trembling, that we might drink the cup of salvation—the cup of infinite favor. He was treated according to our deserts, that we might be treated according to His.

Such is the wondrous truth illustrated by the ceremonial act of imposition of hands. When the worshiper had laid his hand upon the head of the burnt-offering, it ceased to be a question as to what he was or what He deserved, and became entirely a question of what the offering was in the judgment of Jehovah. If the offering was without blemish, so was the offerer; if the offering was accepted, so was the offerer. They were perfectly identified. The act of laying on of hands constituted them one in God's view. He looked at the offerer through the medium of the offering. Thus it was in the case of the burnt-offering. But in the sin-offering, when the offerer had laid his hand upon the head of the offering, it became a question of what the offerer was, and what he deserved; the offering was treated according to the deserts of the offerer. They were perfectly identified. The act of laying on of hands constituted them one in the judgment of God. The sin of the offerer was dealt with in the sin-offering; the person of the offerer was accepted in the burnt-offering. This made a vast difference. Hence, though the act of laying on of hands was common to both types, and, moreover, though it was expressive, in the case of each, of identification, yet were the consequences as different as possible. The just treated as the unjust; the unjust accepted in the just.—"Christ hath once suffered for sins, the just for the unjust, that He might bring us to God." This is the doctrine. Our sins brought Christ to the cross, but He brings us to God. And if He brings us to God, it is in His own acceptableness, as risen from the dead, having put away our sins, according to the perfectness of His own work. He bore away our sins far from the sanctuary of God, in order that He might bring us nigh, even into the holiest of all, in full confidence of heart, having the conscience purged by His precious blood from every stain of sin.

Now, the more minutely we compare all the details of the burnt-offering and the sin-offering, the more clearly shall we apprehend the truth of what has been above stated in reference to the laying on of hands and the results thereof in each case.

In the first chapter of this volume, we noticed the fact that "the sons of Aaron" are introduced in the burnt-offering, but not in the sin-offering. As priests, they were privileged to stand around the altar and behold the flame of an acceptable sacrifice ascending to the Lord. But in the sin-offering, in its primary aspect, it was a question of the solemn judgment of sin, and not of priestly worship or admiration, and therefore the sons of Aaron do not appear. It is as convicted sinners that we have to do with Christ as the Antitype of the sin-offering: it is as worshiping priests, clothed in garments of salvation, that we contemplate Christ as the Antitype of the burnt-offering.

But, further, my reader may observe that the burnt-offering was "flayed," the sin-offering was not; the burnt-offering was "cut into his pieces," the sin-offering was not; "the inwards and the legs" of the burnt-offering were "washed in water," which act was entirely omitted in the sin-offering. Lastly, the burnt-offering was burnt upon the altar, the sin-offering was burnt without the camp. These are weighty points of difference, arising simply out of the distinctive character of the offerings. We know there is nothing in the Word of God without its own specific meaning; and every intelligent and careful student of Scripture will notice the above points of difference, and when he notices them, he will naturally seek to ascertain their real import. *Ignorance* of this import there may be, but *indifference* to it there should not. In any section of inspiration, but especially one so rich as that which lies before us, to pass over a single point would be to offer dishonor to the divine Author, and to deprive

our own souls of much profit. We should hang
over the most minute details, either to adore God's
wisdom in them, or to confess our own ignorance
of them. To pass them by, in a spirit of indifference, is to imply that the Holy Ghost has taken the
trouble to write what we do not deem worthy of the
desire to understand. This is what no right-minded
Christian would presume to think. If the Spirit, in
writing upon the ordinance of the sin-offering, has
omitted the various rites above alluded to—rites
which get a prominent place in the ordinance of
the burnt-offering, there must assuredly be some
good reason for, and some important meaning in,
His doing so. These we should seek to apprehend,
and no doubt they arise out of the special design of
the divine mind in each offering. The sin-offering
sets forth that aspect of Christ's work in which He
is seen taking judicially the place which belonged
to us morally. For this reason we could not look
for that intense expression of what He was in all
His secret springs of action, as unfolded in the
typical act of "flaying." Neither could there be
that enlarged exhibition of what he was, not merely
as a whole, but in the most minute features of his
character, as seen in the act of "cutting it into his
pieces." Nor yet could there be that manifestation
of what He was personally, practically, and intrinsically, as set forth in the significant act of "washing the inwards and legs in water."

All these things belonged to the burnt-offering
phase of our blessed Lord, and to that alone, be-

cause in it we see Him offering Himself to the eye,
to the heart, and to the altar of Jehovah, without
any question of imputed sin, of wrath, or of judgment.   In the sin-offering, on the contrary, instead
of having, as the great prominent idea, what Christ
is, we have what sin is,—instead of the preciousness
of Jesus, we have the odiousness of sin.   In the
burnt-offering, inasmuch as it is Christ Himself
offered to and accepted by God, we have every
thing done that could possibly make manifest what
He was in every respect.   In the sin-offering, because it is sin as judged by God, the very reverse
is the case.   All this is so plain as to need no effort
of the mind to understand it.   It naturally flows
out of the distinctive character of the type.

However, although the leading object in the sin-
offering is to shadow forth what Christ became for
us, and not what He was in Himself, there is nevertheless one rite connected with this type which most
fully expresses His personal acceptableness to Jehovah.   This rite is laid down in the following words:
"And he shall take off from it all the fat of the
bullock for the sin-offering; the fat that covereth
the inwards, and all the fat that is upon the inwards,
and the two kidneys, and the fat that is upon them,
which is by the flanks, and the caul above the liver,
with the kidneys, it shall he take away, as it was
taken off from the bullock of the sacrifice of peace-
offering; and the priest shall burn them upon the
altar of the burnt-offering." (Chap. iv. 8–10.)
Thus the intrinsic excellency of Christ is not

omitted even in the sin-offering. The fat burnt
upon the altar is the apt expression of the divine
appreciation of the preciousness of Christ's Person,
no matter what place He might, in perfect grace,
take on our behalf or in our stead. He was made
sin for us, and the sin-offering is the divinely appointed shadow of Him in this respect; but inasmuch as it was the Lord Jesus Christ—God's Elect,
His Holy One—His pure, His spotless, His eternal
Son that was made sin, therefore the fat of the
sin-offering was burnt upon the altar, as a proper
material for that fire which was the impressive
exhibition of divine holiness.

But even in this very point we see what a contrast
there is between the sin-offering and the burnt-
offering. In the case of the latter, it was not
merely the fat, but the whole sacrifice that was
burnt upon the altar, because it was Christ, without
any question of sin-bearing whatever. In the case
of the former, there was nothing but the fat to be
burnt upon the altar, because it was a question of
sin-bearing, though Christ was the Sin-bearer. The
divine glories of Christ's Person shine out even
from amid the darkest shades of that cursed tree
to which He consented to be nailed as a curse for
us. The hatefulness of that with which, in the
exercise of divine love, He connected His blessed
Person on the cross, could not prevent the sweet
odor of His preciousness from ascending to the
throne of God. Thus have we unfolded to us the
profound mystery of God's face hidden from that

which Christ *became,* and God's heart refreshed by
what Christ *was.* This imparts a peculiar charm
to the sin-offering. The bright beams of Christ's
Personal glory shining out from amid the awful
gloom of Calvary—His Personal worth set forth in
the very deepest depths of His humiliation—God's
delight in the One from whom He had, in vindication of His inflexible justice and holiness, to hide
His face—all this is set forth in the fact that the fat
of the sin-offering was burnt upon the altar.

Having thus endeavored to point out, in the first
place, what was done with "the blood," and, in the
second place, what was done with "the fat," we
have now to consider what was done with "the
flesh." "And the skin of the bullock, and *all his
flesh,* . . . . even *the whole bullock* shall he carry
forth without the camp unto a clean place, where the
ashes are poured out, and burn him on the wood
with fire: where the ashes are poured out shall he
be burnt." (Ver. 11, 12.) In this act, we have the
main feature of the sin-offering—that which distinguished it both from the burnt-offering and the
peace-offering. Its flesh was not burnt upon the
altar as in the burnt-offering, neither was it eaten
by the priest or the worshiper as in the peace-
offering; it was wholly burnt without the camp.*
"No sin-offering, whereof any of the blood is
brought into the tabernacle of the congregation to

---

*The statement in the text refers only to the sin-offerings of
which the blood was brought into the holy place. There were sin-
offerings of which Aaron and his *sons* partook. (See Lev. vi. 26,
29; Numb. xviii. 9, 10.)

reconcile withal in the holy place, shall be eaten:
it shall be burnt in the fire.'' (Lev. vi. 30.) ''For
the bodies of those beasts, whose blood is brought
into the sanctuary by the high-priest for sin, are
burned without the camp. Wherefore Jesus also,
that He might sanctify the people with His own
blood, suffered without the gate.''(Heb. xiii. 11, 12.)

Now, in comparing what was done with the
''blood'' with what was done with the ''flesh,'' or
''body,'' of the sacrifice, two great branches of
truth present themselves to our view, namely, worship and discipleship. The blood brought into the
sanctuary is the foundation of the former; the body
burnt outside the camp is the foundation of the
latter. Before ever we can worship in peace of
conscience and liberty of heart, we must know, on
the authority of the Word, and by the power of the
Spirit, that the entire question of *sin* has been forever settled by the blood of the divine Sin-offering—
that His blood has been sprinkled perfectly before
the Lord—that all God's claims, and all our necessities as ruined and guilty sinners, have been forever
answered. This gives perfect peace; and, in the
enjoyment of this peace, we worship God. When
an Israelite of old had offered his sin-offering, his
conscience was set at rest, in so far as the offering
was capable of imparting rest. True, it was but a
temporary rest, being the fruit of a temporary sacrifice; but, clearly, whatever kind of rest the offering
was fitted to impart, that the offerer might enjov.
Hence, therefore, our Sacrifice being divine and

eternal, our rest is divine and eternal also. As
is the sacrifice, such is the rest which is founded
thereon. A Jew never had an eternally purged
conscience, simply because he had not an eternally
efficacious sacrifice. He might, in a certain way,
have his conscience purged for a day, a month, or
a year; but he could not have it purged forever.
"But Christ being come a High-Priest of good
things to come, by a greater and more perfect
tabernacle, not made with hands, that is to say,
not of this building; neither by the blood of goats
and calves, but by His own blood He entered in
once into the holy place, having obtained *eternal*
redemption. For if the blood of bulls and of goats,
and the ashes of a heifer sprinkling the unclean,
sanctifieth to the purifying of the flesh; how much
more shall the blood of Christ, who through the
eternal Spirit offered Himself without spot to God,
purge your conscience from dead works to serve
the living God?" (Heb. ix. 11–14.)

Here, we have the full, explicit statement of the
doctrine. The blood of goats and calves procured
a temporary redemption: the blood of Christ pro-
cures eternal redemption. The former purified
outwardly; the latter, inwardly. That purged the
flesh for a time; this, the conscience forever. The
whole question hinges, not upon the character or
condition of the offerer, but upon the value of the
offering. The question is not, by any means,
whether a Christian is a better man than a Jew,
but whether the blood of Christ is better than the

blood of a bullock. Assuredly, it is better. How
much better? Infinitely better. The Son of God
imparts all the dignity of His own divine Person to
the sacrifice which He offered; and if the blood of
a bullock purified the flesh for a year, "how much
more" shall the blood of the Son of God purge the
conscience forever?—if that took away *some* sin,
how much more shall this take away "*all*"?

Now, why was the mind of a Jew set at rest, for
the time being, when he had offered his sin-offering?
How did he know that the special sin for which he
had brought his sacrifice was forgiven? Because
God had said, "It shall be forgiven him." His peace
of heart, in reference to that particular sin, rested
upon the testimony of the God of Israel and the
blood of the victim. So now, the peace of the
believer, in reference to "ALL SIN," rests upon the
authority of God's word and "the precious blood of
Christ." If a Jew had sinned, and neglected to
bring his sin-offering, he should have been "cut off
from among his people;" but when he took his
place as a sinner—when he laid his hand upon the
head of a sin-offering, then the offering was "cut
off" instead of him, and he was free, so far. The
offering was treated as the offerer deserved; and
hence, for him not to know that his sin was forgiven
him, would have been to make God a liar, and to
treat the blood of the divinely appointed sin-offering
as nothing.

And if this were true in reference to one who had
only the blood of a goat to rest upon, "how much

more'' powerfully does it apply to one who has the precious blood of Christ to rest upon? The believer sees in Christ One who has been judged for all his sin—One who, when He hung upon the cross, sustained the entire burden of his sin—One who, having made Himself responsible for that sin, could not be where He now is if the whole question of sin had not been settled according to all the claims of Infinite Justice. So absolutely did Christ take the believer's place on the cross—so entirely was he identified with Him—so completely was all the believer's sin imputed to Him, there and then, that all question of the believer's liability—all thought of his guilt—all idea of his exposure to judgment and wrath, is eternally set aside.* It was all settled on the cursed tree, between Divine Justice and the spotless Victim. And now the believer is as absolutely identified with Christ on the throne, as Christ was identified with him on the cross. Justice has no charge to bring against the believer, because it has no charge to bring against Christ. Thus it stands forever. If a charge could be preferred against the believer, it would be calling in question the reality of Christ's identification with him on the cross, and the perfectness of Christ's work on his behalf. If, when the worshiper of old was on his way back,

---

*We have a singularly beautiful example of the divine accuracy of Scripture in 2 Cor. v. 21.—"He hath *made* Him to be sin [$\dot{\alpha}\mu\alpha\rho\tau\iota\alpha\nu$ $\epsilon\pi o\iota\eta\delta\epsilon\nu$] for us, that we might *become* [$\gamma\iota\nu\omega\mu\epsilon\theta\alpha$] the righteousness of God in Him." The English reader might suppose that the word which is rendered "made" is the same in each clause of the passage. This is not the case.

after having offered his sin-offering, any one had
charged him with that special sin for which his sacrifice had bled, what would have been his reply?
Just this: The sin has been rolled away by the
blood of the victim, and Jehovah has pronounced
the words, "It shall be forgiven him." The victim
had died instead of him, and he lived instead of the
victim.

Such was the type. And as to the Antitype, when
the eye of faith rests on Christ as the Sin-offering, it
beholds Him as One who having assumed a perfect
human life, gave up that life on the cross, because
sin was there and then attached to it by imputation.
But it beholds Him also as One who having in Himself the power of divine and eternal life, rose from
the tomb therein, and who now imparts this His
risen, His divine, His eternal life to all who believe
in His name. The sin is gone, because the life to
which it was attached is gone. And now, instead of
the life to which sin was attached, all true believers
possess the life to which righteousness attaches.
The question of sin can never once be raised, in
reference to the risen and victorious life of Christ;
but this is the life which believers possess. There
is no other life. All beside is death, because all
beside is under the power of sin. "He that hath
the Son hath life," and he that hath life hath righteousness also. The two things are inseparable, because Christ is both the one and the other. If
the judgment and death of Christ upon the cross
were realities, then the life and righteousness of the

believer are realities; if imputed sin was a reality
to Christ, imputed righteousness is a reality to the
believer. The one is as real as the other; for if
not, Christ would have died in vain. The true and
irrefragable ground of peace is this,—that the claims
of God's nature have been perfectly met as to sin.
The death of Jesus has satisfied them all—satisfied
them forever. What is it that proves this to the
satisfaction of the awakened conscience? The great
fact of resurrection. A risen Christ declares the full
deliverance of the believer—his perfect discharge
from every possible demand.—"He was delivered
for our offenses, and raised again for our justification." (Rom. iv. 25.) For a Christian not to know
that his sin is gone, and gone forever, is to cast a
slight upon the blood of his divine Sin-offering; it
is to deny that there has been the perfect presentation—the sevenfold sprinkling of the blood before
the Lord.

And now, ere turning from this fundamental point
which has been occupying us, I would desire to make
an earnest and a most solemn appeal to my reader's
heart and conscience. Let me ask you, dear friend,
have you been led to repose on this holy and happy
foundation? Do you know that the question of your
sin has been forever disposed of? Have you laid
your hand, by faith, on the head of the Sin-offering?
Have you seen the atoning blood of Jesus rolling
away all your guilt, and carrying it into the mighty
waters of God's forgetfulness? Has Divine Justice
any thing against you? Are you free from the un-

utterable horrors of a guilty conscience? Do not,
I pray you, rest satisfied until you can give a joyous
answer to these inquiries. Be assured of it, it is
the happy privilege of the feeblest babe in Christ to
rejoice in a full and everlasting remission of sins,
on the ground of a finished atonement; and hence,
for any to teach otherwise, is to lower the sacrifice
of Christ to the level of "goats and calves." If we
cannot know that our sins are forgiven, then where
are the glad tidings of the gospel? Is a Christian
in no wise better off, in the matter of a sin-offering,
than a Jew? The latter was privileged to know that
his matters were set straight for a year, by the blood
of an annual sacrifice. Can the former not have
any certainty at all? Unquestionably. Well, then,
if there is any certainty, it must be eternal, inasmuch as it rests on an eternal sacrifice.

This, and this alone, is the basis of worship. The
full assurance of sin put away ministers, not to a
spirit of self-confidence, but to a spirit of praise,
thankfulness, and worship. It produces, not a spirit
of self-complacency, but of Christ-complacency,
which, blessed be God, is the spirit which shall
characterize the redeemed throughout eternity. It
does not lead one to think little of sin, but to think
much of the grace which has perfectly pardoned it,
and of the blood which has perfectly canceled it.
It is impossible that any one can gaze on the cross
—can see the place which Christ took—can meditate
upon the sufferings which He endured—can ponder
on those three terrible hours of darkness, and at the

same time think lightly of sin. When all these
things are entered into, in the power of the Holy
Ghost, there are two results which must follow,
namely, an abhorrence of sin in all its forms, and a
genuine love to Christ, His people, and His cause.

Let us now consider what was done with the
"flesh," or "body," of the sacrifice, in which, as
has been stated, we have the true ground of discipleship. "The whole bullock shall he carry forth,
without the camp, unto a clean place, where the
ashes are poured out, and burn him on the wood
with fire." (Chap. iv. 12.) This act is to be viewed
in a double way; first, as expressing the place which
the Lord Jesus took for us as bearing sin; secondly,
as expressing the place into which He was cast by a
world which had rejected Him. It is to this latter
point that I would here call my reader's attention.

The use which the apostle, in Heb. xiii, makes
of Christ's having "suffered without the gate," is
deeply practical.—"Let us go forth therefore *unto
Him* without the camp, *bearing His reproach*." If
the sufferings of Christ have secured us an entrance
into heaven, the place where He suffered expresses
our rejection from earth. His death has procured
us a city on high; the place where He died divests
us of a city below.* "He suffered without the

---

*The epistle to the Ephesians furnishes the most elevated view of
the Church's place above, and gives it to us, not merely as to the
title, but also as to the mode. The title is assuredly the blood; but
the mode is thus stated: "But God, who is rich in mercy, for His
great love wherewith He loved us, even when we were dead in
sins, hath quickened us together with Christ, (by grace ye are
saved;) and hath raised us up together, and made us sit together
in heavenly places in Christ Jesus." (Eph. ii. 4-6.)

gate," and, in so doing, He set aside Jerusalem as the present centre of divine operation. There is no such thing now as a consecrated spot on the earth. Christ has taken His place, as a suffering One, outside the range of this world's religion, its politics, and all that pertains to it. The world hated Him and cast Him out. Wherefore, the word is, "*Go forth.*" This is the motto as regards every thing that men would set up here in the form of a "camp," no matter what that camp may be. If men set up "a holy city," you must look for a rejected Christ "without the gate." If men set up a religious camp, call it by what name you please, you must "go forth" out of it, in order to find a rejected Christ. It is not that blind superstition will not grope amid the ruins of Jerusalem in search of relics of Christ. It assuredly will do so, and has done so. It will affect to find out and do honor to the site of His cross and to His sepulchre. Nature's covetousness, too, taking advantage of nature's superstition, has carried on for ages a lucrative traffic, under the crafty plea of doing honor to the so-called sacred localities of antiquity. But a single ray of light from Revelation's heavenly lamp is sufficient to enable us to say that you must "go forth" of all these things, in order to find and enjoy communion with a rejected Christ.

However, my reader will need to remember that there is far more involved in the soul-stirring call to "go forth" than a mere escape from the gross absurdities of an ignorant superstition, or the designs

of a crafty covetousness. There are many who can
powerfully and eloquently expose all such things,
who are very far indeed from any thought of re-
sponding to the apostolic summons. When men set
up a "camp," and rally round a standard on which
is emblazoned some important dogma of truth, or
some valuable institution—when they can appeal to
an orthodox creed—an advanced and enlightened
scheme of doctrine—a splendid ritual, capable of
satisfying the most ardent aspirations of man's de-
votional nature—when any or all of these things
exist, it demands much spiritual intelligence to
discern the real force and proper application of the
words, "Let us go forth," and much spiritual energy
and decision to act upon them. They should, however, be discerned and acted upon, for it is perfectly
certain that the atmosphere of a camp, let its ground
or standard be what it may, is destructive of personal communion with a rejected Christ; and no
so-called religious advantage can ever make up for
the loss of that communion. It is the tendency of
our hearts to drop into cold stereotyped forms.
This has ever been the case in the professing church.
These forms may have originated in real power;
they may have resulted from positive visitations of
the Spirit of God. The temptation is to stereotype
the form when the spirit and power have all departed. This is, in principle, to set up a camp.
The Jewish system could boast a divine origin. A
Jew could triumphantly point to the temple, with
its splendid system of worship, its priesthood, its

sacrifices, its entire furniture, and show that it had all been handed down from the God of Israel. He could give chapter and verse, as we say, for every thing connected with the system to which he was attached. Where is the system, ancient, medieval, or modern, that could put forth such lofty and powerful pretensions, or come down upon the heart with such an overwhelming weight of authority? And yet, the command was to "GO FORTH."

This is a deeply solemn matter. It concerns us all, because we are all prone to slip away from communion with a living Christ and sink into dead routine. Hence the practical power of the words, "Go forth therefore unto *Him*." It is not, Go forth from one system to another—from one set of opinions to another—from one company of people to another. No; but, Go forth from every thing that merits the appellation of a camp, "*to Him*" who "suffered without the gate." The Lord Jesus is as thoroughly outside the gate now as He was when He suffered there eighteen centuries ago. What was it that put Him outside? "The religious world" of that day; and the religious world of that day is, in spirit and principle, the religious world of the present moment. The world is the world still. "There is nothing new under the sun." Christ and the world are not one. The world has covered itself with the cloak of Christianity; but it is only in order that its hatred to Christ may work itself up into more deadly forms underneath. Let us not deceive ourselves. If we will walk with a rejected Christ, we must be a rejected people. If our Master "suffered *without* the gate," we cannot expect to reign *within* the gate. If we walk in His footsteps, whither will they lead us? Surely, not to the high places of this Godless, Christless world.

> "His path, uncheered by earthly smiles,
>   Led only to the cross."

He is a despised Christ—a rejected Christ—a Christ outside the camp. Oh, then, dear Christian reader, let us go forth to Him, bearing His reproach. Let us not bask in the sunshine of this world's favor, seeing it crucified, and still hates with an unmitigated hatred, the beloved One to whom we owe our present and eternal all, and who loves us with a love which many waters cannot quench. Let us not, directly or indirectly, accredit that thing which calls itself by His sacred name, but, in reality, hates His Person, hates His ways, hates His truth, hates the bare mention of His advent. Let us be faithful to an absent Lord. Let us live for Him who died for us. While our consciences repose in His blood, let our heart's affections entwine themselves around His Person; so that our separation from "this present evil world" may not be merely a matter of cold principle, but an affectionate separation, because the object of our affections is not here. May the Lord deliver us from the influence of that consecrated, prudential selfishness so common at the present time, which would not be without religiousness, but is the enemy of the cross of Christ. What we want, in order to make a successful stand,

against this terrible form of evil, is not peculiar
views, or special principles, or curious theories, or
cold intellectual accuracy: we want a deep-toned
devotedness to the Person of the Son of God, a
whole-hearted consecration of ourselves—body,
soul, and spirit—to His service, an earnest longing
for His glorious advent. These, my reader, are
the special wants of the times in which you and I
live. Will you not, then, join in uttering, from the
very depths of your heart, the cry, "O Lord, revive
Thy work!"—"Accomplish the number of Thine
elect!"—"Hasten Thy kingdom!"—"Come, Lord
Jesus, come!"

CHAPTER V. 14—VI. 7

THESE verses contain the doctrine of the trespass-
offering, of which there were two distinct kinds,
namely, trespass against *God*, and trespass against
man. "If a soul commit a trespass, and sin *through
ignorance*, in the holy things of the Lord, then shall
he bring for his trespass unto the Lord a ram without blemish out of the flocks, with thy estimation
by shekels of silver, after the shekel of the sanctuary, for a trespass-offering." Here we have a
case in which a positive wrong was done, in the
holy things which pertained unto the Lord; and,
albeit this was done "through ignorance," yet could
it not be passed over. God can forgive all manner
of trespass, but He cannot pass over a single jot or
tittle. His grace is perfect, and therefore He can

forgive *all:* His holiness is perfect, and therefore
He cannot pass over any thing. He cannot sanction
iniquity, but He can blot it out; and that, moreover, according to the perfection of His grace, and
according to the perfect claims of His holiness.

It is a very grave error to suppose that, provided
a man acts up to the dictates of his conscience, he
is all right and safe. The peace which rests upon
such a foundation as this will be eternally destroyed
when the light of the judgment-seat shines in upon
the conscience. God could never lower His claim
to such a level. The balances of the sanctuary
are regulated by a very different scale from that
afforded by the most sensitive conscience. We
have had occasion to dwell upon this point before,
in the notes on the sin-offering. It cannot be too
strongly insisted upon. There are two things involved in it,—first, a just perception of what the
holiness of God really is; and secondly, a clear
sense of the ground of a believer's peace in the
divine presence.

Whether it be a question of my condition or my
conduct—my nature or my acts—God alone can be
the Judge of what suits Himself, and of what befits
His holy presence. Can human ignorance furnish
a plea when divine requirements are in question?
God forbid. A wrong has been done "in the holy
things of the Lord," but man's conscience has not
taken cognizance of it. What then? Is there to
be nothing more about it? Are the claims of God
to be thus lightly disposed of? Assuredly not.

This would be subversive of every thing like divine relationship. The righteous are called to give thanks at the remembrance of God's holiness. (Ps. xcvii. 12.) How can they do this? Because their peace has been secured on the ground of the full vindication and perfect establishment of that holiness. Hence, the higher their sense of what that holiness is, the deeper and more settled must be their peace. This is a truth of the most precious nature. The unregenerate man could never rejoice in the divine holiness. His aim would be to lower that holiness, if he could not ignore it altogether. Such an one will console himself with the thought that God is good, God is gracious, God is merciful; but you will never find him rejoicing in the thought that God is holy. He has unholy thoughts respecting God's goodness, His grace, and His mercy. He would fain find in those blessed attributes an excuse for his continuing in sin.

On the contrary, the renewed man exults in the holiness of God. He sees the full expression thereof in the cross of the Lord Jesus Christ. It is that holiness which has laid the foundation of his peace; and not only so, but he is made a partaker of it, and he delights in it, while he hates sin with a perfect hatred. The instincts of the divine nature shrink from it, and long after holiness. It would be impossible to enjoy true peace and liberty of heart if one did not know that all the claims connected with "the holy things of the Lord" had been perfectly met by our divine Trespass-offering.

There would ever be springing up in the heart the painful sense that those claims had been slighted, through our manifold infirmities and shortcomings. Our very best services, our holiest seasons, our most hallowed exercises, may present something of trespass "in the holy things of the Lord"— "something that ought not to be done." How often are our seasons of public worship and private devotion infringed upon and marred by barrenness and distraction! Hence it is that we need the assurance that our trespasses have all been divinely met by the precious blood of Christ. Thus, in the ever-blessed Lord Jesus, we find One who has come down to the full measure of our necessities as sinners by nature, and trespassers in act. We find in Him the perfect answer to all the cravings of a guilty conscience, and to all the claims of Infinite Holiness, in reference to *all* our sins and *all* our trespasses; so that the believer can stand, with an uncondemning conscience and emancipated heart, in the full light of that holiness which is too pure to behold iniquity or look upon sin.

"And he shall make amends for the harm that he hath done in the holy thing, and shall add the fifth part thereto, and give it unto the priest; and the priest shall make an atonement for him with the ram of the trespass-offering, and it shall be forgiven him." (Chap. v. 16.) In the addition of "the fifth part," as here set forth, we have a feature of the true Trespass-offering which, it is to be feared, is but little appreciated. When we think of all the

wrong and all the trespass which we have done
against the Lord, and, further, when we remember
how God has been wronged of His rights in this
wicked world, with what interest can we contemplate
the work of the cross as that wherein God has not
merely received back what was lost, but whereby
He is an actual gainer.   He has gained more by
redemption than ever He lost by the fall.   He reaps
a richer harvest of glory, honor, and praise in the
fields of redemption than ever He could have reaped
from those of creation.   "The sons of God" could
raise a loftier song of praise around the empty tomb
of Jesus than ever they raised in view of the Creator's accomplished work.   The wrong has not only
been perfectly atoned for, but an eternal advantage
has been gained by the work of the cross.   This is
a stupendous truth.   God is a gainer by the work
of Calvary.   Who could have conceived this?   When
we behold man, and the creation of which he was
lord, laid in ruins at the feet of the enemy, how
could we conceive that, from amid those ruins,
God should gather richer and nobler spoils than
any which our unfallen world could have yielded?
Blessed be the name of Jesus for all this !   It is to
Him we owe it all.   It is by His precious cross that
ever a truth so amazing, so divine, could be enun-
ciated.   Assuredly, that cross involves a mysterious
wisdom "which none of the princes of this world
knew ; for had they known it, they would not have
crucified the Lord of glory." (1 Cor. ii. 8.)   No
marvel, therefore, that around that cross, and around

Him who was crucified thereon, the affections of patriarchs, prophets, apostles, martyrs, and saints have ever entwined themselves. No marvel that the Holy Ghost should have given forth that solemn, but just, decree, "If any man love not the Lord Jesus Christ, let him be Anathema Maran-atha." (1 Cor. xvi. 22.) Heaven and earth shall echo forth a loud and an eternal amen to this anathema. No marvel that it should be the fixed and immutable purpose of the divine mind, that "at the name of Jesus every knee should bow, of things in heaven, and things in earth, and things under the earth; and that every tongue should confess that Jesus Christ is Lord, to the glory of God the Father." (Phil. ii. 10, 11.)

The same law in reference to "the fifth part" obtained in the case of a trespass committed against a man, as we read, "If a soul sin, and commit a trespass *against the Lord,** and lie unto his neighbor in that which was delivered him to keep, or in fellowship, or in a thing taken away by violence, or hath deceived his neighbor; or have found that which was lost, and lieth concerning it, and sweareth falsely; in any of all these that a man doeth,

---

* There is a fine principle involved in the expression, "against the Lord." Although the matter in question was a wrong done to one's neighbor, yet the Lord looked upon it as a trespass against Himself. Every thing must be viewed in reference to the Lord. It matters not who may be affected, Jehovah must get the first place. Thus, when David's conscience was pierced by the arrow of conviction, in reference to his treatment of Uriah, he exclaims, "I have sinned *against the Lord.*" (2 Sam. xii. 13.) This principle does not in the least interfere with the injured man's claim.

sinning therein: then it shall be, because he hath
sinned, and is guilty, that he shall restore that which
he took violently away, or the thing which he hath
deceitfully gotten, or that which was delivered him
to keep, or the lost thing which he found, or all that
about which he hath sworn falsely; he shall even
restore it in the principal, *and shall add the fifth
part more thereto*, and give it unto him to whom it
appertaineth, in the day of his trespass-offering.''
(Chap. vi. 2-5.)

Man, as well as God, is a positive gainer by the
cross. The believer can say, as he gazes upon that
cross, Well, it matters not how I have been wronged
—how I have been trespassed against—how I have
been deceived—what ills have been done to me, I
am a gainer by the cross. I have not merely received back all that was lost, but much more beside.

Thus, whether we think of the injured or the
injurer, in any given case, we are equally struck
with the glorious triumphs of redemption, and the
mighty practical results which flow from that gospel
which fills the soul with the happy assurance that
''all trespasses'' are ''forgiven,'' and that the root
from whence those trespasses have sprung has been
judged. ''The gospel of the glory of the blessed
God'' is that which alone can send forth a man into
the midst of a scene which has been the witness of
his sins, his trespasses, and his injurious ways—
can send him back to all who in any wise have been
sufferers by his evil doings, furnished with grace,
not only to repair the wrongs, but far more, to

allow the full tide of practical benevolence to flow forth in all his ways—yea, to love his enemies, to do good to them that hate him, and to pray for them that despitefully use him and persecute him. Such is the precious grace of God that acts in connection with our great Trespass-offering! such are its rich, rare, and refreshing fruits!

What a triumphant answer to the caviler who could say, "Shall we continue in sin, that grace may abound?" Grace not merely cuts up sin by the roots, but transforms the sinner from a curse, into a blessing—from a moral plague, into a channel of divine mercy—from an emissary of Satan, into a messenger of God—from a child of darkness, into a son of the light—from a self-indulgent pleasure-hunter, into a self-denying lover of God—from a slave of vile, selfish lusts, into a willing-hearted servant of Christ—from a cold, narrow-hearted miser, into a benevolent minister to the need of his fellow-man. Away, then, with the oft-repeated taunts, "Are we to do nothing?"—"That is a marvelously easy way to be saved."—"According to this gospel, we may live as we list." Let all who utter such language behold yonder thief transformed into a liberal donor, and let them be silent forever. (See Eph. iv. 28.) They know not what grace means; they have never felt its sanctifying and elevating influences. They forget that, while the blood of the trespass-offering cleanses the conscience, the law of that offering sends the trespasser back to the one whom he has wronged, with "the

principal" and "the fifth" in his hand. Noble
testimony this, both to the grace and righteousness
of the God of Israel! Beauteous exhibition of the
results of that marvelous scheme of redemption,
whereby the injurer is forgiven, and the injured
becomes an actual gainer! If the conscience has
been set to rights, by the blood of the cross, in
reference to the claims of God, the conduct must
be set to rights, by the holiness of the cross, in
reference to the claims of practical righteousness.
These things must never be separated; God has
joined them together, and let not man put them
asunder. The hallowed union will never be dissolved by any mind which is governed by pure
gospel morality. Alas! it is easy to profess the
principles of grace, while the practice and power
thereof are completely denied,—it is easy to talk of
resting in the blood of the Trespass-offering, while
"the principal" and "the fifth" are not forthcoming. This is vain, and worse than vain. "He that
doeth not righteousness is not of God." (1 John
iii. 10.)

Nothing can be more dishonoring to the pure
grace of the gospel than the supposition that a man
may belong to God while his conduct and character
exhibit not the fair traces of practical holiness.
"Known unto God are all His works," no doubt;
but He has given us, in His holy Word, those evidences by which we can discern those that belong
to Him. "The foundation of God standeth sure,
having this seal, 'The Lord knoweth them that are

his.' And, 'Let every one that nameth the name of
Christ depart from iniquity.'" (2 Tim. ii. 19.) We
have no right to suppose that an evil-doer belongs
to God. The holy instincts of the divine nature are
shocked by the mention of such a thing. People
sometimes express much difficulty in accounting for
such and such evil practices on the part of those
whom they cannot help regarding in the light of
Christians. The Word of God settles the matter so
clearly and so authoritatively, as to leave no possible ground for any such difficulty.—"In this the
children of God are manifest, and the children of
the devil: whosoever doeth not righteousness is
not of God, neither he that loveth not his brother."
It is well to remember this, in this day of laxity
and self-indulgence. There is a fearful amount of
easy, uninfluential profession abroad, against which
the genuine Christian is called upon to make a firm
stand, and bear a severe testimony—a testimony
resulting from the steady exhibition of "the fruits
of righteousness which are by Jesus Christ unto the
glory and praise of God." It is most deplorable
to see so many going along the beaten path—the
well-trodden highway of religious profession, and
yet manifesting not a trace of love or holiness in
their conduct. Christian reader, let us be faithful;
let us rebuke, by a life of self-denial and genuine
benevolence, the self-indulgence and culpable in-
activity of evangelical, yet worldly, profession. May
God grant unto all His true-hearted people abundant grace for these things!

Let us now proceed to compare the two classes of trespass-offering; namely, the offering on account of trespass "in the holy things of the Lord," and that which had reference to a trespass committed in the common transactions and relations of human life. In so doing, we shall find one or two points which demand our attentive consideration.

And first, the expression, "if a soul sin through ignorance," which occurs in the former, is omitted in the latter. The reason of this is obvious. The claims which stand connected with the holy things of the Lord must pass infinitely beyond the reach of the most elevated human sensibility. Those claims may be continually interfered with—continually trespassed upon, and the trespasser not be aware of the fact. Man's consciousness can never be the regulator in the sanctuary of God. This is an unspeakable mercy. God's holiness alone must fix the standard when God's rights are in question.

On the other hand, the human conscience can readily grasp the full amount of a human claim, and can readily take cognizance of any interference with such claim. How often may we have wronged God, in His holy things, without ever taking a note of it in the tablet of conscience—yea, without having the competency to detect it. (See Mal. iii. 8.) Not so, however, when man's rights are in question. The wrong which the human eye can see, and the human heart feel, the human conscience can take notice of. A man, "through ignorance" of the laws which governed the sanctuary of old, might commit a trespass against those laws without being aware of it, until a higher light had shone in upon his conscience; but a man could not "through ignorance" tell a lie, swear falsely, commit an act of violence, deceive his neighbor, or find a lost thing and deny it. These were all plain and palpable acts, lying within the range of the most sluggish sensibility. Hence it is that the expression, "through ignorance" is introduced in reference to "the holy things of the Lord," and omitted in reference to the common affairs of men. How blessed it is to know that the precious blood of Christ has settled all questions, whether with respect to God or man— our sins of ignorance or our known sins! Here lies the deep and settled foundation of the believer's peace. The cross has divinely met ALL.

Again, when it was a question of trespass "in the holy things of the Lord," the unblemished sacrifice was first introduced; and afterward, "the principal" and "the fifth." This order was reversed when it was a question of the common affairs of life. (Comp. chap. v. 15, 16 with chap. vi. 4–7.) The reason of this is equally obvious. When the divine rights were infringed, the blood of atonement was made the great prominent matter; whereas when human rights were interfered with, restitution would naturally assume the leading place in the mind. But inasmuch as the latter involved the question of the soul's relation with God as well as the former, therefore the sacrifice is introduced, though it be last in order. If I wrong my fellow-man, that wrong will undoubtedly interfere with my communion with God; and that communion can only be restored on the ground of atonement. Mere restitution would not avail; it might satisfy the injured man, but it could not form the basis of restored communion with God. I might restore "the principal" and add "the fifth" ten thousand times over, and yet my sin remain, for "without shedding of blood is no remission." (Heb. ix. 22.) Still, if it be a question of injury done to my neighbor, then restitution must first be made.—"If thou bring thy gift to the altar, and there rememberest that thy brother hath aught against thee, leave there thy gift before the altar, and go thy way; first be reconciled to thy brother, and then come and offer thy gift." (Matt. v. 23, 24.)*

There is far more involved in the divine order prescribed in the trespass-offering than might at first sight appear. The claims which arise out of our human relations must not be disregarded; they must ever get their proper place in the heart. This

---

*From a comparison of Matt. v. 23, 24 with Matt. xviii. 21, 22, we may learn a fine principle as to the way in which wrongs and injuries are to be settled between two brothers. The injurer is sent back from the altar, in order to have his matters set straight with the injured one; for there can be no communion with the Father so long as my brother "hath aught against me." But then, mark the beauteous way in which the injured one is taught to receive the injurer.—"'Lord, how oft shall my brother sin against me, and I forgive him? till seven times?' Jesus saith unto him, 'I say not unto thee, Until seven times; but, *Until seventy times seven.*'" Such is the divine mode of settling all questions between brethren. "Forbearing one another, and forgiving one another, if any man have a quarrel against any: even as Christ forgave you, so also do ye." (Col. iii. 13.)

is distinctly taught in the trespass-offering. When an Israelite had, by an act of trespass, deranged his relation with Jehovah, the order was, sacrifice and restitution: when he had, by an act of trespass, deranged his relation with his neighbor, the order was, restitution and sacrifice. Will any one undertake to say this is a distinction without a difference? Does the change of the order not convey its own appropriate, because divinely appointed, lesson? Unquestionably. Every point is pregnant with meaning, if we will but allow the Holy Ghost to convey that meaning to our hearts, and not seek to grasp it by the aid of our poor vain imaginings. Each offering conveys its own characteristic view of the Lord Jesus and His work, and each is presented in its own characteristic order; and, we may safely say, it is at once the business and the delight of the spiritual mind to apprehend both the one and the other. The very same character of mind which would seek to make nothing of the peculiar order of each offering, would also set aside the idea of a peculiar phase of Christ in each. It would deny the existence of any difference between the burnt-offering and the sin-offering, and between the sin-offering and the trespass-offering, and between any or all of these and the meat-offering or the peace-offering. Hence, it would follow that the first seven chapters of the book of Leviticus are all a vain repetition, each successive chapter going over the same thing. Who could cede aught so monstrous as this? What Christian mind could suffer such an

insult to be offered to the sacred page? A German
rationalist or neologian may put forth such vain and
detestable notions, but those who have been divinely
taught that "all scripture is given by inspiration of
God," will be led to regard the various types, in
their specific order, as so many variously-shaped
caskets, in which the Holy Ghost has treasured up,
for the people of God, "the unsearchable riches of
Christ." There is no tedious repetition, no redun-
dancy. All is rich, divine, heavenly variety; and
all we need is to be personally acquainted with the
great Antitype, in order to enter into the beauties
and seize the delicate touches of each type. Directly
the heart lays hold of the fact that it is Christ we
have in each type, it can hang with spiritual interest over the most minute details, it sees meaning and beauty in every thing, it finds Christ in
all. As, in the kingdom of nature, the telescope
and the microscope present to the eye their own
special wonders, so with the Word of God; whether
we look at it as a whole, or scrutinize each clause,
we find that which elicits the worship and thanksgiving of our hearts.

Christian reader, may the name of the Lord Jesus
ever be more precious to our hearts! Then shall we
value every thing that speaks of Him—every thing
that sets Him forth—every thing affording a fresh
insight into His peculiar excellency and matchless
beauty.

NOTE.—The remainder of chapter vi, together

with the whole of chapter vii, is occupied with the law of the various offerings, to which reference has already been made. There are, however, some points presented in the law of the sin-offering and the trespass-offering which may be noticed ere we leave this copious section of our book.

In none of the offerings is Christ's personal holiness more strikingly presented than in the sin-offering. "Speak unto Aaron and to his sons, saying, This is the law of the sin-offering: In the place where the burnt-offering is killed shall the sin-offering be killed before the Lord: *it is most holy*. . . . . Whatsoever shall touch the flesh thereof *shall be holy*. . . . . All the males among the priests shall eat thereof: *it is most holy*." (Chap. vi. 25–29.) So also in speaking of the meat-offering, "It is most holy, *as is the sin-offering*, and as the trespass-offering." This is most marked and striking. The Holy Ghost did not need to guard with such jealousy the personal holiness of Christ in the burnt-offering; but lest the soul should, by any means, lose sight of that holiness while contemplating the place which the blessed One took in the sin-offering, we are again and again reminded of it by the words, "It is most holy." Truly edifying and refreshing it is to behold the divine and essential holiness of the Person of Christ shining forth in the midst of Calvary's profound and awful gloom. The same point is observable "in the law of the trespass-offering." (See chap. vii. 1, 6.) Never was the Lord Jesus more fully seen to be "the Holy One of God"

than when He was "made sin" upon the cursed tree.
The vileness and blackness of that with which He
stood identified on the cross, only served to show
out more clearly that He was "most holy." Though
a sin-bearer, He was sinless; though enduring the
wrath of *God*, He was the *Father's* delight; though
deprived of the light of *God's* countenance, He dwelt
in the *Father's* bosom. Precious mystery! Who can
sound its mighty depths? How wonderful to find it
so accurately shadowed forth in "the law of the sin-
offering"!

Again, my reader should seek to apprehend the
meaning of the expression, "All the *males* among
the priests shall eat thereof." The ceremonial act of
eating the sin-offering or the trespass-offering was
expressive of full identification; but to eat the sin-
offering—to make another's sin one's own, demanded
a higher degree of priestly energy, such as was expressed in "the *males* among the priests." "And
the Lord spake unto Aaron, 'Behold, I also have
given thee the charge of Mine heave-offerings of all
the hallowed things of the children of Israel; unto
thee have I given them by reason of the anointing,
and *to thy sons*, by an ordinance forever. This shall
be thine of the most holy things, reserved from the
fire: every oblation of theirs, every meat-offering of
theirs, and every sin-offering of theirs, and every
trespass-offering of theirs, which they shall render
unto Me, shall be most holy for thee and for *thy
sons*. In the most holy place shalt thou eat it; *every
male* shall eat it: i. shall be holy unto thee. And

this is thine; the heave-offering of their gift, witl. aii the wave-offerings of the children of Israel: I have given them unto thee, and to thy sons and to *thy daughters* with thee, by a statute forever: *every one that is clean* in thy house shall eat of it." (Numb. xviii. 8–11.)

It demanded a larger measure of priestly energy to eat of the sin or trespass-offering than merely to partake of the heave and wave-offerings of gift. The "daughters" of Aaron could eat of the latter: none but the "sons" could eat of the former. In general, "the male" expresses a thing according to the divine idea; "the female," according to human development. The former gives you the thing in full energy; the latter, in its imperfections. How few of us have sufficient priestly energy to enable us to make another's sin or trespass our own! The blessed Lord Jesus did this perfectly. He made His people's sins His own, and bore the judgment thereof, on the cross. He fully identified Himself with us, so that we may know, in full and blessed certainty, that the whole question of sin and trespass has been divinely settled. If Christ's identification was perfect, then the settlement was perfect likewise; and that it was perfect, the scene enacted at Calvary declares. All is accomplished. The sin, the trespasses, the claims of God, the claims of man —all have been eternally settled; and now, perfect peace is the portion of all who, by grace, accept as true the record of God. It is as simple as God could make it, and the soul that believes it is made happy. The peace and happiness of the believer depend wholly upon the perfection of Christ's sacrifice. It is not a question of his mode of receiving it, his thoughts about it, or his feelings respecting it; it is simply a question of his crediting, by faith, the testimony of God as to the value of the sacrifice. The Lord be praised for His own simple and perfect way of peace! May many troubled souls be led by the Holy Spirit into an understanding thereof?

We shall here close our meditations upon one of the richest sections in the whole canon of inspiration. It is but little we have been enabled to glean from it. We have hardly penetrated below the surface of an exhaustless mine. If, however, the reader has, for the first time, been led to view the offerings as so many varied exhibitions of the great Sacrifice, and if he is led to cast himself at the feet of the great Teacher, to learn more of the living depths of these things, I cannot but feel that an end has been gained for which we may well feel deeply thankful.

CHAPTERS VIII. & IX

HAVING considered the doctrine of sacrifice, as unfolded in the first seven chapters of this book, we now approach the subject of priesthood. The two subjects are intimately connected. The sinner needs a *sacrifice;* the believer needs a *priest.* We have both the one and the other in Christ, who, having offered Himself without spot to God, entered upon the sphere of His priestly ministry in the sanctuary above. We need no other sacrifice, no other priest: Jesus is divinely sufficient. He imparts the dignity and worth of His own Person to every office He sustains, and to every work He performs. When we see Him as a sacrifice, we know that we have in Him all that a perfect sacrifice could be; and when we see Him as a priest, we know that every function of the priesthood is perfectly discharged by Him. As a sacrifice, He introduces His people into a settled relationship with God; and as a priest, He maintains them therein, according to the perfectness of what He is. Priesthood is designed for those who already stand in a certain relationship with God. As sinners, by nature and by practice, we are "brought nigh to God by the blood of the cross;" we are brought into an established relationship with Him; we stand before Him as the fruit of His own work. He has put away our sins in such a manner as suits Himself, so that we might be before Him to the praise of His name, as the exhibition of what He can accomplish through the power of death and resurrection.

But though so fully delivered from every thing that could be against us—though so perfectly accepted in the Beloved—though so complete in Christ —though so highly exalted, yet are we, in ourselves, while down here, poor feeble creatures, ever prone to wander, ready to stumble, exposed to manifold temptations, trials, and snares. As such, we need the ceaseless ministry of our "great High-Priest," whose very presence in the sanctuary above maintains us in the full integrity of that place and relationship in which, through grace, we stand. "He ever liveth to make intercession for us." (Heb. vii. 25.) We could not stand for a moment down here if He were not living for us up there. "Because I live, ye shall live also." (John xiv. 19.) "For if, when we were enemies, we were reconciled to God by the death of His Son, much more, being reconciled, we shall be saved by His life." (Rom. v. 10.) The "death" and the "life" are inseparably connected in the economy of grace. But, be it observed, the life comes after the death. It is Christ's life as risen from the dead, and not His life down here, that the apostle refers to in the last-quoted passage. This distinction is eminently worthy of my reader's attention. The life of our blessed Lord Jesus while down here was, I need hardly remark, infinitely precious; but He did not enter upon His sphere of priestly service until He had accomplished the work of redemption. Nor could He have done so, inasmuch as "it is evident that our Lord sprang out of Juda, of which tribe Moses spake nothing concerning priesthood." (Heb. vii. 14.) "For every high-priest is ordained to offer gifts and sacrifices: wherefore it is of necessity that this Man have somewhat also to offer. For if He were on earth, He should not be a priest, seeing that there are priests that offer gifts according to the law." (Heb. viii. 3, 4.) "But Christ being come a high-priest of good things to come, by a greater and more perfect tabernacle, not made with hands, that is to say, not of this building; neither by the blood of goats and calves, but by His own blood He entered in once into the holy place, having obtained eternal redemption. . . . . For Christ is not entered into the holy places made with hands, which are the figures of the true; but into heaven itself, now to appear in the presence of God for us." (Heb. ix. 11, 12, 24.)

Heaven, not earth, is the sphere of Christ's priestly ministry; and on that sphere He entered when He had offered Himself without spot to God. He never appeared as a priest in the temple below. He ofttimes went up to the temple to teach, but never to sacrifice or burn incense. There never was any one ordained of God to discharge the functions of the priestly office on earth save Aaron and his sons. "If He were on earth, He should not be a priest." This is a point of much interest and value in connection with the doctrine of priesthood. Heaven is the sphere, and accomplished redemption the basis, of Christ's priesthood. Save in the sense that all believers are priests (1 Pet. ii. 5.), there is no such thing as a priest upon earth. Unless a man can show his descent from Aaron—unless he can trace his pedigree up to that ancient source, he has no right to exercise the priestly office. Apostolic succession itself, could it be proved, would be of no possible value here, inasmuch as the apostles themselves were not priests, save in the sense above referred to. The feeblest member of the household of faith is as much a priest as the apostle Peter himself. He is a spiritual priest,—he worships in a spiritual temple, he stands at a spiritual altar, he offers a spiritual sacrifice, he is clad in spiritual vestments. "Ye also, as lively stones, are built up a spiritual house, a holy priesthood, to offer up spiritual sacrifices, acceptable to God by Jesus Christ." (1 Pet. ii. 5.) "By Him, therefore, let us offer the sacrifice of praise to God continually, that is, the fruit of our lips, giving thanks to His name. But to do good and to communicate forget not, for with such sacrifices God is well pleased." (Heb. xiii. 15, 16.)

If one of the direct descendants of the house of Aaron were converted to Christ, he would enter upon an entirely new character and ground of priestly service. And be it observed, that the passages just quoted present the two great classes of spiritual sacrifice which the spiritual priest is privileged to offer. There is the sacrifice of praise to God, and the sacrifice of benevolence to man. There is a double stream continually going forth from the believer who is living in the realization of his priestly place—a stream of grateful praise ascending to the throne of God, and a stream of active benevolence flowing forth to a needy world. The spiritual priest stands with one hand lifted up to God in the presentation of the incense of grateful praise, and the other opened wide to minister, in genuine beneficence, to every form of human need. Were these things more distinctly apprehended, what hallowed elevation and what moral grace would they not impart to the Christian character! Elevation, inasmuch as the heart would ever be lifted up to the infinite Source of all that is capable of elevating; moral grace, inasmuch as the heart would ever be kept open to all demands upon its sympathies. The two things are inseparable. Immediate occupation of heart with God must, of necessity, elevate and enlarge; but, on the other hand, if one walks at a distance from God, the heart will become groveling and contracted. Intimacy of communion with God—the habitual realization of our priestly dignity, is the only effectual remedy for the downward and selfish tendencies of the old nature.

Having said thus much on the subject of priesthood in general, both as to its primary and secondary aspects, we shall proceed to examine the contents of the eighth and ninth chapters of the book of Leviticus.

"And the Lord spake unto Moses, saying, 'Take Aaron and his sons with him, and the garments, and the anointing oil, and a bullock for the sin-offering, and two rams, and a basket of unleavened bread; and gather thou all the congregation together unto the door of the tabernacle of the congregation.' And Moses did as the Lord commanded him; and the assembly was gathered together unto the door of the tabernacle of the congregation." There is special grace unfolded here. The whole assembly is convened at the door of the tabernacle of the congregation, in order that all might have the

privilege of beholding the one who was about to be
intrusted with the charge of their most important
interests.   In the twenty-eighth and twenty-ninth
of Exodus we are taught the same general truth
with respect to the vestments and sacrifices connected with the priestly office; but in Leviticus, the
the congregation is introduced, and allowed to look
on at every movement in the solemn and impressive
service of consecration.   The humblest member of
the assembly had his own place.   Each one—the
lowest as well as the highest—was permitted to gaze
upon the person of the high-priest, upon the sacrifice which he offered, and upon the robes which he
wore.   Each one had his own peculiar need, and
the God of Israel would have each to see and know
that his need was fully provided for by the varied
qualifications of the high-priest who stood before
him.   Of these qualifications the priestly robes were
the apt typical expression.   Each portion of the
dress was designed and adapted to set forth some
special qualification in which the assembly as a
whole, and each individual member, would, of necessity, be deeply interested.   The coat, the girdle,
the robe, the ephod, the breastplate, the Urim and
the Thummim, the mitre, the holy crown—all told
out the varied virtues, qualifications, and functions
of the one who was to represent the congregation
and maintain the interests thereof in the divine
presence.

Thus it is the believer can, with the eye of faith,
behold his great High-Priest in the heavens, and

see in Him the divine realities of which the Aaronic vestments were but the shadows. The Lord Jesus Christ is the holy One, the anointed One, the mitred One, the girded One. He is all these, not in virtue of outward garments to be put on or off, but in virtue of the divine and eternal graces of His Person, the changeless efficacy of His work, and the imperishable virtue of His sacred offices. This is the special value of studying the types of the Mosaic economy. The enlightened eye sees Christ in all. The blood of the sacrifice and the robe of the high-priest both point to Him—both were designed of God to set Him forth. If it be a question of conscience, the blood of the sacrifice meets it, according to the just claims of the sanctuary. Grace has met the demand of holiness. And then, if it be a question of the need connected with the believer's position down here, he can see it all divinely answered in the official robes of the high-priest.

And here let me say, there are two ways in which to contemplate the believer's position—two ways in which that position is presented in the Word, which must be taken into account ere the true idea of priesthood can be intelligently laid hold of. The believer is represented as being part of a body of which Christ is the Head. This body, with Christ its Head, is spoken of as forming one man, complete in every respect. It was quickened with Christ, raised with Christ, and in Christ seated in the heavens. It is one with Him, complete in Him, accepted in Him, possessing His life, and

standing in His favor before God. All trespasses
are blotted out. There is no spot. All is fair
and lovely beneath the eye of God. (See 1 Cor.
xii. 12, 13; Eph. ii. 5-10; Col. ii. 6-15; 1 John
iv. 17.)

Then, again, the believer is contemplated as in
the place of need, weakness, and dependence down
here in this world. He is ever exposed to temptation, prone to wander, liable to stumble and fall.
As such, he continually stands in need of the perfect sympathy and powerful ministrations of the
High-Priest, who ever appears in the presence of
God in the full value of His Person and work, and
who represents the believer and maintains his cause
before the throne.

Now, my reader should ponder both these aspects
of the believer, in order that he may see, not only
what a highly exalted and privileged place he occupies with Christ on high, but also what ample provision there is for him in reference to his every
need and weakness here below. This distinction
might further be developed in this way:—The believer is represented as being *of the Church*, and *in
the kingdom*. As the former, heaven is his place,
his home, his portion, the seat of his affections: as
the latter, he is on earth, in the place of trial,
responsibility, and conflict. Hence, therefore,
priesthood is a divine provision for those who
though being of the Church, and belonging to
heaven, are nevertheless in the kingdom, and walking on the earth. This distinction is a very simple

one, and, when apprehended, explains a vast number of passages of Scripture in which many minds encounter considerable difficulty.*

In looking into the contents of the chapters which lie open before us, we may remark three things put prominently forward, namely, the authority of the Word, the value of the blood, the power of the Spirit. These are weighty matters—matters of unspeakable importance—matters which must be regarded by every Christian as unquestionably vital and fundamental.

And, first, as to the authority of the Word, it is of the deepest interest to see that in the consecration of the priests, as well as in the entire range of the sacrifices, we are brought immediately under the authority of the Word of God.—"And Moses said unto the congregation, '*This is the thing which the Lord* commanded to be done.'" (Chap. viii. 5.) And again, "Moses said, '*This is the thing which the Lord commanded* that ye should do: *and the glory of the Lord shall appear unto you.*'" (Chap. ix. 6.) Let these words sink down into our ears; let them be carefully and prayerfully pondered: they are priceless words.—"*This* is *the* thing which *the Lord* commanded." He did not say, This is the thing which is expedient, agreeable, or suitable; neither did he say, This is the thing which has been

---

*A comparison of the epistle to the Ephesians with the first epistle of Peter will furnish the reader with much valuable instruction in reference to the double aspect of the believer's position. The former shows him as seated in heaven; the latter, as a pilgrim and a sufferer on earth.

arranged by the voice of the fathers, the decree of
the elders, or the opinion of the doctors. Moses
knew nothing of such sources of authority. To him
there was one holy, elevated, paramount source of
authority, and that was, the Word of Jehovah, and
he would bring every member of the assembly into
direct contact with that blessed source. This gave
assurance to the heart, and fixedness to all the
thoughts. There was no room left for tradition,
with its uncertain sound, or for man, with his
doubtful disputations. All was clear, conclusive,
and authoritative. Jehovah had spoken; and all
that was needed was to hear what He had said, and
obey. Neither tradition nor expediency has any
place in the heart that has learnt to prize, to reverence, and to obey the Word of God.

And what was to be the result of this strict adherence to the Word of God? A truly blessed
result indeed.—"The glory of the Lord shall appear
unto you." Had the Word been disregarded, the
glory would not have appeared. The two things
were intimately connected. The slightest deviation
from "Thus saith Jehovah" would have prevented
the beams of the divine glory from appearing to the
congregation of Israel. Had there been the introduction of a single rite or ceremony not enjoined
by the Word, or had there been the omission of
aught which that Word commanded, Jehovah would
not have manifested His glory. He could not sanction by the glory of His presence the neglect or
rejection of His Word. He can bear with ignorance

and infirmity, but He cannot sanction neglect or disobedience.

Oh that all this were more solemnly considered, in this day of tradition and expediency! I would, in earnest affection, and in the deep sense of personal responsibility to my reader, exhort him to give diligent heed to the importance of close—I had almost said severe—adherence and reverent subjection to the Word of God. Let him try every thing by that standard, and reject all that comes not up to it,—let him weigh every thing in that balance, and cast aside all that is not full weight,—let him measure every thing by that rule, and refuse all deviation. If I could only be the means of awakening one soul to a proper sense of the place which belongs to the Word of God, I should feel I had not written my book for naught or in vain.

Reader, pause, and, in the presence of the Searcher of hearts, ask yourself this plain, pointed question: Am I sanctioning by my presence, or adopting in my practice, any departure from, or neglect of, the Word of God? Make this a solemn, personal matter before the Lord. Be assured of it, it is of the very deepest moment—the very last importance. If you find that you have been in any wise connected with, or involved in, aught that wears not the distinct stamp of divine sanction, reject it at once and forever. Yes, reject it, though arrayed in the imposing vestments of antiquity, accredited by the voice of tradition, and putting forward the almost irresistible plea of expediency. If you cannot say,

in reference to every thing with which you stand
connected, "This is the thing which the Lord hath
commanded," then away with it unhesitatingly,
away with it forever. Remember these words, "*As*
He hath done this day, *so* the Lord hath commanded
to do." Yes, remember the "as" and the "so;"
see that you are connecting them in your ways and
associations, and let them never be separated.

"So Aaron and his sons did *all* things *which the
Lord commanded* by the hand of Moses." (Chap.
viii. 36.) "And Moses and Aaron went into the
tabernacle of the congregation, and came out, and
blessed the people: and the glory of the Lord appeared unto all the people. And there came a fire
out from before the Lord, and consumed upon the
altar the burnt-offering and the fat; which, when all
the people saw, they shouted and fell on their faces."
(Chap. ix. 23, 24.) Here we have an "eighth day"
scene—a scene of resurrection-glory. Aaron, having offered the sacrifice, lifted up his hands in
priestly benediction upon the people; and then
Moses and Aaron retire into the tabernacle, and
disappear, while the whole assembly is seen in waiting outside. Finally, Moses and Aaron, represent-
ing Christ in His double character as Priest and
King, come forth, and bless the people; the glory
appears in all its splendor, the fire consumes the
sacrifice, and the entire congregation falls prostrate
in worship before the presence of the Lord of all
the earth.

Now, all this was literally enacted at the conse-

cration of Aaron and his sons; and, moreover, all
this was the result of strict adherence to the Word
of Jehovah. But ere I turn from this branch of the
subject, let me remind the reader that all that these
chapters contain is but "a shadow of good things
to come." This, indeed, holds good in reference to
the entire Mosaic economy. (Heb. x. 1.) Aaron
and his sons together represent Christ and His
priestly house; Aaron alone represents Christ in
His sacrificial and intercessory functions; Moses
and Aaron together represent Christ as King and
Priest; "the eighth day" represents the day of
resurrection-glory, when the congregation of Israel
shall see the Messiah, seated as a Royal Priest upon
His throne, and when the glory of Jehovah shall fill
the whole earth, as the waters cover the sea. These
sublime truths are largely unfolded in the Word,
they glitter like gems of celestial brilliancy all along
the inspired page; but lest they should, to any
reader, wear the suspicious aspect of novelty, I
shall refer him to the following direct Scripture
proofs; viz., Num. xiv. 21; Isaiah ix. 6, 7; xi.;
xxv. 6–12; xxxii. 1, 2; xxxv.; xxxvii. 31, 32; xl.
1–5; liv.; lix. 16–21; lx.–lxvi.; *passim*, Jer. xxiii.
5–8; xxx. 10–24; xxxiii. 6–22; Ezek. xlviii. 35;
Dan. vii. 13, 14; Hos. xiv. 4–9; Zeph. iii. 14–20;
Zech. iii. 8–10; vi. 12, 13; xiv.

Let us now consider the second point presented
in our section, namely, the efficacy of the blood.
This is unfolded with great fullness, and put forward in great prominence. Whether we contem-

plate the doctrine of sacrifice or the doctrine of priesthood, we find the shedding of blood gets the same important place. "And he brought the bullock for the sin-offering; and Aaron and his sons laid their hands upon the head of the bullock for the sin-offering. And he slew it; and Moses took the blood, and put it upon the horns of the altar round about with his finger, and purified the altar, and poured the blood at the bottom of the altar, and sanctified it, to make reconciliation upon it." (Chap. viii. 14, 15.) "And he brought the ram for the burnt-offering; and Aaron and his sons laid their hands upon the head of the ram. And he killed it; and Moses sprinkled the blood upon the altar round about." (Ver. 18, 19.) "And he brought the other ram, the ram of consecration; and Aaron and his sons laid their hands upon the head of the ram. And he slew it; and Moses took of the blood of it, and put it upon the tip of Aaron's right ear, and upon the thumb of his right hand, and upon the great toe of his right foot. And he brought Aaron's sons, and Moses put of the blood upon the tip of their right ear, and upon the thumbs of their right hands, and upon the great toes of their right feet; and Moses sprinkled the blood upon the altar round about." (Ver. 22–24.)

The import of the various sacrifices has been, in some degree, developed in the opening chapters of this volume; but the passages just quoted serve to show the prominent place which the blood occupies in the consecration of the priests. A blood-stained *ear* was needed to hearken to the divine communications, a blood-stained *hand* was needed to execute the services of the sanctuary, and a blood-stained *foot* was needed to tread the courts of the Lord's house. All this is perfect in its way. The shedding of blood was the grand foundation of all sacrifice for sin, and it stood connected with all the vessels of the ministry and with all the functions of the priesthood. Throughout the entire range of Levitical service, we observe the value, the efficacy, the power, and the wide application of the blood. "Almost all things are by the law purged with blood." (Heb. ix. 22.) Christ has entered, by His own blood, into heaven itself. He appears on the throne of the Majesty in the heavens in the value of all that He has accomplished on the cross. His presence on the throne attests the worth and acceptableness of His atoning blood. He is there *for us.* Blessed assurance! He ever liveth. He never changeth; and we are in Him, and as He is. He presents us to the Father in His own eternal perfectness; and the Father delights in us as thus presented, even as He delights in the One who presents us. This identification is typically set forth in "Aaron and his sons" laying their hands upon the head of each of the sacrifices. They all stood before God in the value of the same sacrifice. Whether it were the "bullock for the sin-offering," "the ram for the burnt-offering," or "the ram of consecration," they jointly laid their hands on all. True, Aaron alone was anointed before the blood

was shed,—he was clad in his robes of office and
anointed with the holy oil before ever his sons were
clothed or anointed.   The reason of this is obvious.
Aaron, when spoken of by himself, typifies Christ
in His own peerless excellency and dignity; and,
as we know, Christ appeared in all His own personal
worth and was anointed by the Holy Ghost previous
to the accomplishment of His atoning work.   In all
things He has the pre-eminence. (Col. i.)   Still,
there is the fullest identification afterwards between
Aaron and his sons, as there is the fullest identification between Christ and His people.   "The Sancti-
fier and the sanctified are all of one." (Heb. ii.)
The personal distinctness enhances the value of the
mystic oneness.

This truth of the distinctness and yet oneness of
the Head and members leads us naturally to our
third and last point, namely, the power of the
Spirit.   We may remark how much takes place
between the anointing of Aaron and the anointing
of his sons with him.   The blood is shed, the fat
consumed on the altar, and the breast waved before
the Lord.   In other words, the Sacrifice is perfected,
the sweet odor thereof ascends to God, and the One
who offered it ascends in the power of resurrection,
and takes His place on high.   All this comes in between the anointing of the Head and the anointing
of the members.   Let us quote and compare the
passages.   First, as to Aaron alone, we read, "And
he put upon him the coat, and girded him with the
girdle, and clothed him with the robe, and put the

ephod upon him, and he girded him with the curious girdle of the ephod, and bound it unto him therewith. And he put the breastplate upon him; also he put in the breastplate the Urim and the Thummim. And he put the mitre upon his head; and upon the mitre, even upon his forefront, did he put the golden plate, the holy crown; as the Lord commanded Moses. And Moses took the anointing oil, and anointed the tabernacle and all that was therein, and sanctified them. And he sprinkled thereof upon the altar seven times, and anointed the altar and all his vessels, both the laver and his foot, to sanctify them. And he poured of the anointing oil upon Aaron's head, and anointed him, to sanctify him." (Chap. viii. 7–12.)

Here we have Aaron presented alone. The anointing oil is poured upon his head, and that, too, in immediate connection with the anointing of all the vessels of the tabernacle. The whole assembly was permitted to behold the high-priest clothed in his official robes, mitred and anointed; and not only so, but as each garment was put on—as each act was performed—as each ceremony was enacted, it was seen to be immediately founded upon the authority of the Word. There was nothing vague, nothing arbitrary, nothing imaginative: all was divinely stable. The need of the congregation was fully met, and met in such a way as that it could be said, "This is the thing which Jehovah commanded to be done."

Now, in Aaron anointed alone, previous to the

shedding of the blood, we have a type of Christ, who, until He offered Himself upon the cross, stood entirely alone. There could be no union between Him and His people save on the ground of death and resurrection. This all-important truth has already been referred to, and, in some measure, developed in connection with the subject of sacrifice; but it adds force and interest to it to see it so distinctly presented in connection with the question of priesthood. Without shedding of blood there was no remission—the sacrifice was not completed. So, also, without shedding of blood Aaron and his sons could not be anointed together. Let the reader note this fact; let him be assured of it, it is worthy of his deepest attention. We must ever beware of passing lightly over any circumstance in the Levitical economy. Every thing has its own specific voice and meaning; and the One who designed and developed the order can expound to the heart and understanding what that order means.

"And Moses took of the anointing *oil*, and of the *blood* which was upon the altar, and sprinkled it upon Aaron, and upon his garments, and upon his sons, and upon his sons' garments *with him;* and sanctified Aaron, and his garments, and his sons, and his sons' garments *with him*." (Chap. viii. 30.) Why were not Aaron's sons anointed with him at verse 12? Simply because the blood had not been shed. When "the blood" and "the oil" could be connected together, then Aaron and his sons could be "anointed" and "sanctified" together, but not

until then. "And for their sakes I sanctify Myself,
that they also might be sanctified through the truth."
(John xvii. 19.) The reader who could lightly pass
over so marked a circumstance, or say it meant nothing, has yet to learn to value aright the types of
the Old Testament scriptures — "the shadows of
good things to come;" and, on the other hand,
the one who admits that it does mean something,
but yet refuses to inquire and understand what that
something is, is doing serious damage to his own
soul, and manifesting but little interest in the precious oracles of God.

"And Moses said unto Aaron and to his sons,
'Boil the flesh at the door of the tabernacle of the
congregation; and there eat it with the bread that
is in the basket of consecrations, as I commanded,
saying, Aaron and his sons shall eat it. And that
which remaineth of the flesh and of the bread shall
ye burn with fire. And ye shall not go out of the
door of the tabernacle of the congregation in seven
days, until the days of your consecration be at an
end; for seven days shall He consecrate you. As
He hath done this day, so the Lord hath commanded
to do, to make an atonement for you. Therefore
shall ye abide at the door of the tabernacle of the
congregation day and night seven days, and keep
the charge of the Lord, that ye die not; for so I am
commanded.'" (Ver. 31–35.) These verses furnish
a fine type of Christ and His people feeding together
upon the results of accomplished atonement. Aaron
and his sons, having been anointed together on the

ground of the shed blood, are here presented to our
view as shut in within the precincts of the tabernacle
during "seven days." A striking figure of the
present position of Christ and His members during
the entire of this dispensation—shut in with God,
and waiting for the manifestation of the glory.
Blessed position! Blessed portion! Blessed hope!
To be associated with Christ, shut in with God,
waiting for the day of glory, and, while waiting for
the glory, feeding upon the riches of divine grace,
in the power of holiness, are blessings of the most
precious nature—privileges of the very highest
order. Oh, for a capacity to take them in, a heart
to enjoy them, a deeper sense of their magnitude!
May our hearts be withdrawn from all that pertains
to this present evil world, so that we may feed upon
the contents of "the basket of consecrations,"
which is our proper food as priests in the sanctuary
of God.

"And it came to pass *on the eighth day*, that Moses
called Aaron, and his sons, and *the elders of Israel.*
And he said unto Aaron, 'Take thee a young calf
for a sin-offering, and a ram for a burnt-offering,
without blemish, and offer them before the Lord.
And unto *the children of Israel* thou shalt speak,
saying, Take ye a kid of the goats for a sin-offering;
and a calf and a lamb, both of the first year, without
blemish, for a burnt-offering; also a bullock and a
ram for peace-offerings, to sacrifice before the Lord;
and a meat-offering mingled with oil; for TO-DAY
THE LORD WILL APPEAR UNTO YOU.'" (Chap. ix. 1–4.)

The "seven days" being over, during which Aaron and his sons were shut in in the retirement of the tabernacle, the whole congregation is now introduced, and the glory of Jehovah unfolds itself. This gives great completeness to the whole scene. The shadows of good things to come are here passing before us, in their divine order. "The "eighth day" is a shadow of that bright millennial morning which is about to dawn upon this earth, when the congregation of Israel shall behold the true Priest coming forth from the sanctuary, where He is now hidden from the eyes of men, and with Him a company of priests—the companions of His retirement, and the happy participators of His manifested glory. In short, nothing, as a type or shadow, could be more complete. In the first place, Aaron and his sons washed with water—a type of Christ and His people, as viewed in God's eternal decree, sanctified together in purpose. (Chap. viii. 6.) Then we have the mode and order in which this purpose was to be carried out. Aaron, in solitude, is robed and anointed—a type of Christ as sanctified and sent into the world, and anointed by the Holy Ghost. (Ver. 7–12; comp. Luke iii. 21, 22; John x. 36; xii. 24.) Then we have the presentation and acceptance of the sacrifice, in virtue of which Aaron and his sons were anointed and sanctified *together* (ver. 14–29.)—a type of the cross, in its application to those who now constitute Christ's priestly household, who are united to Him, anointed with Him, hidden with Him, and expecting with Him "the eighth day," when He with them

shall be manifested in all the brightness of that glory
which belongs to Him in the eternal purpose of God.
(John xiv. 19; Acts ii. 33; xix. 1–7; Col. iii. 1–4.)
Finally, we have Israel brought into the full enjoyment of the results of accomplished atonement.
They are gathered before the Lord; "and Aaron
lifted up his hand toward the people, and blessed
them, and came down from offering of the sin-offering, and the burnt-offering, and peace-offerings."
(See chap. ix. 1–22.)

What, now, we may legitimately inquire, remains
to be done? Simply that the top-stone should be
brought forth with shoutings of victory and hymns
of praise. "And Moses and Aaron went into the
tabernacle of the congregation, and came out, and
blessed the people: and *the glory of the Lord appeared unto all the people.* And there came a fire
out from before the Lord, and consumed upon the
altar the burnt-offering and the fat: which when all
the people saw, THEY SHOUTED, AND FELL
ON THEIR FACES." (Ver. 23, 24.) This was
the shout of victory—the prostration of worship.
All was complete. The sacrifice, the robed and
mitred priest, the priestly family associated with
their head, the priestly benediction, the appearance
of the king and priest; in short, nothing was lacking, and therefore the divine glory appeared, and
the whole assembly fell prostrate in adoring worship.
It is altogether a truly magnificent scene—a marvelously beautiful shadow of good things to come.
And be it remembered, that all which is here shad-

owed forth will ere long be fully actualized. Our
great High-Priest has passed into the heavens, in
the full value and power of accomplished atonement.
He is hidden there now, and with Him all the members of His priestly family; but when the "seven
days" have run their course, and "the eighth day"
casts its beams upon the earth, then shall the remnant of Israel—a repentant and an expectant people—hail, with a shout of victory, the manifested
presence of the Royal Priest; and in immediate
association with Him shall be seen a company of
worshipers, occupying the most exalted position.
These are "the good things to come"—things,
surely, well worth waiting for—things worthy of
God to give—things in which He shall be eternally
glorified, and His people eternally blessed.

CHAPTER X.

THE page of human history has ever been a sadly
    blotted one. It is a record of failure from
first to last. Amid all the delights of Eden, man
hearkened to the tempter's lie (Gen. iii.); when
preserved from judgment by the hand of electing
love, and introduced into a restored earth, he was
guilty of the sin of intemperance (Gen. ix.); when
conducted, by Jehovah's outstretched arm, into the
land of Canaan, he "forsook the Lord, and served
Baal and Ashtaroth" (Judges ii. 13.); when placed
at the very summit of earthly power and glory, with

untold wealth at his feet, and all the resources of
the world at his command, he gave his heart to the
uncircumcised stranger. (1 Kings xi.) No sooner
had the blessings of the gospel been promulgated
than it became needful for the Holy Ghost to
prophesy concerning "grievous wolves," "apostacy," and all manner of failure. (Acts xx. 29;
1 Tim. iv. 1–3; 2 Tim. iii. 1–5; 2 Pet. ii.; Jude.)
And, to crown all, we have the prophetic record
of human apostacy from amid all the splendors of
millennial glory. (Rev. xx. 7–10.)

Thus, man spoils every thing. Place him in a
position of highest dignity, and he will degrade
himself; endow him with the most ample privileges,
and he will abuse them; scatter blessings around
him in richest profusion, and he will prove ungrate-
ful, place him in the midst of the most impressive
institutions, and he will corrupt them. Such is
man! Such is nature in its fairest forms and under
the most favorable circumstances!

Hence, therefore, we are in a measure prepared
for the words with which our chapter opens—"And
Nadab and Abihu, the sons of Aaron, took either
of them his censer, and put fire therein, and put
incense thereon, and offered strange fire before the
Lord, which He commanded them not." What a
contrast to the scene with which our last section
closed! There, all was done "as the Lord commanded," and the result was, manifested glory;
here, something is done "which the Lord commanded them not," and the result is, judgment.

Hardly had the echo of the shout of victory died away ere the elements of a spurious worship were prepared,—hardly had the divine position been assumed ere it was deliberately abandoned, through neglect of the divine commandment. No sooner were those priests inaugurated than they grievously failed in the discharge of their priestly functions.

And in what did their failure consist? Were they spurious priests? were they mere pretenders? By no means. They were genuine sons of Aaron—true members of the priestly family—duly appointed priests. Their vessels of ministry, and their priestly garments too, would seem to have been all right. What, then, was their sin? Did they stain the curtains of the tabernacle with human blood? or pollute the sacred precincts with some crime which shocks the moral sense? We have no proof of their having done so. Their sin was this: "They offered strange fire before the Lord, which He commanded them not." Here was their sin. They departed in their worship from the plain word of Jehovah, who had fully and plainly instructed them as to the mode of their worship. We have already alluded to the divine fullness and sufficiency of the word of the Lord, in reference to every branch of priestly service. There was no room left for man to introduce what he might deem desirable or expedient. "This is the thing which the Lord hath commanded" was quite sufficient. It made all very plain and very simple. Nothing was needed on man's part save a spirit of implicit obedience to the divine command.

But herein they failed. Man has always proved himself ill-disposed to walk in the narrow path of strict adherence to the plain word of God. The by-path has ever seemed to present resistless charms to the poor human heart. "Stolen waters are sweet, and bread eaten in secret is pleasant." (Prov. ix. 17.) Such is the enemy's language; but the lowly, obedient heart knows full well that the path of subjection to the Word of God is the only one that leads to "waters" that are really "sweet," or to "bread" that can be rightly called "pleasant." Nadab and Abihu might have deemed one kind of "fire" as good as another, but it was not their province to decide as to that. They should have acted according to the word of the Lord; but instead of this, they took their own way and reaped the awful fruits thereof. "He knoweth not that the dead are there; and that her guests are in the depths of hell."

"And there went out fire from the Lord, and devoured them, and they died before the Lord." How deeply solemn! Jehovah was dwelling in the midst of His people, to govern, to judge, and to act, according to the claims of His nature. At the close of chapter ix, we read, "And there came a fire out from before the Lord, and consumed upon the altar the burnt-offering and the fat." This was Jehovah's acceptance of a true sacrifice; but in chapter x, it is His judgment upon erring priests. It is a double action of the same fire. The burnt-offering went up as a sweet ordor: the "strange fire" was rejected as an abomination. The Lord was glorified in the former; but it would have been a dishonor to accept the latter. Divine grace accepted and delighted in that which was a type of Christ's most precious sacrifice: divine holiness rejected that which was the fruit of man's corrupt will—a will never more hideous and abominable than when active in the things of God.

"Then Moses said unto Aaron, 'This is it that the Lord spake, saying, I will be sanctified in them that come nigh Me, and before all the people I will be glorified.'" The dignity and glory of the entire economy depended upon the strict maintenance of Jehovah's righteous claims. If these were to be trifled with, all was forfeited. If man were permitted to defile the sanctuary of the divine presence by "strange fire," there was an end to every thing. Nothing could be permitted to ascend from the priestly censer but the pure fire, kindled from off the altar of God, and fed by the "pure incense beaten small." Beauteous type of true saintly worship, of which the Father is the object, Christ the material, and the Holy Ghost the power. Man must not be allowed to introduce his devices into the worship of God. All his efforts can only issue in the presentation of "strange fire"—unhallowed incense—false worship. His very best attempts are an absolute abomination in the sight of God.

I speak not here of the honest struggles of earnest spirits searching after peace with God,—of the sincere efforts of upright, though unenlightened, consciences to attain to a knowledge of the forgive-

ness of sins by works of law or the ordinances of
symtematic religion; all such will doubtless issue,
through the exceeding goodness of God, in the clear
light of a known and an enjoyed salvation. They
prove very clearly that peace is earnestly sought;
though, at the same time, they prove just as clearly
that peace has not yet been found. There never
yet was one who honestly followed the faintest glim-
merings of light which fell upon his understanding
who did not, in due time, receive more. "To him
that hath shall more be given." And again, "The
path of the just is as the shining light, which shin-
eth more and more unto the perfect day."

All this is as plain as it is encouraging; but it
leaves wholly untouched the question of the human
will, and its impious workings in connection with
the service and worship of God. All such workings must inevitably call down, sooner or later, the
solemn judgment of a righteous God, who cannot
suffer His claims to be trifled with. "I will be
sanctified in them that come nigh Me, and before
all the people I will be glorified." Men will be
dealt with according to their profession. If men
are honestly seeking, they will assuredly find; but
when men approach as worshipers, they are no
longer to be regarded as seekers, but as those who
profess to have found; and then, if their priestly
censer smokes with unhallowed fire—if they offer
unto God the elements of a spurious worship—if
they profess to tread His courts, unwashed, un-
sanctified, unsubdued—if they place on His altar

the workings of their own corrupt will, what must
be the result? Judgment! Yes, sooner or later,
judgment must come. It may linger, but it will
come. It could not be otherwise. And not only
must judgment come at last, but there is, in every
case, the immediate rejection on the part of Heaven
of all worship which has not the Father for its object,
Christ for its material, and the Holy Ghost for its
power. God's holiness is as quick to reject all
"strange fire" as His grace is ready to accept the
faintest, feeblest breathings of a true heart. He
must pour out His righteous judgment upon all
false worship, though He will never "quench the
smoking flax nor break the bruised reed." The
thought of this is most solemnizing, when one calls
to mind the thousands of censers smoking with
strange fire throughout the wide domain of chris-
tendom. May the Lord, in His rich grace, add to
the number of true worshipers, who worship the
Father in spirit and in truth. (John iv.) It is infinitely happier to think of the true worship ascending from honest hearts to the throne of God, than
to contemplate, even for a moment, the spurious
worship on which the divine judgments must ere
long be poured out. Every one who knows, through
grace, the pardon of his sins through the atoning
blood of Jesus, can worship the Father in spirit and
in truth. He knows the proper ground, the proper
object, the proper title, the proper capacity of worship. These things can only be known in a divine
way. They do not belong to nature or to earth.

They are spiritual and heavenly.　Very much of
that which passes among men for the worship of
God is but "strange fire" after all.　There is neither
the pure fire nor the pure incense, and therefore
Heaven accepts it not; and albeit the divine judgment is not seen to fall upon those who present
such worship as it fell upon Nadab and Abihu of
old, this is only because "God is in Christ reconciling the world unto Himself, not imputing their
trespasses unto them."　It is not because the worship is acceptable to God, but because God is gracious.　The time, however, is rapidly approaching
when the strange fire will be quenched forever—
when the throne of God shall no longer be insulted
by clouds of impure incense ascending from unpurged worshipers—when all that is spurious shall
be abolished, and the whole universe shall be as
one vast and magnificent temple, in which the one
true God—Father, Son, and Holy Ghost—shall be
worshiped throughout the everlasting ages.

"Grateful incense this, ascending
　　Ever to the Father's throne;
Every knee to Jesus bending,
　　All the mind in heaven is one.

All the Father's counsels claiming
　　Equal honors to the Son,
All the Son's effulgence beaming
　　Makes the Father's glory known.

By the Spirit all pervading,
　　Hosts unnumbered round the Lamb,
Crowned with light and joy unfading,
　　Hail Him as the great 'I AM.'"

For this the redeemed are waiting; and, blessed be God, it is but a little while when all their longing desires shall be fully met, and met forever—yea, met after such a fashion as to elicit from each and all the touching confession of Sheba's queen that "the half was not told me." May the Lord hasten the happy time !

We must now return to our solemn chapter, and, lingering a little longer over it, endeavor to gather up and bear away with us some of its salutary teaching; for truly salutary it is, in an age like the present, when there is so much "strange fire" abroad.

There is something unusually arresting and im-pressive in the way in which Aaron received the heavy stroke of divine judgment.—"*Aaron held his peace.*" It was a solemn scene. His two sons struck dead at his side—smitten down by the fire of divine judgment.* He had but just seen them

---

* Lest any reader should be troubled with a difficulty in reference to the souls of Nadab and Abihu, I would say that no such question ought ever to be raised. In such cases as Nadab and Abihu in Leviticus x, Korah and his company in Numbers xvi, the whole congregation, Joshua and Cable excepted, whose carcases fell in the wilderness (Numb. xiv. and Heb. iii.), Achan and his family (Josh. vii.), Ananias and Sapphira (Acts v.), those who were judged for abuses at the Lord's table (1 Cor. xi.),—in all such cases, the question of the soul's salvation is never raised. We are simply called to see in them the solemn actings of God in government in the midst of His people. This relieves the mind from all difficulty. Jehovah dwelt, of old, between the cherubim, to judge His people in every thing; and God the Holy Ghost dwells now in the Church, to order and govern according to the perfection of His presence. He was so really and personally present that Ananias and Sapphira could lie to Him, and He could execute judgment upon them. It was as positive and as immediate an exhibition of His actings in

clothed in their garments of glory and beauty—washed, robed, and anointed. They had stood with him before the Lord to be inaugurated into the priestly office; they had offered, in company with him, the appointed sacrifices; they had seen the beams of the divine glory darting from the shekinah; they had seen the fire of Jehovah fall upon the sacrifice and consume it; they had heard the shout of triumph issuing from an assembly of adoring worshipers;—all this had but recently passed before him; and now, alas! his two sons lie at his side in the grasp of death. The fire of the Lord, which so recently fed upon an acceptable sacrifice, had now fallen in judgment upon them, and what could he say? Nothing. "Aaron held his peace." "I was dumb and opened not my mouth, because Thou didst it." It was the hand of God; and although it might, in the judgment of flesh and blood, seem to be a very heavy hand, yet he had only to bow his head in silent awe and reverent acquiescence. "*I* was dumb . . . . . because *Thou* didst it." This was the suited attitude in the presence of the divine visitation. Aaron doubtless

government as we have in the matter of Nadab and Abihu, or Achan, or any other.

This is a great truth to get hold of. God is not only *for* His people, but *with* them, and *in* them. He is to be counted upon for every thing, whether it be great or small. He is present to comfort and help. He is there to chasten and judge; He is there "for exigence of every hour." He is sufficient. Let faith count upon Him. "Where two or three are gathered together in My name, there am I." (Matt. xviii. 20.) And, assuredly, where He is, we want no more.

felt that the very pillars of his house were shaken
by the thunder of divine judgment, and he could
only stand in silent amazement in the midst of the
soul-subduing scene.   A father bereaved of his two
sons, and in such a manner, and under such circumstances, was no ordinary case.   It furnished a
deeply impressive commentary upon the words of
the Psalmist, "God is greatly to be feared in the
assembly of the saints, and to be had in reverence
of all them that are about Him." (Psalm lxxxix.)
"Who would not fear Thee, O Lord, and glorify
Thy name?"   May we learn to walk softly in the
divine presence—to tread Jehovah's courts with
unshod foot and reverent spirit.   May our priestly
censer ever bear upon it the one material—the
beaten incense of Christ's manifold perfections, and
may the power of the Spirit kindle up the hallowed
flame.   All else is not only worthless, but vile.
Every thing that springs from nature's energy,
every thing produced by the actings of the human
will—the most fragrant incense of man's devising—
the most intense ardor of natural devotion, will all
issue in "strange fire," and evoke the solemn judgment of the Lord God Almighty.   Oh for a thoroughly truthful heart and worshiping spirit, in the
presence of our God and Father, continually!

But let not any upright, though timid, heart be
discouraged or alarmed.   It is too often the case
that those who really ought to be alarmed take no
heed, while those for whom the Spirit of grace
would only design a word of comfort and encour-

agement apply to themselves in a wrong way the
startling warnings of holy Scripture. No doubt,
the meek and contrite heart that trembles at the
word of the Lord is in a safe condition; but then
we should remember that a father warns his child,
not because he does not regard him as his child,
but because he does, and one of the happiest proofs
of the relationship is the disposition to receive and
profit by the warning. The parental voice, even
though its tone be that of solemn admonition, will
reach the child's heart, but certainly not to raise in
that heart a question as to its relationship with the
one who speaks. If a son were to question his sonship whenever his father warns, it would be a poor
affair indeed. The judgment which had just fallen
upon Aaron's house did not make him doubt that
he was really a priest; it merely had the effect of
teaching him how to conduct himself in that high
and holy position.

"And Moses said unto Aaron, and unto Eleazar
and unto Ithamar, his sons, 'Uncover not your
heads, neither rend your clothes; lest ye die, and
lest wrath come upon all the people: but let your
brethren, the whole house of Israel, bewail the
burning which the Lord hath kindled. And ye shall
not go out from the door of the tabernacle of the
congregation, lest ye die; for the anointing oil of
the Lord is upon you.' And they did according to
the word of Moses."

Aaron, Eleazar, and Ithamar were to remain un-
moved in their elevated place — their holy dignity

—their position of priestly sanctity. Neither the failure nor yet the judgment consequent thereon was to be allowed to interfere with those who wore the priestly robes and were anointed with "the oil of the Lord." That holy oil had placed them in a sacred inclosure, where the influences of sin, of death, and of judgment could not reach them. Those who were outside, who were at a distance from the sanctuary, who were not in the position of priests, they might "bewail the burning;" but as for Aaron and his sons, they were to go on in the discharge of their hallowed functions as though nothing had happened. Priests in the sanctuary were not to bewail, but to worship—they were not to weep, as in the presence of death, but to bow their anointed heads in the presence of the divine visitation. "The fire of the Lord" might act, and do its solemn work of judgment; but to a priest it mattered not what that "fire" had come to do—whether to express the divine approval by consuming a sacrifice, or the divine displeasure by consuming the offerers of "strange fire"—he had but to worship. That "fire" was a well-known manifestation of the divine presence in Israel of old, and whether it acted in "mercy or in judgment," the business of all true priests was to worship. "I will sing of mercy and of judgment; unto Thee, O Lord, will I sing."

There is a deep and holy lesson for the soul in all this. Those who are brought nigh to God, in the power of the blood, and by the anointing of the

Holy Ghost, must move in a sphere beyond the range of nature's influences. Priestly nearness to God gives the soul such an insight into all His ways, such a sense of the rightness of all His dispensations, that one is enabled to worship in His presence, even though the stroke of His hand has removed from us the object of tender affection. It may be asked, Are we to be Stoics? I ask, Were Aaron and his sons Stoics? Nay, they were priests. Did they not feel as men? Yes; but they worshiped as priests. This is profound. It opens up a region of thought, feeling, and experience in which nature can never move—a region of which, with all its boasted refinement and sentimentality, nature knows absolutely nothing. We must tread the sanctuary of God in true priestly energy, in order to enter into the depth, meaning, and power of such holy mysteries.

The prophet Ezekiel was called, in his day, to sit down to this difficult lesson. "Also the word of the Lord came unto me, saying, 'Son of man, behold, I take away from thee the desire of thine eyes with a stroke: yet neither shalt thou mourn nor weep, neither shall thy tears run down. Forbear to cry, make no mourning for the dead, bind the tire of thine head upon thee, and put on thy shoes upon thy feet, and cover not thy lips, and eat not the bread of *men*.' . . . . And I did in the morning as I was commanded." (Ez. xxiv. 16–18.) It will be said that all this was as "a sign" to Israel. True; but it proves that in prophetic testimony, as well

as in priestly worship, we must rise superior to all
the claims and influences of nature and of earth.
Aaron's sons and Ezekiel's wife were cut down with
a stroke, and yet neither the priest nor the prophet
was to uncover his head or shed a tear.

Oh, my reader, how far have you and I progressed
in this profound lesson? No doubt both reader and
writer have to make the same humiliating confession. Too often, alas! we "walk as men" and "eat
the bread of men"—too often are we robbed of our
high priestly privileges by the workings of nature
and the influences of earth. These things must be
watched against.   Nothing save realized priestly
nearness to God can ever preserve the heart from
the power of evil or maintain its spiritual tone. All
believers are priests unto God, and nothing can possibly deprive them of their position as such; but
though they cannot lose their position, they may
grievously fail in the discharge of their functions.
These things are not sufficiently distinguished.
Some there are who, while looking at the precious
truth of the believer's security, forget the possibility of his failing in the discharge of his priestly
functions: others, on the contrary, looking at the
failure, venture to call in question the security.

Now, I desire that my reader should keep clear
of both the above errors. He should be fully established in the divine doctrine of the eternal security
of every member of the true priestly house; but he
should also bear in mind the possibility of failure,
and the constant need of watchfulness and prayer,

lest he should fail. May all those who have been
brought to know the hallowed elevation of priests
unto God be preserved, by His heavenly grace, from
every species of failure, whether it be personal defilement or the presentation of any of the varied
forms of "strange fire," which abound so in the
professing church.

"And the Lord spake unto Aaron, saying, 'Do
not drink wine nor strong drink, thou, nor thy sons
with thee, when ye go into the tabernacle of the
congregation, lest ye die : it shall be a statute forever throughout your generations : and that ye may
put difference between holy and unholy, and between unclean and clean ; and that ye may teach
the children of Israel all the statutes which the Lord
hath spoken unto them by the hand of Moses.'"
(Ver. 8–11.)

The effect of wine is to excite nature, and all
natural excitement hinders that calm, well-balanced
condition of soul which is essential to the proper
discharge of the priestly office. So far from using
any means to excite nature, we should treat it as a
thing having no existence. Thus only shall we be
in a moral condition to serve in the sanctuary, to
form a dispassionate judgment between clean and
unclean, and to expound and communicate the mind
of God. It devolves upon each one to judge for
himself what, in his special case, would act as
"wine or strong drink."* The things which excite

---

* Some have thought that, owing to the special place which this
direction about wine occupies, Nadab and Abihu must have been

mere nature are manifold indeed—wealth, ambition, politics, the varied objects of emulation around us in the world. All these things act with exciting power upon nature, and entirely unfit us for every department of priestly service. If the heart be swollen with feelings of pride, covetousness, or emulation, it is utterly impossible that the pure air of the sanctuary can be enjoyed, or the sacred functions of priestly ministry discharged. Men speak of the versatility of genius, or a capacity to turn quickly from one thing to another; but the most versatile genius that was ever possessed could not enable a man to pass from an unhallowed arena of literary, commercial, or political competition, into the holy retirement of the sanctuary of the divine presence; nor could it ever adjust the eye that had become dimmed by the influence of such scenes, so as to enable it to discern, with priestly accuracy, the difference "between holy and unholy, and be-

---

under the influence of strong drink when they offered the "strange fire." But be this as it may, we have to be thankful for a most valuable principle in reference to our conduct as spiritual priests. We are to refrain from every thing which would produce the same effect upon our spiritual man as strong drink produces upon the physical man.

It needs hardly to be remarked that the Christian should be *most jealous* over himself as to the use of wine or strong drink. Timothy, as we know, needed an apostolic recommendation to induce him even to touch it for his health's sake. (1 Tim. v.) A beauteous proof of Timothy's habitual self-denial, and of the thoughtful love of the Spirit in the apostle. I must confess that one's moral sense is offended by seeing Christians making use of strong 'rink in cases where it is very manifestly not medicinal. I rarely, ever, see a spiritual person indulge in such a thing. One trembles to see a Christian the mere slave of a habit, whatever that habit may be. It proves that he is not keeping his body in subjection.

tween unclean and clean.'' No, my reader, God's priests must keep themselves apart from ''wine and strong drink.'' Theirs is a path of holy separation and abstraction. They are to be raised far above the influence of earthly joy as well as earthly sorrow. If they have aught to do with ''strong wine,'' it is only that it may ''be poured unto the Lord for a drink-offering, in the holy place.'' (Numb. xxviii. 7.) In other words, the joy of God's priests is not the joy of earth, but the joy of heaven—the joy of the sanctuary. ''The joy of the Lord is their strength.''

Would that all this holy instruction were more deeply pondered by us! We surely stand much in need of it. If our priestly responsibilities are not duly attended to, all must be deranged. When we contemplate the camp of Israel, we may observe three circles, and the innermost of these circles had its centre in the sanctuary. There was first the circle of men of war (Numb, i, ii.); then the circle of Levites round about the tabernacle (Numb. iii, iv.); and lastly, the innermost circle of priests, ministering in the holy place. Now, let it be remembered that the believer is called to move in all those circles. He enters into conflict, as a man of war (Eph. vi. 11–17; 1 Tim. i. 18; vi. 12; 2 Tim. iv. 7.); he serves, as a Levite, in the midst of his brethren, according to his measure and sphere (Matt. xv. 14. 15; Luke xix. 12, 13.); finally, he sacrifices and worships, as a priest, in the holy place (Heb. xiii. 15, 16; 1 Pet. ii. 5, 9.). The last of these shall endure forever. And, moreover, it is

as we are enabled now to move aright in that holy
circle that all other relations and responsibilities are
rightly discharged. Hence, every thing that inca-
pacitates us for our priestly functions—every thing
that draws us off from the centre of that innermost
circle, in which it is our privilege to move—every
thing, in short, that tends to derange our priestly
relation, or dim our priestly vision, must, of necessity, unfit us for the service which we are called to
render, and for the warfare which we are called to
wage.

These are weighty considerations. Let us dwell
upon them. The heart must be kept right, the conscience pure, the eye single, the spiritual vision
undimmed. The soul's business in the holy place
must be faithfully and diligently attended to, else
we shall go all wrong. Private communion with
God must be kept up, else we shall be fruitless as
servants, and defeated as men of war. It is vain
for us to bustle about, and run hither and thither in
what we call service, or indulge in vapid words about
Christian armor and Christian warfare. If we are not
keeping our priestly garments unspotted, and if we
are not keeping ourselves free from all that would
excite nature, we shall assuredly break down. The
priest must keep his heart with all diligence, else
the *Levite* will fail, and the *warrior* will be defeated.

It is, let me repeat it, the business of each one to
be fully aware of what it is that to him proves to be
"wine and strong drink"—what it is that produces
excitement—that blunts his spiritual perception, or

dims his priestly vision. It may be an auction-mart, a cattle-show, a newspaper,—it may be the merest trifle. But no matter what it is, if it tends to excite, it will disqualify us for priestly ministry; and if we are disqualified as priests, we are unfit for every thing, inasmuch as our success in every department and in every sphere must ever depend upon our cultivating a spirit of worship.

Let us, then, exercise a spirit of self-judgment— a spirit of watchfulness over our habits, our ways, and our associations; and when we, by grace, discover aught that tends, in the smallest, degree to unfit us for the elevated exercises of the sanctuary, let us put it away from us, cost what it may. Let us not suffer ourselves to be the slaves of a habit. Communion with God should be dearer to our hearts than all beside; and just in proportion as we prize that communion, shall we watch and pray against any thing that would rob us of it—every thing that would excite, ruffle, or unhinge.*

" And Moses spake unto Aaron, and unto Eleazar,

---

* Some, perhaps, may think that the wording of Leviticus x. 9 affords a warrant for *occasional* indulgence in those things which tend to excite the natural mind, inasmuch as it is said, " Do not drink wine nor strong drink . . . . *when* ye go into the tabernacle of the congregation." To this we may reply that the sanctuary is not a place which the Christian is *occasionally* to visit, but a place in which he is *habitually* to serve and worship. It is the sphere in which he should "live, and move, and have his being." The more we live in the presence of God, the less can we bear to be out of it; and no one who knows the deep joy of being there could lightly indulge in aught that would take or keep him thence. There is not that object within the compass of earth which would, in the judgment of a spiritual mind, be an equivalent for one hour's fellowship with God.

and unto Ithamar, his sons that were left, 'Take the meat-offering that remaineth of the offerings of the Lord made by fire, and eat it without leaven beside the altar; for it is most holy: and ye shall eat it in the holy place, because it is thy due, and thy sons' due, of the sacrifices of the Lord made by fire; for so I am commanded.'" (Ver. 12, 13.)

There are few things in which we are more prone to fail than in the maintenance of the divine standard when human failure has set in. Like David, when the Lord made a breach upon Uzzah because of his failure in putting his hand to the ark, "he was afraid of God that day, saying, 'How shall I bring the ark of God home to me?'" (1 Chron. xiii. 12.) It is exceedingly difficult to bow to the divine judgment and, at the same time, to hold fast the divine ground. The temptation is to lower the standard—to come down from the lofty elevation—to take human ground. We must ever carefully guard against this evil, which is all the more dangerous as wearing the garb of modesty, self-distrust, and humility. Aaron and his sons, notwithstanding all that had occurred, were to eat the meat-offering in the holy place. They were to do so, not because all had gone on in perfect order, but "because it is thy due," and "so I am commanded." Though there had been failure, yet their place was in the tabernacle; and those who were there had certain "dues" founded upon the divine commandment. Though man had failed ten thousand times over, the word of the Lord could not fail; and that word had secured certain privileges for all true priests, which it was their place to enjoy. Were God's priests to have nothing to eat —no priestly food, because failure had set in? Were those that were left to be allowed to starve, because Nadab and Abihu had offered "strange fire"? This would never do. God is faithful, and He can never allow any one to be empty in His blessed presence. The prodigal may wander and squander and come to poverty, but it must ever hold good that "in my Father's house is bread enough and to spare."

"And the wave breast and the heave shoulder shall ye eat in a clean place; thou, and thy sons, and thy daughters with thee: for they be thy due, and thy sons' due, which are *given* out of the sacrifices of peace-offerings of the children of Israel . . . . by *a statute forever, as the Lord hath commanded.*" (Ver. 14, 15.) What strength and stability we have here! All the members of the priestly family, "daughters" as well as "sons"—all, whatever be the measure of energy or capacity, are to feed upon "the breast" and "the shoulder"—the affections and the strength of the true Peace-offering, as raised from the dead, and presented, in resurrection, before God. This precious privilege is theirs as "given by a statute forever, as the Lord hath commanded." This makes all "sure and steadfast," come what may. Men may fail and come short, strange fire may be offered, but God's priestly family must never be deprived of the rich and gracious portion which divine love has provided and divine faithfulness secured "by a statute forever."

However, we must distinguish between those privileges which belonged to all the members of Aaron's family, "daughters" as well as "sons," and those which could only be enjoyed by the male portion of the family. This point has already been referred to in the notes on the offerings. There are certain blessings which are the common portion of all believers, simply as such; and there are those which demand a higher measure of spiritual attainment and priestly energy to apprehend and enjoy. Now, it is worse than vain, yea, it is impious, to set up for the enjoyment of this higher measure when we really have it not. It is one thing to hold fast the privileges which are "given" of God, and can never be taken away, and quite another to assume a measure of spiritual capacity to which we have never attained. No doubt, we ought to desire earnestly the very highest measure of priestly communion—the most elevated order of priestly privilege; but then desiring a thing, and assuming to have it, are very different.

This thought will throw light upon the closing paragraph of our chapter. "And Moses diligently sought the goat of the sin-offering, and, behold, it was burnt: and he was angry with Eleazar and Ithamar, the sons of Aaron which were left, saying, 'Wherefore have ye not eaten the sin-offering in the holy place, seeing it is most holy, and God hath given it to you to bear the iniquity of the congrega-

tion, to make atonement for them before the Lord ?
Behold, the blood of it was not brought in within the
holy place : ye should indeed have eaten it in the
holy place, as I commanded.' And Aaron said unto
Moses, 'Behold, this day have they offered their sin-
offering and their burnt-offering before the Lord ;
and such things have befallen me : and if I had
eaten the sin-offering to-day, should it have been
accepted in the sight of the Lord ?' And when Moses
heard that, he was content."

The "daughters" of Aaron were not permitted to
eat of "the sin-offering." This high privilege belonged only to the "sons," and it was a type of the
most elevated form of priestly service. To eat of
the sin-offering was the expression of full identification with the offerer, and this demanded an amount
of priestly capacity and energy which found its type
in "the sons of Aaron." On the occasion before
us, however, it is very evident that Aaron and his
sons were not in a condition to rise to this high and
holy ground. They ought to have been, but they
were not. "Such things have befallen me," said
Aaron. This, no doubt, was to be deplored ; but
yet, "when Moses heard that, he was content." It is
far better to be real in the confession of our failure
and shortcoming, than to put forth pretensions to
spiritual power which are wholly without foundation.

Thus, then, the tenth chapter of the book of
Leviticus opens with positive sin and closes with
negative failure. Nadab and Abihu offered "strange
fire," and Eleazar and Ithamar were unable to eat

the sin-offering.   The former was met by divine
judgment; the latter, by divine forbearance.   There
could be no allowance for "strange fire."   It was
positively flying in the face of God's plain commandment.   There is obviously a wide difference
between a deliberate rejection of a plain command
and mere inability to rise to the height of a divine
privilege.   The former is open dishonor done to
God; the latter is a forfeiture of one's own bless·
ing.   There should be neither the one nor the other,
but the difference between the two is easily traced.

May the Lord, in His infinite grace, ever keep u
abiding in the secret retirement of His holy pres
ence, abiding in His love, and feeding upon His
truth.   Thus shall we be preserved from "strange
fire" and "strong drink"—from false worship of
every kind and fleshly excitement in all its forms.
Thus, too, shall we be enabled to carry ourselves
aright in every department of priestly ministration,
and to enjoy all the privileges of our priestly position.   The communion of a Christian is like a sensitive plant.   It is easily hurt by the rude influences
of an evil world.   It will expand beneath the genial
action of the air of heaven, but must firmly shut
itself up from the chilling breath of time and sense.
Let us remember these things, and ever seek to keep
close within the sacred precincts of the divine presence.   There, all is pure, safe, and happy.

> Far from a world of grief and sin,
> With God eternally shut in.

CHAPTER XI

THE book of Leviticus may be termed "The Priest's Guide-book." This is very much its character. It is full of principles for the guidance of such as desire to live in the enjoyment of priestly nearness to God. Had Israel gone on with Jehovah according to the grace in which He had brought them up out of the land of Egypt, they should have been to Him "a kingdom of priests and a holy nation." (Ex. xix. 6.) This, however, they failed to do. They put themselves at a distance; they got under law and failed to keep it. Hence, Jehovah had to take up a certain tribe, and from that tribe a certain family, and from that family a certain man, and to him and to his house was granted the high privilege of drawing nigh as priests unto God.

Now, the privileges of such a position were immense; but it had its heavy responsibilities likewise. There would be the ever-recurring demand for the exercise of a discerning mind. "The priest's lips should keep knowledge, and they should seek the law at his mouth; for he is the messenger of the Lord of hosts." (Mal. ii. 7.) The priest was not only to bear the judgment of the congregation before the Lord, but also to expound the ordinances of the Lord to the congregation. He was to be the ever-ready medium of communication between Jehovah and the assembly. He was not merely to know the mind of God for himself, but be able also to interpret that mind to the people. All this would demand, of necessity, constant watching, constant waiting, constant hanging over the page of inspiration, that he might drink in, to his very soul, all the precepts, the judgments, the statutes, the laws, the commandments, and the ordinances of the God of Israel, so as to be able to instruct the congregation in reference to "those things which ought to be done.

There was no room left for the play of fancy, the working of imagination, the introduction of man's plausible inferences, or the cunning devices of human expediency. Every thing was laid down with the divine precision and commanding authority of a "Thus saith the Lord." Minute and elaborate as was the detail of sacrifices, rites, and ceremonies, nothing was left for man's brain to originate. He was not even permitted to decide upon the kind of sacrifice to be offered upon any given occasion, nor yet as to the mode in which such sacrifice was to be presented. Jehovah took care of every thing. Neither the congregation nor the priest had any authority whatsoever to decree, enact, or suggest so much as a single item throughout all the vast array of ordinances in the Mosaic economy. *The word of the Lord settled all:* man had *only to obey.*

This, to an obedient heart, was nothing short of an unspeakable mercy. It is quite impossible to overestimate the privilege of being permitted to betake one's self to the oracles of God, and there find the most ample guidance as to all the details of one's faith and service day by day. All that we need is a broken will, a mortified mind, a single eye. The divine guide-book is as full as we can possibly desire: we want no more. To imagine for a moment that aught is left for man's wisdom to supply, must be regarded as a flagrant insult offered to the sacred canon. No one can read the book of Leviticus and not be struck with the extraordinary painstaking on the part of Israel's God to furnish His people with the most minute instruction upon every point connected with His service and worship. The most cursory reader of the book might at least bear away with him this touching and interesting lesson.

And truly, if ever there was a time when this self-same lesson needed to be read out in the ears of the professing church, this is the time. On all hands, the divine sufficiency of holy Scripture is called in question. In some cases, this is openly and deliberately done; in others, it is with less frankness hinted, insinuated, implied, and inferred. The Christian mariner is told, directly or indirectly, that the divine chart is insufficient for all the intricate details of his voyage—that such changes have taken place in the ocean of life since that chart was made that in in many cases it is entirely deficient for the purposes of modern navigation. He is told that the currents, tides, coasts, strands, and shores of that ocean are quite different now from what they were some centuries ago, and that, as a necessary consequence, he must have recourse to the aids which modern navi-

gation supplies, in order to make up for the defi-
ciencies in the old chart, which is, as a matter of
course, admitted to have been perfect at the time it
was made.

Now, I earnestly desire that the Christian reader
should be able, with clearness and decision, to meet
this grievous dishonor done to the precious volume
of inspiration, every line of which comes to him
fresh from his Father's bosom, through the pen of
God the Holy Ghost. I desire that he should meet
it whether it comes before him in the shape of a bold
and blasphemous statement or a learned and plausible inference. Whatever garb it wears, it owes its
origin to the enemy of Christ, the enemy of the
Bible, the enemy of the soul. If, indeed, the Word
of God be not sufficient, then where are we? or
whither shall we turn? To whom shall we betake
ourselves for aid if our Father's book be in any
respect defective? God says that His book can
"furnish us *thoroughly* to *all* good works." (2 Tim.
iii. 17.) Man says, No; there are many things
about which the Bible is silent, which, nevertheless,
we need to know. Whom am I to believe? God,
or man? Our reply to any one who questions the
divine sufficiency of Scripture is just this: Either
you are not a "man of God," or else that for which
you want a warrant is not "a good work." This is
plain. No one can possibly think otherwise with
his eye resting on 2 Timothy iii. 17.

Oh for a deeper sense of the fullness, majesty,
and authority of the Word of God! We very much

need to be braced up on this point. We want such a deep, bold, vigorous, influential, and abiding sense of the supreme authority of the divine canon, and of its absolute completeness for every age, every clime, every position, every department—personal, social, and ecclesiastical, as shall enable us to withstand every attempt of the enemy to depreciate the value of that inestimable treasure. May our hearts enter more into the spirit of those words of the Psalmist—"Thy Word is true *from the beginning;* and every one of thy righteous judgments *endureth forever.*" (Psalm cxix. 160.)

The foregoing train of thought is awakened by the perusal of the eleventh chapter of the book of Leviticus. Therein we find Jehovah entering, in most marvelous detail, into a description of beasts, birds, fishes, and reptiles, and furnishing His people with various marks by which they were to know what was clean and what was unclean. We have the summing up of the entire contents of this remarkable chapter in the two closing verses.—"This is the law of the beasts, and of the fowl, and of every living creature that moveth in the waters, and of every creature that creepeth upon the earth; *to make a difference* between the unclean and the clean, and between the beast that may be eaten and the beast that may not be eaten."

With regard to beasts, two things were essential to render them clean—they should chew the cud and divide the hoof. "Whatsoever parteth the hoof, and is cloven-footed, and cheweth the cud among the beasts, that shall ye eat.'' Either of these marks would, of itself, have been wholly insufficient to constitute ceremonial cleanness: the two should go together. Now, while these two marks were quite sufficient for the guidance of an Israelite as to the cleanness or uncleanness of an animal, without any reference as to why or wherefore such marks were given or what they meant, yet is the Christian permitted to inquire into the spiritual truth wrapped up in these ceremonial enactments.

What, then, are we to learn from those two features in a clean animal? The chewing of the cud expresses the natural process of ''inwardly digesting'' that which one eats, while the divided hoof sets forth the character of one's outward walk. There is, as we know, an intimate connection between the two in the Christian life. The one who feeds upon the green pastures of the Word of God, and inwardly digests what he takes in—the one who is enabled to combine calm meditation with prayerful study, will, without doubt, manifest that character of outward walk which is to the praise of Him who has graciously given us His Word to form our habits and govern our ways.

It is to be feared that many who *read the Bible* do not *digest the Word*. The two things are widely different. One may read chapter after chapter, book after book, and not digest so much as a single line. We may read the Bible as part of a dull and profitless routine, but, through lack of the ruminating powers—the digestive organs, we derive no profit whatsoever. This should be carefully looked into. The cattle that browse on the green may teach us a wholesome lesson. They first diligently gather up the refreshing pasture, and then calmly lie down to chew the cud. Striking and beautiful picture of a Christian feeding upon and inwardly digesting the precious contents of the volume of inspiration! Would that there were more of this amongst us! Were we more accustomed to betake ourselves to the Word as the necessary pasture of our souls, we should assuredly be in a more vigorous and healthy condition. Let us beware of reading the Bible as a dead form—a cold duty—a piece of religious routine.

The same caution is needful in reference to the public exposition of the Word. Let those who expound Scripture to their fellows first feed and digest for themselves,—let them read and ruminate in private, not merely for others, but for themselves. It is a poor thing for a man to be continually occupied in procuring food for other people, and he himself dying of starvation. Then, again, let those who attend upon the public ministry of the Word see that they are not doing so mechanically, as by the force of mere religious habit, but with an earnest desire to "read, mark, learn, and inwardly digest" what they hear. Then will both teachers and taught be well-conditioned, the spiritual life nourished and sustained, and the true character of outward walk exhibited.

But be it remembered that the chewing of the cud

must never be separated from the divided hoof. If one but partially acquainted with the priest's guide-book — unpracticed in the divine ceremonial happened to see an animal chewing the cud, he might hastily pronounce him clean. This would have been a serious error. A more careful reference to the divine directory would at once show that he must mark the animal's *walk*—that he must note the impression made by each movement—that he must look for the result of the divided hoof. "Nevertheless these shall ye not eat of them that chew the cud, or of them that divide the hoof; as the camel, because he cheweth the cud, but divideth not the hoof, he is unclean unto you," etc., etc. (Ver. 4–6.)

In like manner the divided hoof was insufficient if not accompanied by the chewing of the cud.— "The swine, though he divide the hoof and be cloven-footed, yet he cheweth not the cud; he is unclean to you." (Ver. 7.) In a word, then, the two things were inseparable in the case of every clean animal; and as to the spiritual application, it is of the very last importance, in a practical point of view. The inward life and the outward walk must go together. A man may profess to love and feed upon—to study and ruminate over the Word of God—the pasture of the soul; but if his footprints along the pathway of life are not such as the Word requires, he is not clean. And on the other hand, a man may seem to walk with pharisaic blamelessness; but if his walk be not the result of the hidden life, it is worse than worthless. There must be the divine principle within, which feeds upon and digests the rich pasture of God's Word, else the impression of the footstep will be of no avail. The value of each depends upon its inseparable connection with the other.

We are here forcibly reminded of a solemn passage in the first epistle of John, in which the apostle furnishes us with the two marks whereby we may know those that are of God.—"In this the children of God are manifest, and the children of the devil: whosoever *doeth not righteousness* is not of God, neither he that *loveth not his brother.*" (1 John iii. 10.) Here we have the two grand characteristics of the eternal life of which all true believers are possessed, namely, "righteousness" and "love"— the outward and the inward. Both must be combined. Some professing Christians are all for love, so called, and some for righteousness. Neither can exist, in a divine way, without the other. If that which is called love exist without practical righteousness, it will, in reality, be but a lax, soft, easy-going habit of mind, which will tolerate all manner of error and evil; and if that which is called righteousness exist without love, it will be a stern, proud, pharisaic, self-sufficient temper of soul, resting upon the miserable basis of personal reputation. But where the divine life is in energy, there will ever be the inward charity combined with genuine practical righteousness. The two elements are essential in the formation of true Christian character. There must be the love that will express itself in reference to the very feeblest development of that which is of God, and, at the same time, the holiness that shrinks, with intense abhorrence, from all that is of Satan.

We shall now pass on to the consideration of that which the Levitical ceremonial taught with respect to "all that are in the waters." Here, again, we find the double mark. "These shall ye eat of all that are in the waters : whatsoever hath fins and scales in the waters, in the seas, and in the rivers, them shall ye eat. And all that have not fins and scales in the seas, and in the rivers, of all that move in the waters, and of any living thing which is in the waters, they shall be an abomination unto you." (Ver. 9, 10.) Two things were necessary to render a fish ceremonially clean, namely, "fins and scales," which obviously set forth a certain fitness for the sphere and element in which the creature had to move.

But doubtless there was more than this. I believe it is our privilege to discern, in the natural properties with which God has endowed those creatures which move in the waters, certain spiritual qualities which belong to the Christian life. If a fish needs a "fin" to enable him to move through the water, and "scales" to resist the action thereof, so does the believer need that spiritual capacity which enables him to move onward through the scene with which he is surrounded, and, at the same time, to resist its influence—to prevent its penetrating—to keep it out. These are precious qualities. The fin and the scale are pregnant with meaning—full of practical instruction to the Christian. They exhibit to us, in ceremonial garb, two things which we specially need, namely, spiritual energy to move onward through the element which surrounds us, and the power to preserve us from its action. The one will not avail without the other. It is of no use to possess a capacity to get on through the world if we are not proof against the world's influence; and though we may seem to be able to keep the world out, yet if we have not the motive-power, we are defective. The "fins" would not do without the "scales," nor the "scales" without the "fins." Both were required, to render a fish ceremonially clean; and we, in order to be properly equipped, require to be incased against the penetrating influence of an evil world, and, at the same time, to be furnished with a capacity to pass rapidly on.

The whole deportment of a Christian should declare him a pilgrim and a stranger here. "*Onward*" must be his motto—ever and only onward. Let his locality and his circumstances be what they may, he is to have his eye fixed on a home beyond this perishing, passing world. He is furnished, by grace, with spiritual ability to go forward—to penetrate energetically through all, and carry out the earnest aspirations of his heaven-born spirit. And while thus vigorously pushing his way onward—while "forcing his passage to the skies," he is to keep his inward man fenced round about and fast closed up against all external influences.

Oh, for more of the onward bent—the upward

tendency! for more holy fixedness of soul and profound retirement from this vain world! We shall have reason to bless the Lord for our meditations amid the ceremonial shadows of the book of Leviticus if we are led thereby to long more intensely after those graces which though so dimly portrayed there are nevertheless so manifestly needful for us.

From verse 13 to verse 24 of our chapter, we have the law with respect to birds. All of the carnivorous kind, that is, all that fed on flesh, were unclean; the omnivorous, or those who could eat any thing, were unclean; all those which though furnished with power to soar into the heavens would nevertheless grovel upon the earth were unclean. As to the latter class, there were some exceptional cases (ver. 21, 22.); but the general rule, the fixed principle, the standing ordinance, was as distinct as possible—"All fowls that creep, going upon all fours, shall be an abomination unto you." (Ver. 20.) All this is very simple in its instruction to us. Those fowls that could feed upon flesh, those that could swallow any thing or every thing, and all groveling fowls, were to be unclean to the Israel of God, because so pronounced by the God of Israel; nor can the spiritual mind have any difficulty in discerning the fitness of such an ordinance. We can not only trace in the habits of the above three classes of fowl the just ground of their being pronounced unclean, but we can also see in them the striking exhibition of that in nature which is to be strenuously guarded against by every true Christian. Such an one is called to refuse every thing of a carnal nature. Moreover, he cannot feed promiscuously upon every thing that comes before him. He must "try the things that differ;" he must "take heed what he hears;" he must exercise a discerning mind, a spiritual judgment, a heavenly taste. Finally, he must use his wings; he must rise on the pinions of faith, and find his place in the celestial sphere to which he belongs. In short, there must be nothing groveling, nothing promiscuous, nothing unclean, for the Christian.

As to "creeping things," the following was the general rule: "And every creeping thing that creepeth upon the earth shall be an abomination; it shall not be eaten." (Ver. 41.) How wonderful to think of the condescending grace of Jehovah! He could stoop to give directions about a crawling reptile. He would not leave His people at a loss as to the most trivial affair. The priest's guide-book contained the most ample instructions as to every thing. He desired to keep His people free from the defilement consequent upon touching, tasting, or handling aught that was unclean. They were not their own, and hence they were not to do as they pleased. They belonged to Jehovah; His name was called upon them; they were identified with Him. His Word was to be their grand regulating standard in every case. From it they were to learn the ceremonial *status* of beasts, birds, fishes, and creeping things. They were not to think their own thoughts, to exercise their own reasoning powers, or

be guided by their own imaginations in such matters. *God's Word was to be their sole directory.*
Other nations might eat what they pleased, but
Israel enjoyed the high privilege of eating that only
which was pleasing to Jehovah.

Nor was it as to the mere matter of *eating* aught
that was unclean that the people of God were so
jealously guarded. Bare *contact* was forbidden.
(See ver. 8, 24, 26–28, 31–41.) It was impossible
for a member of the Israel of God to touch that
which was unclean without contracting defilement.
This is a principle largely unfolded both in the law
and the prophets.—"Thus saith the Lord of hosts,
'Ask ye now the priests concerning the law, saying,
If one bear holy flesh in the skirt of his garment,
and with his skirt do touch bread, or pottage, or
wine, or oil, or any meat, shall it be holy?' And the
priests answered and said, 'No.' Then said Haggai,
'If one that is unclean by a dead body *touch* any of
these, shall it be unclean?' And the priests answered and said, 'It shall be unclean.'" (Hag. ii.
11–13.) Jehovah would have His people holy in all
things. They were neither to eat nor touch aught
that was unclean.—"Ye shall not make yourselves
abominable with any creeping thing that creepeth,
neither shall ye make yourselves unclean with them,
that ye should be defiled thereby." Then follows
the powerful reason for all this careful separation.—
"*For I am the Lord your God:* ye shall therefore
sanctify yourselves, and ye shall be holy; *for I am
holy:* neither shall ye defile yourselves with any

manner of creeping thing that creepeth upon the earth. For I am the Lord that bringeth you up out of the land of Egypt, to be *your God:* ye shall therefore be holy, *for I am holy.*'' (Ver. 43–45.)

It is well to see that the personal holiness of God's people—their entire separation from all manner of uncleanness, flows out of their relationship to Him. It is not upon the principle of "Stand by thyself: I am holier than thou;" but simply this: "God is holy," and therefore all who are brought into association with Him must be holy likewise. It is in every way worthy of God that *His* people should be holy. "Thy testimonies are very sure: holiness becometh Thy house, O Lord, forever." What else save holiness could become the house of such an One as Jehovah? If any one had asked an Israelite of old, Why do you shrink so from that reptile which crawls along the path? He would have replied, Jehovah is holy, and I belong to Him. He has said, "Touch not." So also now, if a Christian be asked why he walks apart from the ten thousand things in which the men of this world participate, his answer is simply to be, *My Father is holy.* This is the true foundation of personal holiness. The more we contemplate the divine character, and enter into the power of our relationship to God, in Christ, by the energy of the Holy Ghost, the holier we must, of necessity, be. There can be no progress in the condition of holiness into which the believer is introduced, but there is and ought to be progress in the apprehension, experience, and practical exhibition of that holiness. These things should never be confounded. All believers are in the same condition of holiness or sanctification, but their practical measure may vary to any conceivable degree. This is easily understood. The condition arises out of our *being brought* nigh to God by the blood of the cross; the practical measure will depend upon our *keeping* nigh by the power of the Spirit. It is not a man setting up for something superior in himself—for a greater degree of personal sanctity than is ordinarily possessed—for being in any wise better than his neighbors. All such pretensions are utterly contemptible in the judgment of every right-thinking person. But then, if God, in His exceeding grace, stoop down to our low estate and lift us into the holy elevation of His blessed presence, in association with Christ, has He not a right to prescribe what our character is to be as thus brought nigh? Who could think of calling in question a truth so obvious? And further, are we not bound to aim at the maintenance of that character which He prescribes? Are we to be accused of presumption for so doing? Was it presumption in an Israelite to refuse to touch "a creeping thing"? Nay, it would have been presumption of the most daring and dangerous character to have done so. True, he might not have been able to make an uncircumcised stranger understand or appreciate the reason of his conduct; but this was not his province. Jehovah had said, "Touch not," not because an Israelite was holier in himself than a stranger, but because Jehovah was holy, and

Israel belonged to Him. It needed the eye and the heart of a circumcised disciple of the law of God, in order to discern what was clean and what was not. An alien knew no difference. Thus it must ever be. It is only Wisdom's children that can justify her and approve her heavenly ways.

Ere turning from the eleventh chapter of Leviticus, my reader might, with much spiritual profit, compare it with the tenth chapter of Acts, ver. 11–16. How strange it must have appeared to one who had, from his earliest days, been taught the principles of the Mosaic ritual, to see a vessel descending from heaven, "wherein were *all manner* of four-footed beasts of the earth, and wild beasts, and *creeping things*, and fowls of the air;" and not only to see such a vessel so filled, but also to hear a voice, saying, "Rise, Peter; kill and eat." How wonderful! No examination of hoofs or habits! There was no need of this. The vessel and its contents had come from heaven. This was enough. The Jew might ensconce himself behind the narrow inclosures of the Jewish ritual, and exclaim, "Not so, Lord; for I have never eaten any thing that is common or unclean;" but then the tide of divine grace was rising majestically above all such inclosures, in order to embrace, in its mighty compass, "all manner" of objects, and bear them upward to heaven, in the power and on the authority of those precious words, "What God hath cleansed, that call not thou common." It mattered not what was in the vessel if God had cleansed it. The Author

of the book of Leviticus was about to raise the
thoughts of His servant above the barriers which
that book had erected, into all the magnificence of
Heaven's grace. He would teach him that true
cleanness—the cleanness which Heaven demanded—
was no longer to consist in chewing the cud, divid-
ing the hoof, or any such ceremonial marks, but
in being washed in the blood of the Lamb, which
cleanseth from all sin, and renders the believer clean
enough to tread the sapphire pavement of the heavenly courts.

This was a noble lesson for a Jew to learn; it
was a divine lesson, before the light of which the
shadows of the old economy must pass away. The
hand of sovereign grace has thrown open the door
of the kingdom, but not to admit aught that is unclean. This could not be. Nothing unclean can
enter heaven. But then, a cloven hoof was no
longer to be the criterion, but *"what God hath
cleansed."* When God cleanses a man, he must
needs be clean. Peter was about to be sent to open
the kingdom to the Gentiles, as he had already
opened it to the Jews, and his Jewish heart needed
to be enlarged. He needed to get above the dark
shadows of a by-gone age, into the meridian light
that was shining from an open heaven, in virtue of
a completed sacrifice. He needed to get out of the
narrow current of Jewish prejudices, and be borne
upon the bosom of that mighty tide of grace which
was about to roll through the length and breadth
of a lost world. He had to learn, too, that the

standard by which true cleanness must be regulated was no longer carnal, ceremonial, and earthly, but spiritual, moral, and heavenly. Assuredly, we may say, these were noble lessons for the apostle of the circumcision to learn upon the housetop of Simon the tanner. They were eminently calculated to soften, to expand, and elevate a mind which had been trained amid the contracting influences of the Jewish system. We bless the Lord for these precious lessons. We bless Him for the large and wealthy place in which He has set us, by the blood of the cross. We bless Him that we are no longer hemmed round about by "Touch not this; taste not that; handle not the other thing;" but that His Word assures us that "every creature of God is good, and nothing to be refused, if it be received with thanksgiving; for it is sanctified by the Word of God and prayer." (1 Tim. iv. 4, 5.)

CHAPTER XII

THIS brief section reads out to us, after its own peculiar fashion, the double lesson of "man's ruin and God's remedy." But though the fashion is peculiar, the lesson is most distinct and impressive. It is, at once, deeply humbling and divinely comforting. The effect of all Scripture, when interpreted to one's own soul directly by the power of the Holy Ghost, is to lead us out of self to Christ. Wherever we see our fallen nature, at whatever stage of its history we contemplate it—whether in its conception, at its birth, or at any point along its whole career, from the womb to the coffin, it wears the double stamp of infirmity and defilement. This is sometimes forgotten amid the glitter and glare, the pomp and fashion, the wealth and splendor, of human life. The mind of man is fruitful in devices to cover his humiliation. In various ways he seeks to ornament and gild, and put on an appearance of strength and glory, but it is all vain. He has only to be seen as he enters this world, a poor helpless creature, or as he passes away from it, to take his place with the clod of the valley, in order to have a most convincing proof of the hollowness of all his pride, the vanity of all his glory. Those whose path through this world has been brightened by what man calls glory, have entered in nakedness and helplessness, and retreated amid disease and death.

Nor is this all. It is not merely helplessness that belongs to man—that characterizes him as he enters this life: there is defilement also. "Behold," says the Psalmist, "I was shapen in iniquity, and in sin did my mother conceive me." (Ps. li. 5.) "How can he be clean that is born of a woman?" (Job xxv. 4.) In the chapter before us, we are taught that the conception and birth of "a man-child" involved "seven days" of ceremonial defilement to the mother, together with thirty-three days of separation from the sanctuary; and these periods were doubled in the case of "a maid-child." Has this no voice? Can we not read herein a humbling

lesson? Does it not declare to us, in language not
to be misunderstood, that man is "an unclean thing,"
and that he needs the blood of atonement to cleanse
him? Truly so. Man may imagine that he can
work out a righteousness of his own, he may vainly
boast of the dignity of human nature, he may put
on a lofty air and assume a haughty bearing as he
moves across the stage of life; but if he would just
retire for a few moments and ponder over the short
section of our book which now lies open before us,
his pride, pomp, dignity, and righteousness would
speedily vanish, and instead thereof, he might find
the solid basis of all true dignity, as well as the
ground of divine righteousness, in the cross of our
Lord Jesus Christ.

The shadow of this cross passes before us in a
double way in our chapter; first, in the circumcision
of the "man-child," whereby he became enrolled as
a member of the Israel of God; and secondly, in
the burnt-offering and sin-offering, whereby the
mother was restored from every defiling influence,
rendered fit once more to approach the sanctuary
and to come in contact with holy things. "And
when the days of her purifying are fulfilled, for a
son or for a daughter, she shall bring a lamb of the
first year for a burnt-offering, and a young pigeon
or a turtle-dove for a sin-offering, unto the door of
the tabernacle of the congregation, unto the priest;
who shall offer it before the Lord, and make an
atonement for her; and she shall be cleansed from
the issue of her blood. This is the law for her that

hath born a male or a female.'' (Ver. 6, 7.) The death of Christ in its two grand aspects is here introduced to our thoughts as the only thing which could possibly meet and perfectly remove the defilement connected with man's natural birth. The burnt-offering presents the death of Christ according to the divine estimate thereof; the sin-offering, on the other hand, presents the death of Christ as bearing upon the sinner's need.

"And if she be not able to bring a lamb, then she shall bring two turtles, or two young pigeons; the one for a burnt-offering and the other for a sin-offering; and the priest shall make an atonement for her, and she shall be clean.'' Nothing but blood-shedding could impart cleanness. The cross is the only remedy for man's infirmity and man's defilement. Wherever that glorious work is apprehended, by faith, there is perfect cleanness enjoyed. Now, the apprehension may be feeble, the faith may be but wavering, the experience may be shallow; but let the reader remember, for his soul's joy and comfort, that it is not the depth of his experience, the stability of his faith, or the strength of his apprehension, but the divine value, the changeless efficacy, of the blood of Jesus. This gives great rest to the heart. The sacrifice of the cross is the same to every member of the Israel of God whatever be his *status* in the assembly. The tender considerateness of our ever-gracious God is seen in the fact that the blood of a turtle-dove was as efficacious for the poor as the blood of a bullock for the rich. The

full value of the atoning work was alike maintained
and exhibited in each.   Had it not been so, the
humble Israelite, if involved in ceremonial defilement, might, as she gazed upon the well-stocked
pastures of some wealthy neighbor, exclaim, Alas!
what shall I do? how shall I be cleansed? how shall
I get back to my place and privilege in the assembly?
I have neither flock nor herd: I am poor and needy.
But, blessed be God, the case of such an one was
fully met.   A pigeon or turtle-dove was quite sufficient.   The same perfect and beautiful grace shines
forth in the case of the leper in chapter xiv. of our
book—"And *if he be poor and cannot get so much*,
then he shall take, etc. . . . . And he shall offer
the one of the turtle-doves, or of the young pigeons,
such as he can get; even such as he is able to get.
. . . . This is the law of him in whom is the plague
of leprosy, *whose hand is not able to get* that which
pertaineth to his cleansing." (Ver. 21, 30–32.)

Grace meets the needy one just where he is and
as he is.   The atoning blood is brought within the
reach of the very lowest, the very poorest, the very
feeblest.   All who need it can have it.   "If he be
poor"—what then? Let him be cast aside? Ah, no;
Israel's God could never so deal with the poor and
needy.   There is ample provision for all such in the
gracious expression, "Such as he can get; even such
as he is able to get."   Most exquisite grace! "To
the poor the gospel is preached."   None can say,
The blood of Jesus was beyond me. Each can be
challenged with the inquiry, How near would you

have it brought to you? "I bring *near* My right-eousness." How "near"? So near, that it is "to him that worketh not, but believeth on Him that justifieth the ungodly." (Rom. iv. 5.) Again, "The Word is *nigh* thee." How "nigh"? So nigh, "that if thou shalt confess with thy mouth the Lord Jesus, and shalt believe in thine heart that God hath raised Him from the dead, thou shalt be saved." (Rom. x. 9.) So also that most touching and beautiful invitation, "Ho, every one that thirsteth, come ye to the waters, and *he that hath no money.*" (Is. lv. 1.)

What matchless grace shines in the expressions, "To him that *worketh not,*" and, "He that hath *no money*"! They are as like God as they are unlike man. Salvation is as free as the air we breathe. Did we create the air? did we mingle its component parts? No; but we enjoy it, and, by enjoying it, get power to live and act for Him who made it. So is it in the matter of salvation. We get it without a fraction, without an effort. We feed upon the wealth of another, we rest in the work finished by another; and, moreover, it is by so feeding and resting that we are enabled to work for Him on whose wealth we feed and in whose work we rest. This is a grand gospel paradox, perfectly inexplicable to legality, but beautifully plain to faith. Divine grace delights in making provision for those who are "not able" to make provision for themselves.

But there is another invaluable lesson furnished by this twelfth chapter of Leviticus. We not only read herein the grace of God to the poor, but, by

comparing its closing verse with Luke ii. 24, we
learn the amazing depth to which God stooped in
order to manifest that grace. The Lord Jesus
Christ—God manifest in the flesh—the pure and
spotless Lamb—the Holy One, who knew no sin,
was "made of a woman," and that woman (wondrous mystery!), having borne in her womb, and
brought forth, that pure and perfect, that holy and
spotless, human body, had to undergo the usual
ceremonial, and accomplish the days of her purification, according to the law of Moses. And not
only do we read divine grace in the fact of her having thus to purify herself, but also the mode in which
this was accomplished.—"And to offer a sacrifice
according to that which is said in the law of the
Lord, *a pair of turtle-doves or to young pigeons.*"
From this simple circumstance we learn that the
reputed parents of our blessed Lord Jesus were so
poor as to be obliged to take advantage of the gracious provision made for those whose means did not
afford "a lamb for a burnt-offering." What a
thought! The Lord of glory, the most high God,
Possessor of heaven and earth, the One to whom
pertained "the cattle upon a thousand hills"—yea,
the wealth of the universe, appeared in the world
which His hands had made, in the narrow circumstances of humble life. The Levitical economy had
made provision for the poor, and the mother of Jesus
availed herself thereof. Truly there is a profound
lesson in this for the human heart. The Lord Jesus
did not make His appearance in this world in con-

nection with the great or the noble. He was pre-
eminently a poor man. He took His place with the
poor.—"For ye know the grace of our Lord Jesus
Christ, that though He was rich, yet for our sakes
He became poor, that ye through His poverty might
be rich." (2 Cor. viii. 9.)

May it ever be our joy to feed upon this precious
grace of our Lord Jesus Christ, by which we have
been made rich for time and for eternity. He emptied Himself of all that love could give, that we
might be filled; He stripped Himself that we might
be clothed; He died that we might live. He, in the
greatness of His grace, traveled down from the
height of divine wealth into the depth of human
poverty, in order that we might be raised from the
dunghill of nature's ruin, to take our place amid the
princes of His people forever. Oh that the sense
of this grace, wrought in our hearts by the power of
the Holy Ghost, may constrain us to a more unre-
served surrender of ourselves to Him, to whom we
owe our present and everlasting felicity, our riches,
our life, our all!

CHAPTERS XIII. & XIV

OF all the functions which, according to the Mosaic ritual, the priest had to discharge, none
demanded more patient attention or more strict
adherence to the divine guide-book than the discernment and proper treatment of leprosy. This
fact must be obvious to every one who studies, with

any measure of care, the very extensive and important section of our book at which we have now arrived.

There were two things which claimed the priest's vigilant care, namely, the purity of the assembly, and the grace which could not admit of the exclusion of any member save on the most clearly established grounds. Holiness could not permit any one to remain in who ought to be out; and on the other hand, grace would not have any one out who ought to be in. Hence, therefore, there was the most urgent need, on the part of the priest, of watchfulness, calmness, wisdom, patience, tenderness, and enlarged experience. Things might seem trifling which in reality were serious, and things might look like leprosy which were not it at all. The greatest care and coolness were needed. A judgment rashly formed, a conclusion hastily arrived at, might involve the most serious consequences, either as regards the assembly or some individual member thereof.

This will account for the frequent occurrence of such expressions as the following; namely, "The priest shall look"—"The priest shall shut up him that hath the plague *seven days*"—"And the priest shall look on him the seventh day"—"Then the priest shall shut him up *seven days more*"—"And the priest shall *look on him again* the seventh day" —"And the priest shall *see him*"—"Then the priest shall *consider.*" No case was to be hastily judged or rashly decided. No opinion was to be formed from mere hearsay. Personal observation, priestly discernment, calm reflection, strict adherence to the written Word—the holy, infallible guide-book—all these things were imperatively demanded of the priest if he would form a sound judgment of each case. He was not to be guided by his own thoughts, his own feelings, his own wisdom, in any thing. He had ample guidance in the Word, if only he was subject thereto. Every point, every feature, every movement, every variation, every shade and character, every peculiar symptom and affection—all was provided for, with divine fullness and forethought, so that the priest only needed to be acquainted with and subject to the Word in all things, in order to be preserved from ten thousand mistakes.

Thus much as to the priest and his holy responsibilities.

We shall now consider the disease of leprosy, as developed in a person, in a garment, or in a house.

Looking at this disease in a physical point of view, nothing can possibly be more loathsome; and being, so far as man is concerned, totally incurable, it furnishes a most vivid and appalling picture of sin—sin in one's nature, sin in his circumstances, sin in an assembly. What a lesson for the soul in the fact that such a vile and humiliating disease should be used as a type of moral evil, whether in a member of God's assembly, in the circumstances of any member, or in the assembly itself!

I. And first, then, as to leprosy in a person; or in other words, the working of moral evil, or of that

which might seem to be evil, in any member of the
assembly. This is a matter of grave and solemn
import—a matter demanding the utmost vigilance
and care on the part of all who are concerned in the
good of souls and in the glory of God, as involved
in the well-being and purity of His assembly as a
whole or of each individual member thereof.

It is important to see that while the broad principles of leprosy and its cleansing apply in a secondary
sense to any sinner, yet in the scripture now before
us, the matter is presented in connection with those
who were God's recognized people. The person who
is here seen as the subject of priestly examination
is a member of the assembly of God. It is well to
apprehend this. God's assembly must be kept pure,
because it is His dwelling-place. No leper can be
allowed to remain within the hallowed precincts of
Jehovah's habitation.

But then, mark the care, the vigilance, the perfect
patience, inculcated upon the priest, lest aught that
was not leprosy might be treated as such, or lest
aught that really was leprosy might be suffered to
escape. Many things might appear "in the skin"—
the place of manifestation—"like the plague of leprosy," which, upon patient, priestly investigation,
would be found to be merely superficial. This was
to be carefully attended to. Some blemish might
make its appearance upon the surface, which, though
demanding the jealous care of the one who had to
act for God, was not, in reality, defiling. And yet,
that which seemed but a superficial blemish might

prove to be something deeper than the skin, something below the surface, something affecting the hidden springs of the constitution. All this claimed the most intense care on the part of the priest. (See ver. 2–11.) Some slight neglect, some trifling oversight, might lead to disastrous consequences. It might lead to the defilement of the assembly, by the presence of a confirmed leper, or to the expulsion, for some superficial blemish, of a genuine member of the Israel of God.

Now, there is a rich fund of instruction in all this for the people of God. There is a difference between personal infirmity and the positive energy of evil— between mere defects and blemishes in the outward character, and the activity of sin in the members. No doubt it is important to watch against our infirmities; for, if not watched, judged, and guarded against, they may become the source of positive evil. (See ver. 14–28.) Every thing of nature must be judged and kept down. We must not make any allowance for personal infirmity *in ourselves*, though we should make ample allowance for it *in others.* Take, for example, the matter of an irritable temper. I should judge it in myself; I should make allowance for it in another. It may, like "the burning boil" in the case of an Israelite (ver. 19, 20.), prove the source of real defilement—the ground of exclusion from the assembly. Every form of weakness must be watched, lest it become an occasion of sin. "A bald forehead" was not leprosy, but it was that in which leprosy might appear, and hence it had to

be watched. There may be a hundred things which
are not in themselves sinful, but which may become
the occasion of sin if not diligently looked after.
Nor is it merely a question of what, in our estimation, may be termed blots, blemishes, and personal
infirmities, but even of what our hearts might feel
disposed to boast of. Wit, humor, vivacity of spirit
and temper—all these may become the source and
centre of defilement. Each one has something to
guard against—something to keep him ever upon
the watch-tower. How happy it is that we have a
Father's heart to come to and count on with respect
to all such things! We have the precious privilege
of coming, at all times, into the presence of unre-
buking, unupbraiding love, there to tell out all, and
obtain grace to help in all, and full victory over all.
We need not be discouraged so long as we see such
a motto inscribed on the door of our Father's treasury—"He giveth more grace." Precious motto!
It has no limit: it is bottomless and boundless.

We shall now proceed to inquire what was done
in every case in which the plague of leprosy was
unquestionably and unmistakably defined. The God
of Israel could bear with infirmity, blemish, and failure; but the moment it became a case of defilement,
whether in the head, the beard, the forehead, or any
other part, it could not be tolerated in the holy
assembly. "The leper in whom the plague is, his
clothes shall be rent, and his head bare, and he shall
put a covering upon his upper lip, and shall cry,
Unclean, unclean. All the days wherein the plague

shall be in him he shall be defiled; he is unclean:
he shall dwell alone; without the camp shall his
habitation be." (Ver. 45, 46.) Here was the leper's
condition, the leper's occupation, the leper's place.
With rent garments, bare head, and covered lip;
crying, "Unclean, unclean;" and dwelling outside,
in the dreary solitude—the dismal desert waste.
What could be more humiliating, what more de-
pressing, than this? "He shall dwell alone." He
was unfit for communion or companionship. He
was excluded from the only spot in all the world in
which Jehovah's presence was known or enjoyed.

Reader, behold, in the poor, solitary leper, a vivid
type of one in whom sin is working. This is really
what it means. It is not, as we shall see presently,
a helpless, ruined, guilty, convicted sinner, whose
guilt and misery have come thoroughly out, and who
is, therefore, a fit subject for the love of God and
the blood of Christ. No; we see in the excluded
leper one in whom sin is actually working—one in
whom there is the positive energy of evil. This is
what defiles and shuts out from the enjoyment of
the divine presence and the communion of saints.
So long as sin is working, there can be no fellowship
with God or with His people. "He shall dwell
alone; without the camp shall his habitation be."
How long? "All the days wherein *the plague* shall
be *in* him." This is a great practical truth. The
energy of evil is the death-blow to communion.
There may be the outward appearance—the mere
form—the hollow profession, but communion there

can be none so long as the energy of evil is there. It matters not what the character or amount of the evil may be—if it were but the weight of a feather— if it were but some foolish thought, so long as it continues to work, it must hinder communion—it must cause a suspension of fellowship. It is when it rises to a head—when it comes to the surface— when it is brought thoroughly out that it can be perfectly met and put away by the grace of God and by the blood of the Lamb.

This leads us to a deeply interesting point in connection with the leper—a point which must prove a complete paradox to all save those who understand God's mode of dealing with sinners. "And if a leprosy break out abroad in the skin, and the leprosy cover all the skin of him that hath the plague, from his head even to his foot, wheresoever the priest looketh; then the priest shall consider; and, behold, if the leprosy have covered all his flesh, he shall pronounce him clean that hath the plague: it is all turned white: he is clean." (Chap. xiii. 12, 13.) The moment a sinner is in his true place before God, the whole question is settled: directly his real character is fully brought out, there is no further difficulty. He may have to pass through much painful exercise ere he reaches this point—exercise consequent upon his refusal to take his true place— to bring out "all the truth" with respect to what he is; but the moment he is brought to say, from his heart, "*Just as I am*," the free grace of God flows down to him. "When I kept silence, my bones

waxed old through my roaring all the day long.
For day and night Thy hand was heavy upon me:
my moisture is turned into the drought of summer."
(Ps. xxxii. 3, 4.)   How long did this painful exercise continue ?   Until the whole truth was brought
out—until all that which was working inwardly
came fully to the surface.—"I acknowledged my
sin unto Thee, and mine iniquity have I not hid.
I said, 'I will confess my transgressions unto the
Lord,' and Thou forgavest the iniquity of my sin."
(Ver. 5.)

It is deeply interesting to mark the progress of
the Lord's dealing with the leprous man, from the
moment that the suspicion is raised, by certain
features in the place of manifestation, until the
disease covers the whole man, "from the crown of
the head unto the sole of the foot."   There was no
haste and no indifference.   God ever enters the
place of judgment with a slow and measured pace ;
but when He does enter, He must act according to
the claims of His nature.   He can patiently investigate.   He can wait for "seven days ;" and should
there be the slightest variation in the symptoms, He
can wait "seven days more ;" but the moment it is
found to be the positive working of leprosy, there
can be no toleration.   "Without the camp shall his
habitation be."   How long ?   Until the disease comes
fully to the surface.   "If the leprosy have covered
all his flesh, he shall pronounce him clean."   This
is a most precious and interesting point.   The very
smallest speck of leprosy was intolerable to God ;

and yet when the whole man was covered, from
head to foot, he was pronounced clean—that is, he
was a proper subject for the grace of God and the
blood of atonement.

Thus is it, in every case, with the sinner.   God is
"of purer eyes than to behold evil, and cannot look
upon iniquity" (Hab. i. 13.); and yet the moment
a sinner takes his true place, as one thoroughly lost,
guilty, and undone—as one in whom there is not so
much as a single point on which the eye of Infinite
Holiness can rest with complacency—as one who is
so bad that he cannot possibly be worse, there is an
immediate, a perfect, a divine settlement of the
entire matter.   The grace of God deals with sinners,
and when I know myself to be a sinner, I know
myself to be one whom Christ came to save.   The
more clearly any one can prove me to be a sinner,
the more clearly he establishes my title to the love
of God and the work of Christ.   "For Christ also
hath once suffered for sins, the just for the unjust,
that He might bring us to God." (1 Pet. iii. 18.)
Now, if I am "unjust," I am one of those very
people for whom Christ died, and I am entitled to
all the benefits of His death.   "There is not a just
man upon earth;" and inasmuch as I am "upon
earth," it is plain that I am "unjust," and it is
equally plain that Christ died for me—that He suffered for my sins.   Since, therefore, Christ died for
me, it is my happy privilege to enter into the immediate enjoyment of the fruits of His sacrifice.   This
is as plain as plainness itself.   It demands no effort

whatsoever. I am not called to be any thing but just what I am. I am not called to feel, to experience, to realize any thing. The Word of God assures me that Christ died for me just as I am; and if He died for me, I am as safe as He is Himself. There is nothing against me: Christ met all. He not only suffered for my "*sins*," but He "made an end of *sin*." He abolished the entire system in which, as a child of the first Adam, I stood, and He has introduced me into a new position, in association with Himself, and there I stand before God, free from all charge of sin and all fear of judgment.

> "Just as I am—without one plea,
>   But that Thy blood was shed for me,
>   And that Thou bid'st me come to Thee,
>   O Lamb of God, I come!"

How do I know that His blood was shed for me? By the Scriptures. Blessed, solid, eternal ground of knowledge! Christ suffered for sins: I have gotten sins. Christ died, "the just for the unjust:" I am unjust. Wherefore the death of Christ appropriates itself to me as fully, as immediately, and as divinely as though I were the only sinner upon earth. It is not a question of my appropriation, realization, or experience. Many souls harass themselves about this. How often has one heard such language as the following: "Oh, I believe that Christ died for sinners, but I cannot *realize* that my sins are forgiven. I cannot apply, I cannot appropriate, I do not experience the benefit of Christ's death"! All this is self, and not Christ; it is feeling, and not

Scripture. If we search from cover to cover of the blessed volume, we shall not find a syllable about being saved by realization, experience, or appropriation. The gospel applies itself to all who are on the ground of being lost. Christ died for sinners. That is just what I am; wherefore He died for me. How do I know this? is it because I feel it? By no means. How then? By the Word of God. "Christ died for our sins according to the Scriptures; He was buried, and rose again the third day according to the Scriptures." (1 Cor. xv. 3, 4.) Thus it is all "according to the Scriptures." If it were according to our feelings, we should be in a deplorable way, for our feelings are hardly the same for the length of a day, but the Scriptures are ever the same. "Forever, O Lord, Thy Word is settled in heaven."—"Thou hast magnified Thy Word above all Thy name."

No doubt it is a very happy thing to realize, to feel, and to experience; but if we put these things in the place of Christ, we shall neither have them nor the Christ that yields them. If I am occupied with Christ, I shall realize; but if I put my realization in place of Christ, I shall have neither the one nor the other. This is the sad condition of thousands. Instead of resting on the stable authority of "the Scriptures," they are ever looking into their own hearts, and hence they are always uncertain and, as a consequence, always unhappy. A condition of doubt is a condition of torture; but how can I get rid of my doubt? Simply by relying on the divine authority of "the Scriptures." Of what do the Scriptures testify? Of Christ. (John v.) They declare that Christ died for our sins, and that He was raised again for our justification. (Rom. iv.) This settles every thing. The self-same authority that tells me I am unjust tells me also that Christ died for me. Nothing can be plainer than this. If I were aught else than unjust, the death of Christ would not be for me at all; but being unjust, it is divinely fitted, divinely intended, and divinely applied to me. If I am occupied with any thing in, of, or about myself, it is plain I have not entered into the full spiritual application of Leviticus xiii. 12, 13—I have not come to the Lamb of God "*just as I am.*" It is when the leper is covered from head to foot that he is on the true ground. It is there and there alone that grace can meet him. "Then the priest shall consider; and, behold, if the leprosy have covered all his flesh, he shall pronounce him clean that hath the plague: it is all turned white: he is clean." Precious truth! "Where sin abounded, grace did much more abound." So long as I think there is a single spot which is not covered with the direful disease, I have not come to the end of myself. It is when my true condition is fully disclosed to my view that I really understand the meaning of salvation by grace.

The force of all this will be more fully apprehended when we come to consider the ordinances connected with the cleansing of the leper, in chapter xiv. of our book. We shall now briefly enter upon the question of leprosy in a garment, as presented in chapter xiii. 47–59.

II. The garment or skin suggests to the mind the idea of a man's circumstances or habits. This is a deeply practical point. We are to watch against the working of evil in our ways just as carefully as against evil in ourselves. The same patient investigation is observable with respect to a garment as in the case of a person. There is no haste, neither is there any indifference.—"The priest shall look upon the plague, and shut up it that hath the plague seven days." There must be no indifference, no indolence, no carelessness. Evil may creep into our habits and circumstances in numberless ways, and hence the moment we perceive aught of a suspicious nature, it must be submitted to a calm, patient process of priestly investigation. It must be "shut up seven days," in order that it may have full time to develop itself perfectly.

"And he shall look on the plague on the seventh day: if the plague be spread in the garment, either in the warp, or in the woof, or in a skin, or in any work that is made of skin, the plague is a fretting leprosy; it is unclean. He shall therefore burn that garment." The wrong habit must be given up the moment I discover it. If I find myself in a thoroughly wrong position, I must abandon it. The burning of the garment expresses the act of judgment upon evil, whether in a man's habits or circumstances. There must be no trifling with evil. In certain cases the garment was to be "washed," which expresses the action of the Word of God upon a man's habits. "Then the priest shall command that they wash the thing wherein the plague is, and he shall shut it up *seven days more.*" There is to be patient waiting, in order to ascertain the effect of the Word. "And the priest shall look on the plague, after that it is washed; and, behold, if the plague have not changed, ... thou shalt burn it in the fire. When there is any thing radically and irremediably bad in one's position or habits, the whole thing is to be given up. "And if the priest look, and, behold, the plague be somewhat dark after the washing of it; then he shall rend it out of the garment." The Word may produce such an effect as that the wrong features in a man's character, or the wrong points in his position, shall be given up, and the evil be got rid of; but if the evil continue after all, the whole thing must be condemned and set aside.

There is a rich mine of practical instruction in all this. We must look well to the position which we occupy, the circumstances in which we stand, the habits we adopt, the character we wear. There is special need of watchfulness. Every suspicious symptom and trait must be sedulously guarded, lest it should prove, in the sequel, to be "a fretting" or "spreading leprosy," whereby we ourselves and many others may be defiled. We may be placed in a position attached to which there are certain wrong things which can be given up without entirely abandoning the position; and on the other hand, we may find ourselves in a situation in which it is impossible to "abide with God." Where the eye is single, the path will be plain. Where the one desire of the heart is to enjoy the divine presence, we shall easily discover those things which tend to deprive us of that unspeakable blessing.

May our hearts be tender and sensitive; may we cultivate a deeper, closer walk with God; and may we carefully guard against every form of defilement, whether in person, in habit, or in association.

We shall now proceed to consider the beauteous and significant ordinances connected with the cleansing of the leper, in which we shall find some of the most precious truths of the gospel presented to us.

"And the Lord spake unto Moses, saying, 'This shall be the law of the leper in the day of his cleansing: he shall be brought unto the priest: and the priest shall go forth out of the camp." (Chap. xiv. 1–3.) We have already seen the place which the leper occupied. He was outside the camp, in the place of moral distance from God—from His sanctuary and His assembly. Moreover, he dwelt in dreary solitude, in a condition of uncleanness. He was beyond the reach of human aid, and as for himself, he could only communicate defilement to every one and every thing he touched. It was therefore obviously impossible that he could do aught to cleanse himself. If, indeed, he could *only* defile by his very touch, how could he possibly cleanse himself? how could he contribute towards, or co-operate in, his cleansing? Impossible. As an unclean leper, he could not do so much as a single thing for himself; *all* had to be done *for* him. He could not make his way to God, but God could make His way to him. He was shut up to God. There was no help for him either in himself or in his fellow-man. It is clear that one leper could not cleanse another; and it is equally clear that if a leper touched a clean person, he rendered him unclean. His *only* resource was in God. He was to be a debtor to grace for every thing.

Hence, we read, "The priest shall go forth out of the camp." It is not said, The leper shall go. This was wholly out of the question. It was of no use talking to the leper about going or doing. He was consigned to deary solitude; whither could he go? He was involved in helpless defilement; what could he do? He might long for fellowship and long to be clean, but his longings were those of a lonely help-less leper. He might make efforts after cleansing, but his efforts could but prove him unclean, and tend to spread defilement. Before ever he could be pronounced "clean," a work had to be wrought for him—a work which he could neither do nor help to do—a work which had to be wholly accomplished by another. The leper was called to "stand still" and behold the priest doing a work in virtue of which the leprosy could be perfectly cleansed. The priest accomplished *all:* the leper did *nothing.*

"Then shall the priest command to take for him that is to be cleansed, two birds, alive and clean, and cedar-wood, and scarlet, and hyssop. And the

priest shall command that one of the birds be killed
in an earthen vessel over running water." In the
priest going forth from the camp—forth from God's
dwelling-place—we behold the blessed Lord Jesus
coming down from the bosom of the Father, His
eternal dwelling-place, into this polluted world of
ours, where He beheld us sunk in the polluting
leprosy of sin. He, like the good Samaritan, "came
where we were." He did not come half-way merely;
He did not come nine-tenths of the way; He came
all the way. This was indispensable. He could not
consistently with the holy claims of the throne of
God have bidden our leprosy to depart had He remained in the bosom. He could call worlds into
existence by the word of His mouth, but when
leprous sinners had to be cleansed, something more
was needed. "God so loved the world, that He gave
His only begotten Son." When worlds were to be
framed, God had but to speak; when sinners had to
be saved, He had to give His Son. "In this was
manifested the love of God towards us, because that
God sent His only begotten Son into the world, that
we might live through Him. Herein is love, not that
we loved God, but that He loved us, and sent His
Son to be the propitiation for our sins." (1 John
iv. 9, 10.)

But there was far more to be accomplished than
the mission and incarnation of the Son. It would
have availed the leper but little indeed had the priest
merely gone forth from the camp and looked upon
his low and forlorn condition. Blood-shedding was

essentially necessary ere leprosy could be removed. The death of a spotless victim was needed. "Without shedding of blood is no remission." (Heb. ix. 22.) And be it observed that the shedding of blood was the real basis of the leper's cleansing. It was not a mere circumstance, which, in conjunction with others, contributed to the leper's cleansing. By no means. The giving up of the life was the grand and all-important fact. When this was accomplished, the way was open, every barrier was removed, God could deal in perfect grace with the leper. This point should be distinctly laid hold of if my reader would fully enter into the glorious doctrine of the blood.

"And the priest shall command that one of the birds be killed in an earthen vessel over running water." Here we have the acknowledged type of the death of Christ, "who through the eternal Spirit offered Himself without spot to God." "He was crucified in weakness." (Heb. ix.; 2 Cor. xiii.) The greatest, the mightiest, the most glorious, the most momentous work that ever was accomplished, throughout the wide universe of God, was wrought "in weakness." Oh, my reader, how terrible a thing must sin be in the judgment of God when His own beloved Son had to come down from heaven and hang upon yonder cursed tree, a spectacle to men, to angels, and to devils, in order that you and I might be forgiven! And what a type of sin have we in leprosy! Who would have thought that that little "bright spot" appearing on the person of some

member of the congregation was a matter of such
grave consequence? But, ah! that little "bright
spot" was nothing less than the energy of evil in the
place of manifestation. It was the index of the
dreadful working of sin in the nature; and ere that
person could be fitted for a place in the assembly,
or for the enjoyment of communion with a holy
God, the Son of God had to leave those bright
heavens and descend into the lowest parts of the
earth, in order to make a full atonement for that
which exhibited itself merely in the form of a little
"bright spot." Let us remember this. Sin is a
dreadful thing in the estimation of God. He cannot
tolerate so much as a single sinful thought. Before
one such thought could be forgiven, Christ had to
die upon the cross. The most trifling sin (if any
sin can be called trifling,) demanded nothing less
than God's eternal and coequal Son. But, eternal
praise be to God, what sin demanded, redeeming
love freely gave; and now God is infinitely more
glorified in the forgiveness of sins than He could
have been had Adam maintained his original innocency. God is more glorified in the salvation, the
pardon, the justification, the preservation, and final
glorification of guilty man than He could have been
in maintaining an innocent man in the enjoyment of
creation-blessings. Such is the precious mystery of
redemption. May our hearts enter, by the power
of the Holy Ghost, into the living and profound
depths of this wondrous mystery.

"As for the living bird, he shall take it, and the

cedar-wood, and the scarlet, and the hyssop, and shall dip them and the living bird in the blood of the bird that was killed over the running water. And he shall sprinkle upon him that is to be cleansed from the leprosy seven times, and shall pronounce him clean, and shall let the living bird loose into the open field.'' The blood being shed, the priest can enter directly and fully upon his work. Up to this, we read, ''The priest shall command;'' but now he acts immediately himself. The death of Christ is the basis of His priestly ministration. Having entered with His own blood into the holy place, He acts as our great High-Priest, applying to our souls all the precious results of His atoning work, and maintaining us in the full and divine integrity of the position into which His sacrifice has introduced us. ''For every high-priest is ordained to offer gifts and sacrifices: wherefore it is of necessity that this Man have somewhat also to offer. For if He were on earth, He should not be a priest.'' (Heb. viii. 3, 4.)

We could hardly have a more perfect type of the resurrection of Christ than that presented in ''the living bird let loose into the open field.'' It was not let go until after the death of its companion; for the two birds typify one Christ in two stages of His blessed work, namely, death and resurrection. Ten thousand birds let loose would not have availed for the leper. It was that living bird, mounting upward into the open heavens, bearing upon his wing the significant token of accomplished atonement—it was that which told out the great fact that the work was done, the ground cleared, the foundation laid. Thus is it in reference to our blessed Lord Jesus Christ. His resurrection declares the glorious triumph of redemption. "He rose again the third day according to the Scriptures." "He was raised again for our justification." It is this that sets the burdened heart free and liberates the struggling conscience. The Scriptures assure me that Jesus was nailed to the cross under the weight of my sins; but the same Scriptures assure me that He rose from the grave without one of those sins upon Him. Nor is this all. The same Scriptures assure me that all who put their trust in Jesus are as free from all charge of guilt as He is; that there is no more wrath or condemnation for them than for Him; that they are in Him, one with Him, accepted in Him, coquickened, co-raised, co-seated, with Him. Such is the peace-giving testimony of the Scriptures of truth—such the record of God who cannot lie. (See Rom. vi. 6–11; viii. 1–4; 2 Cor. v. 21; Eph. ii. 5, 6; Col. ii. 10–15; 1 John iv. 17.)

But we have another most important truth set before us in verse 6 of our chapter. We not only see our full deliverance from guilt and condemnation, as beautifully exhibited in the living bird let loose, but we see also our entire deliverance from all the attractions of earth and all the influences of nature. "The scarlet" would be the apt expression of the former, while "the cedar-wood and hyssop" would set forth the latter. The cross is the end of all this world's glory. God presents it as such, and the believer recognizes it as such. "God forbid that I should glory, save in the cross of our Lord Jesus Christ, whereby the world is crucified unto me, and I unto the world." (Gal. vi. 14.)

Then, as to the "cedar-wood and hyssop," they present to us, as it were, the two extremes of nature's wide range. Solomon "spake of trees, from the cedar-tree that is in Lebanon even unto the hyssop that springeth out of the wall." (1 Kings iv. 33.) From the lofty cedar which crowns the sides of Lebanon, down to the lowly hyssop—the wide extremes and all that lies between—nature in all its departments is brought under the power of the cross; so that the believer sees in the death of Christ the end of all his guilt, the end of all earth's glory, and the end of the whole system of nature— the entire old creation. And with what is he to be occupied? With Him who is the Antitype of that living bird, with blood-stained feathers, ascending into the open heavens. Precious, glorious, soul-satisfying object! A risen, ascended, triumphant, glorified Christ, who has passed into the heavens, bearing in His sacred Person the marks of an accomplished atonement. It is with Him we have to do: we are shut up to Him. He is God's exclusive object; He is the centre of heaven's joy, the theme of angels' song. We want none of earth's glory, none of nature's attractions. We can behold them all, together with our sin and guilt, forever set aside by the death of Christ. We can well afford to dispense with earth and nature, inasmuch as we have gotten, instead thereof, the "unsearchable riches of Christ."

"And he shall sprinkle upon him that is to be cleansed from the leprosy seven times, and shall pronounce him clean, and shall let the bird loose into the open field." The more deeply we ponder over the contents of chapter xiii, the more clearly we shall see how utterly impossible it was for the leper to do aught towards his own cleansing. All he could do was to "put a covering upon his upper lip;" and all he could say was, "Unclean, unclean." It belonged to God, and to Him alone, to devise and accomplish a work whereby the leprosy could be perfectly cleansed; and further, it belonged to God, and to Him alone, to pronounce the leper "clean." Hence it is written, "The priest shall sprinkle," and "he shall pronounce him clean." It is not said, The leper shall sprinkle and pronounce or imagine himself clean. This would never do. God was the Judge—God was the Healer—God was the Cleanser. He alone knew what leprosy was, how it could be put away, and when to pronounce the leper clean. The leper might have gone on all his days covered with leprosy, and yet be wholly ignorant of what was wrong with him. It was the Word of God—the Scriptures of truth—the divine Record that declared the full truth as to leprosy; and nothing short of the self-same authority could pronounce the leper clean, and that, moreover, only on the solid and indisputable ground of death and resurrection. There is the most precious connection between the three things in verse 7: the blood is sprinkled, the leper pronounced clean, and the living bird let loose. There is not so much as a single syllable about what the leper was to do, to say, to think, or to feel. It was enough that he was a leper—a fully revealed, a thoroughly judged leper, covered from head to foot. This sufficed for him; all the rest pertained to God.

It is of all importance for the anxious inquirer after peace to enter into the truth unfolded in this branch of our subject. So many are tried by the question of *feeling*, *realizing*, and *appropriating*, instead of seeing, as in the leper's case, that the sprinkling of the blood was as independent and as divine as the shedding of it. It is not said, The leper shall apply, appropriate, or realize, and then he shall be clean. By no means. The plan of deliverance was divine; the provision of the sacrifice was divine; the shedding of the blood was divine; the sprinkling of the blood was divine; the record as to the result was divine: in short, it was all divine.

It is not that we should undervalue realization, or, to speak more correctly, communion, through the Holy Ghost, with all the precious results of Christ's work for us. Far from it: we shall see presently the place assigned thereto in the divine economy. But then we are no more saved by realization than the leper was cleansed by it. The gospel, by which we are saved, is that "Christ died for our sins according to the Scriptures; and that He was buried, and that He rose again the third day according to

the Scriptures." There is nothing about realization
here. No doubt it is happy to realize. It is a very
happy thing for one who was just on the point of
being drowned to realize himself in a life-boat; but
clearly he is saved by the boat and not by his realization. So it is with the sinner that believes on
the Lord Jesus Christ. He is saved by death and
resurrection. Is it because he realizes it? No;
but because God says it. It is "*according to the
Scriptures.*" Christ died and rose again, and on
that ground God pronounces him clean.

> "No condemnation, O my soul!
> '*Tis God that speaks the word.*"

This gives immense peace to the soul. I have to do
with God's plain record, which nothing can ever
shake. That record has reference to God's own
work. It is He Himself who has wrought all that
was needful in order to my being pronounced clean
in His sight. My pardon no more depends upon
my realization than upon any "works of righteousness that I have done;" and it no more depends
upon my works of righteousness than it does upon
my crimes. In a word, it depends exclusively upon
the death and resurrection of Christ. How do I
know it? God tells me. It is "according to the
Scriptures."

There are perhaps few things which disclose the
deep-seated legality of our hearts more strikingly
than this oft-raised question of realization. We *will*
have in something of self, and thus so sadly mar
our peace and liberty in Christ. It is mainly because

of this that I dwell at such length upon the beautiful ordinance of the cleansing of the leper, and especially on the truth unfolded in chapter xiv. 7.   It
was the priest that sprinkled the blood, and it was
the priest that pronounced the leper clean. Thus it
is in the case of the sinner. The moment he is on
his true ground, the blood of Christ and the Word
of God apply themselves without any further question or difficulty whatever; but the moment this
harassing question of realization is raised, the peace
is disturbed, the heart depressed, and the mind be-
wildered. The more thoroughly I get done with
self, and become occupied with Christ, as presented
in "the Scriptures," the more settled my peace will
be. If the leper had looked at himself when the
priest pronounced him clean, would he have found
any basis for the declaration? Surely not. The
sprinkled blood was the basis of the divine record,
and not any thing in or connected with the leper.
The leper was not asked how he felt or what he
thought; he was not questioned as to whether he
had a deep sense of the vileness of his disease. He
was an acknowledged leper; that was enough. It
was for such an one the blood was shed, and that
blood made him clean. How did he know this? was
it because he felt it? No; but because the priest,
on God's behalf and by His authority, told him so.
The leper was pronounced clean on the very same
ground that the living bird was let loose. The same
blood which stained the feathers of that living bird
was sprinkled upon the leper. This was a perfect

settlement of the whole affair, and that, too, in a manner entirely independent of the leper, the leper's thoughts, his feelings, and his realization.   Such is the type.   And when we look from the type to the Antitype, we see that our blessed Lord Jesus Christ entered heaven and laid on the throne of God the eternal record of an accomplished work, in virtue of which the believer enters also.   This is a most glorious truth, divinely calculated to dispel from the heart of the anxious inquirer every doubt, every fear, every bewildering thought, and every harassing question.   A risen Christ is God's exclusive object, and He sees every believer in Him. May every awakened soul find abiding repose in this emancipating truth.

"And he that is to be cleansed shall wash his clothes, and shave off all his hair, and wash himself in water, that he may be clean; and after that he shall come into the camp, and shall tarry abroad out of his tent seven days." (Ver. 8.) The leper, being pronounced clean, can begin to do what he could not even have attempted to do before, namely, to cleanse himself, cleanse his habits, shave off all his hair; and, having done so, he is privileged to take his place in the camp—the place of ostensible, recognized, public relationship with the God of Israel, whose presence in that camp it was which rendered the expulsion of the leper needful.   The blood having been applied in its expiating virtue, there is the washing of water, which expresses the action of the Word on the character, the habits, the ways, so as to render the person, not only in God's view, but also in the view of the congregation, morally and practically fit for a place in the public assembly.

But, be it observed, the man, though sprinkled with blood and washed with water, and thus entitled to a position in the public assembly, was not permitted to enter his own tent. He was not permitted to enter upon the full enjoyment of those private, personal privileges which belonged to his own peculiar place in the camp. In other words, though knowing redemption through the shed and sprinkled blood, and owning the Word as the rule according to which his person and all his habits should be cleansed and regulated, he had yet to be brought, in the power of the Spirit, into full, intelligent communion with his own special place, portion, and privileges in Christ.

I speak according to the doctrine of the type; and I feel it to be of importance to apprehend the truth unfolded therein. It is too often overlooked. There are many who own the blood of Christ as the alone ground of pardon, and the Word of God as that whereby alone their habits, ways, and associations are to be cleansed and ordered, who nevertheless are far from entering, by the power of the Holy Ghost, into communion with the preciousness and excellency of that One whose blood has put away their sins and whose Word is to cleanse their practical habits. They are in the place of ostensible and actual relationship, but not in the power of personal communion. It is perfectly true that all believers are in Christ, and, as such, entitled to communion with the very highest truths; moreover, they have the Holy Ghost as the power of communion,—all this is divinely true; but then there is not that entire setting aside of all that pertains to nature, which is really essential to the power of communion with Christ in all the aspects of His character and work. In point of fact, this latter will not be fully known to any until "the eighth day"—the day of resurrection-glory, when we shall know even as we are known. Then, indeed, each one for himself, and all together, shall enter into the full, unhindered power of communion with Christ, in all the precious phases of His Person and features of His character unfolded from verse 10 to 20 of our chapter. Such is the hope set before us; but even now, in proportion as we enter, by faith, through the mighty energy of the indwelling Spirit, into the death of nature and all pertaining thereto, we can feed upon and rejoice in Christ as the portion of our souls, in the place of individual communion.

"But it shall be on the seventh day, that he shall shave all his hair off his head and his beard and his eyebrows, even all his hair he shall shave off; and he shall wash his clothes, also he shall wash his flesh in water, and he shall be clean." (Ver. 9.) Now, it is clear that the leper was just as clean, in God's judgment, on the first day, when the blood was sprinkled upon him in its sevenfold or perfect efficacy, as he was on the seventh day. Wherein, then, was the difference? Not in his actual standing and

condition, but in his personal intelligence and communion. On the seventh day he was called to enter
into the full and complete abolition of all that pertained to nature. He was called to apprehend that
not merely was nature's leprosy to be put away, but
nature's ornaments—yea, all that was natural—all
that belonged to the old condition.

It is one thing to know, as a doctrine, that God
sees my nature to be dead, and it is quite another
thing for me to "reckon" myself as dead—to put
off, practically, the old man and his deeds—to mor-
tify my members which are on the earth.   This,
probably, is what many godly persons mean when
they speak of progressive sanctification. They mean
a right thing, though they do not put it exactly
as the Scriptures do. The leper was pronounced
clean the moment the blood was sprinkled upon
him, and yet he had to cleanse himself. How was
this ?   In the former case, he was clean in the judgment of God ; in the latter, he was to be clean practically, in his own personal intelligence, and in his
manifested character. Thus it is with the believer.
He is, as one with Christ, "washed, sanctified, and
justified"—"accepted"—"complete." (1 Cor. vi.
11; Eph. i. 6; Col. ii. 10.) Such is his unalterable
standing and condition before God. He is as perfectly sanctified as he is justified, for Christ is the
measure of both the one and the other, according
to God's judgment and view of the case. But then
the believer's apprehension of all this in his own
soul, and his exhibition thereof in his habits and

ways, open up quite another line of things. Hence it is we read, "Having therefore these promises, dearly beloved, let us *cleanse ourselves* from all filthiness of the flesh and spirit, perfecting holiness in the fear of God." (2 Cor. vii. 1.) It is because Christ has cleansed us by His precious blood that therefore we are called to "cleanse ourselves" by the application of the Word, through the Spirit. "This is He that came by water and blood, Jesus Christ; not by water only, but by water and blood. And it is the Spirit that beareth witness, because the Spirit is truth. For there are three that bear record, the Spirit, and the water, and the blood; and these three agree in one." (1 John v. 6, 8.) Here we have atonement by the blood, cleansing by the Word, and power by the Spirit—all founded upon the death of Christ, and all vividly foreshadowed in the ordinances connected with the cleansing of the leper.

"And on the eighth day he shall take two he lambs without blemish, and one ewe lamb of the first year without blemish, and three tenth deals of fine flour for a meat-offering, mingled with oil, and one log of oil. And the priest that maketh him clean shall present the man that is to be made clean, and those things, before the Lord, at the door of the tabernacle of the congregation. And the priest shall take one he lamb, and offer him for a trespass-offering, and the log of oil, and wave them for a wave-offering before the Lord." (Ver. 10–12.) The entire range of offerings is here introduced; but it is the trespass-offering which is first killed, inasmuch as the leper is viewed as an actual trespasser. This is true in every case. As those who have trespassed against God, we need Christ as the One who atoned, on the cross, for those trespasses. "Himself bare our *sins* in His own body on the tree." The first view which the sinner gets of Christ is as the Anti-type of the trespass-offering.

"And the priest shall take some of the blood of the trespass-offering, and the priest shall put it upon the tip of the right ear of him that is to be cleansed, and upon the thumb of his right hand, and upon the great toe of his right foot. "The ear,"—that guilty member which had so frequently proved a channel of communication for vanity, folly, and even un-cleanness—that ear must be cleansed by the blood of the trespass-offering. Thus all the guilt which I have ever contracted by that member is forgiven according to God's estimate of the blood of Christ. "*The right hand*," which had so frequently been stretched forth for the execution of deeds of vanity, folly, and even uncleanness, must be cleansed by the blood of the trespass-offering. Thus all the guilt which I have ever contracted by that member is forgiven according to God's estimate of the blood of Christ. "*The foot*, which had so often run in the way of vanity, folly, and even uncleanness, must now be cleansed by the blood of the trespass-offering, so that all the guilt which I have ever contracted by that member is forgiven according to God's estimate of the blood of Christ. Yes; *all*, *all*, *all* is forgiven

—all is canceled—all forgotten—all sunk as lead in the mighty waters of eternal oblivion. Who shall bring it up again? Shall angel, man, or devil be able to plunge into those unfathomed and unfathomable waters, to bring up from thence those trespasses of "foot," "hand," or "ear," which redeeming love has cast thereinto? Oh, no; blessed be God, they are gone, and gone forever! I am better off, by far, than if Adam had never sinned. Precious truth! To be washed in the blood is better far than to be clothed in innocency.

But God could not rest satisfied with the mere blotting out of trespasses by the atoning blood of Jesus. This in itself is a great thing, but there is something greater still.

"And the priest shall take some of the log of oil, and pour it into the palm of his own left hand: and the priest shall dip his right finger in the oil that is in his left hand, and shall sprinkle of the oil with his finger seven times before the Lord. And of the rest of the oil that is in his hand shall the priest put upon the tip of the right ear of him that is to be cleansed, and upon the thumb of his right hand, and upon the great toe of his right foot, upon the blood of the trespass-offering; and the remnant of the oil that is in the priest's hand he shall pour upon the head of him that is to be cleansed; and the priest shall make an atonement for him before the Lord." (Ver. 15–18.) Thus, not only are our members cleansed by the blood of Christ, but also consecrated to God in the power of the Spirit. God's work is not only negative, but positive. The ear is no longer to be the vehicle for communicating defilement, but to be "swift to hear" the voice of the Good Shepherd; the hand is no longer to be used as the instrument of unrighteousness, but to be stretched forth in acts of righteousness, grace, and true holiness; the foot is no longer to tread in folly's paths, but to run in the way of God's holy commandments: and, finally, the whole man is to be dedicated to God in the energy of the Holy Ghost.

It is deeply interesting to see that "the oil" was put "upon the blood of the trespass-offering." The blood of Christ is the divine basis of the operations of the Holy Ghost. The blood and the oil go together. As sinners, we could know nothing of the latter save on the ground of the former. The oil could not have been put upon the leper until the blood of the trespass-offering had first been applied. "In whom also, after that ye believed, ye were sealed with that Holy Spirit of promise." The divine accuracy of the type evokes the admiration of the renewed mind. The more closely we scrutinize it—the more of the light of Scripture we concentrate upon it, the more its beauty, force, and precision are perceived and enjoyed. All, as might justly be expected, is in the most lovely harmony with the entire analogy of the Word of God. There is no need for any effort of the mind. Take Christ as the key to unlock the rich treasury of the types; explore the precious contents by the light of Inspiration's heavenly lamp; let the Holy Ghost be your

Interpreter; and you cannot fail to be edified, enlightened, and blessed.

"And the priest shall offer the sin-offering, and make an atonement for him that is to be cleansed from his uncleanness." Here we have a type of Christ, not only as the Bearer of our trespasses, but also as the One who made an end of *sin*, root and branch; the One who destroyed the entire system of sin—"the Lamb of God, who taketh away the sin of the world"—"the propitiation for the whole world." As the Trespass-offering, Christ put away all my trespasses; as the Sin-offering, He met the great root from whence those trespasses emanated. He met all; but it is as the Trespass-offering I first know Him, because it is as such I first need Him. It is the "conscience of sins" that first troubles me. This is divinely met by my precious Trespass-offering. Then, as I get on, I find that all these sins had a root, a parent stem, and that root or stem I find within me. This, likewise, is divinely met by my precious Sin-offering. The order, as presented in the leper's case, is perfect. It is precisely the order which we can trace in the actual experience of every soul. The trespass-offering comes first, and then the sin-offering.

"And afterward he shall kill the burnt-offering." This offering presents the highest possible aspect of the death of Christ. It is Christ offering Himself without spot to God, without special reference to either trespasses or sin: it is Christ, in voluntary devotedness, walking to the cross, and there offering Himself as a sweet savor to God.

"And the priest shall offer the burnt-offering and the meat-offering upon the altar; and the priest shall make an atonement for him, and he shall be clean." (Ver. 20.) The meat-offering typifies "the Man Christ Jesus" in His perfect human life. It is intimately associated, in the case of the cleansed leper, with the burnt-offering; and so it is in the experience of every saved sinner. It is when we know our *trespasses* are forgiven, and the root or principle of *sin* judged, that we can, according to our measure, by the power of the Spirit, enjoy communion with God about that blessed One who lived a perfect human life down here and then offered Himself without spot to God on the cross. Thus the four classes of offerings are brought before us in their divine order in the cleansing of the leper, namely, the trespass-offering, the sin-offering, the burnt-offering, and the meat-offering, each exhibiting its own specific aspect of our blessed Lord Jesus Christ.

Here closes the record of the Lord's dealings with the leprous man; and, oh, what a marvelous record it is! what an unfolding of the exceeding hatefulness of sin, the grace and holiness of God, the preciousness of Christ's Person, and the efficacy of His work! Nothing can be more interesting than to mark the footprints of divine grace forth from the hallowed precincts of the sanctuary to the defiled place where the leper stood, with bare head, covered lip, and rent garments. God visited the leper where

he was, but He did not leave him there. He went
forth prepared to accomplish a work in virtue of
which He could bring the leper into a higher place
and higher communion than ever he had known
before.   On the ground of this work, the leper
was conducted from his place of defilement and
loneliness to the very door of the tabernacle of the
congregation, the priestly place, to enjoy priestly
privileges. (Comp. Exod. xxix. 20, 21, 32.) How
could he ever have climbed to such an elevation?
Impossible! For aught he could do, he might have
languished and died in his leprosy had not the sovereign grace of the God of Israel stooped to lift him
from the dunghill, to set him among the princes of
his people.   If ever there was a case in which the
question of human effort, human merit, and human
righteousness could be fully tried and perfectly
settled, the leper is unquestionably that case.   Indeed it were a sad loss of time to discuss such a
question in the presence of such a case.   It must
be obvious to the most cursory reader that naught
but free grace reigning through righteousness could
meet the leper's condition and the leper's need.
And how gloriously and triumphantly did that grace
act!   It traveled down into the deepest depths, that
it might raise the leper to the loftiest heights.   See
what the leper lost, and see what he gained!   He
lost all that pertained to nature, and he gained the
blood of atonement and the grace of the Spirit.   I
mean typically.   Truly he was a gainer, to an incalculable amount.   He was infinitely better off than

if he had never been thrust forth from the camp. Such is the grace of God! such the power and value, the virtue and efficacy, of the blood of Jesus!

How forcibly does all this remind us of the prodigal in Luke xv! In him, too, leprosy had wrought and risen to a head. He had been afar off, in the defiled place, where his own sins and the intense selfishness of the far country had created a solitude around him; but, blessed forever be a father's deep and tender love, we know how it ended. The prodigal found a higher place and tasted higher communion than ever he had known before; "the fatted calf" had never been slain for him before; "the best robe" had never been on him before. And how was this? was it a question of the prodigal's merit? Oh, no; it was simply a question of the father's love.

Dear reader, let me ask, can you ponder over the record of God's dealings with the leper in Leviticus xiv, or the father's dealings with the prodigal in Luke xv, and not have an enlarged sense of the love that dwells in the bosom of God, that flows through the Person and work of Christ, that is recorded in the Scriptures of truth, and brought home to the heart by the Holy Ghost? Lord grant us a deeper and more abiding fellowship with Himself!

From verse 21 to 32 we have "the law of him in whom is the plague of leprosy, whose hand is not able to get that which pertaineth to his cleansing." This refers to the sacrifices of "the eighth day," and not to the "two birds alive and clean." These

latter could not be dispensed with in any case, because they set forth the death and resurrection of
Christ as the alone ground on which God can receive
a sinner back to Himself. On the other hand, the
sacrifices of "the eighth day" being connected with
the soul's communion, must, in some degree, be
affected by the measure of the soul's apprehension; but whatever that measure may be, the
grace of God can meet it with those peculiarly
touching words, "*such as he is able to get.*" And
not only so, but the "two turtle-doves" conferred
the same privileges on the "poor" as the two lambs
conferred upon the rich, inasmuch as both the
one and the other pointed to "the precious blood
of Christ," which is of infinite, changeless, and
eternal efficacy in the judgment of God.   All
stand before God on the ground of death and resurrection.   All are brought into the same place of
nearness, but all do not enjoy the same measure
of communion—all have not the same measure of
apprehension of the preciousness of Christ in all the
aspects of His work.   They might, if they would;
but they allow themselves to be hindered in various
ways.   Earth and nature, with their respective influences, act prejudicially: the Spirit is grieved, and
Christ is not enjoyed as He might be.   It is utterly
vain to expect that if we are living in the region of
nature, we can be feeding upon Christ.   No; there
must be self-emptiness, self-denial, self-judgment,
if we would habitually feed upon Christ.   It is not
a question of salvation; it is not a question of the

leper introduced into the camp—the place of recognized relationship. By no means. It is only a
question of the soul's communion, of its enjoyment
of Christ. As to this, the largest measure lies open
to us. We may have communion with the very
highest truths; but if our measure be small, the
unupbraiding grace of our Father's heart breathes
in the sweet words, "*such as he is able to get.*" The
title of all is the same, however our capacity may
vary; and, blessed be God, when we get into His
presence, all the desires of the new nature, in their
utmost intensity, are satisfied; all the powers of the
new nature, in their fullest range, are occupied.
May we prove these things in our soul's happy experience day by day.

We shall close this section with a brief reference
to the subject of leprosy in a house.

III. The reader will observe that a case of leprosy
in a person, or in a garment, might occur in the
wilderness; but in the matter of a house, it was of
necessity confined to the land of Canaan.

"When ye be come into the land of Canaan,
which I give to you for a possession, and I put the
plague of leprosy in a house of the land of your possession, . . . then the priest shall command that
they empty the house, before the priest go into it to
see the plague, that all that is in the house be not
made unclean; and afterward the priest shall go in
to see the house: and he shall look on the plague,
and, behold, if the plague be in the walls of the
house with hollow strakes, greenish or reddish,

which in sight are lower than the wall; then the priest shall go out of the house to the door of the house, and shut up the house seven days.''

Looking at the house as the type of an assembly, we have some weighty principles presented to us as to the divine method of dealing with moral evil, or suspicion of evil, in a congregation. We observe the same holy calmness and perfect patience with respect to the house as we have already seen in reference to the person or the garment. There was no haste and no indifference, either as regards the house, the garment, or the individual. The man who had an interest in the house was not to treat with indifference any suspicious symptoms appearing in the wall thereof; neither was he to pronounce judgment himself upon such symptoms: it belonged to the priest to investigate and to judge. The moment that aught of a questionable nature made its appearance, the priest assumed a judicial attitude with respect to the house. The house was under judgment, though not condemned. The perfect period was to be allowed to run its course ere any decision could be arrived at. The symptoms might prove to be merely superficial, in which case there would be no demand for any action whatever.

''And the priest shall *come again the seventh day*, and shall *look:* and, behold, if the plague be spread in the walls of the house, then the priest shall command that they take away the stones in which the plague is, and they shall cast them into an unclean place without the city.'' The whole house was not to be condemned: the removal of the leprous stones was first to be tried.

"And if the plague come again, and break out in the house, after that he hath taken away the stones, and after that he hath scraped the house, and after that it is plastered; then the priest shall come and look, and, behold, if the plague be spread in the house, it is a fretting leprosy in the house: it is unclean. And he shall break down the house, the stones of it, and the timber thereof, and all the mortar of the house; and he shall carry them forth out of the city into an unclean place." The case was hopeless, the evil irremediable, the whole building was annihilated.

"Moreover, he that goeth into the house all the while that it is shut up shall be unclean until the even. And he that lieth in the house shall wash his clothes; and he that eateth in the house shall wash his clothes." This is a solemn truth. *Contact defiles!* Let us remember this. It was a principle largely inculcated under the Levitical economy, and surely it is not less applicable now.

"And if the priest shall come in, and look upon it, and, behold, the plague hath not spread in the house, after the house was plastered; then the priest shall pronounce the house clean, because the plague is healed." The removal of the defiled stones, etc., had arrested the progress of the evil, and rendered all further judgment needless. The house was no longer to be viewed as in a judicial place; but being cleansed by the application of the blood, it was again fit for occupation.

And now as to the moral of all this. It is at once interesting, solemn, and practical. Look, for example, at the church at Corinth. It was a spiritual house, composed of spiritual stones; but, alas! the eagle eye of the apostle discerned upon its walls certain symptoms of a most suspicious nature. Was he indifferent? Surely not. He had imbibed far too much of the spirit of the Master of the house to admit, for one moment, of any such thing. But he was no more hasty than indifferent. He commanded the leprous stone to be removed, and gave the house a thorough scraping. Having acted thus faithfully, he patiently awaited the result. And what was that result? All that the heart could desire. "Nevertheless God, that comforteth those that are cast down, comforted us by the coming of Titus; and not by his coming only, but by the consolation wherewith he was comforted in you, when he told us your earnest desire, your mourning, your fervent mind toward me; so that I rejoiced the more. . . . . In all things ye have approved yourselves to be clear in this matter." (Comp. 1 Cor. v. with 2 Cor. vii. 11.) This is a lovely instance. The zealous care of the apostle was amply rewarded; the plague was stayed, and the assembly delivered from the defiling influence of unjudged moral evil.

Take another solemn example.—"And to the angel of the church in Pergamos write: 'These things saith He that hath the sharp sword with two edges;

I know thy works, and where thou dwellest, even where Satan's seat is; and thou holdest fast My name, and hast not denied My faith, even in those days wherein Antipas was My faithful martyr, who was slain among you, where Satan dwelleth. But I have a few things against thee, because thou hast there them that hold the doctrine of Balaam, who taught Balak to cast a stumbling-block before the children of Israel, to eat things sacrificed unto idols, and to commit fornication. So hast thou also them that hold the doctrine of the Nicolaitanes, which thing I hate. Repent; or else I will come unto thee quickly, and will fight against them with the sword of My mouth." (Rev. ii. 12–16.) Here the divine Priest stands in a judicial attitude with respect to His house at Pergamos. He could not be indifferent to symptoms so alarming, but He patiently and graciously gives time to repent. If reproof, warning, and discipline prove unavailing, judgment must take its course.

These things are full of practical teaching as to the doctrine of the assembly. The seven churches of Asia afford various striking illustrations of the house under priestly judgment. We should ponder them deeply and prayerfully; they are of immense value. We should never sit down at ease so long as aught of a suspicious nature is making its appearance in the assembly. We may be tempted to say, "It is none of my business;" but it is the business of every one who loves the Master of the house to have a jealous, godly care for the purity of that house:

and if we shrink from the due exercise of this care, it will not be for our honor or profit in the day of the Lord.

I shall not pursue this subject any further in these pages; and shall merely remark, in closing this section, that I do not doubt in the least that this whole subject of leprosy has a great dispensational bearing, not only upon the house of Israel, but also upon the professing church.

CHAPTER XV

THIS chapter treats of a variety of ceremonial uncleannesses of a much less serious nature than leprosy. This latter would seem to be presented as the expression of the deep-seated energy of nature's evil; whereas chapter xv. details a number of things which are merely unavoidable infirmities, but which, as being in any measure the outflow of nature, were defiling, and needed the provisions of divine grace. The divine presence in the assembly demanded a high order of holiness and moral purity. Every movement of nature had to be counteracted. Even things which, so far as man was concerned, might seem to be unavoidable weaknesses, had a defiling influence, and required cleansing, because Jehovah was in the camp. Nothing offensive, nothing unsightly, nothing in any way uncomely, should be suffered within the pure, unsullied, and sacred precincts of the presence of the

God of Israel.   The uncircumcised nations around would have understood nothing of such holy ordinances ; but Jehovah would have Israel holy, because He was Israel's God.   If they were to be privileged and distinguished by having the presence of a holy God, they would need to be a holy people.

Nothing can be more calculated to elicit the soul's admiration than the jealous care of Jehovah over all the habits and practices of His people.   At home and abroad, asleep and awake, by day and by night, He guarded them.   He attended to their food, He attended to their clothing, He attended to their most minute and private concerns.   If some trifling spot appeared upon the person, it had to be instantly and carefully looked into.   In a word, nothing was overlooked which could in any wise affect the well-being or purity of those with whom Jehovah had associated Himself, and in whose midst He dwelt. He took an interest in their most trivial affairs.   He carefully attended to every thing connected with them, whether publicly, socially, or privately.

This, to an uncircumcised person, would have proved an intolerable burden.   For such an one to have a God of infinite holiness about his path by day and about his bed by night, would have involved an amount of restraint beyond all power of endurance ; but to a true lover of holiness—a lover of God, nothing could be more delightful.   Such an one rejoices in the sweet assurance that God is always near, and he delights in the holiness which is at once demanded and secured by the presence of God.

Reader, say, is it thus with you? Do you love the divine presence and the holiness which that presence demands? Are you indulging in any thing incompatible with the holiness of God's presence? Are your habits of thought, feeling, and action such as comport with the purity and elevation of the sanctuary? Remember, when you read this fifteenth chapter of Leviticus, that it was written for your learning. You are to read it in the Spirit, for to you it has a spiritual application. To read it in any other way is to wrest it to your own destruction, or, to use a ceremonial phrase, "to seethe a kid in its mother's milk."

Do you ask, What am I to learn from such a section of Scripture? what is its application to me? In the first place, let me ask, do you not admit that it was written for your learning? This, I imagine, you will not question, seeing the inspired apostle so expressly declares that "*whatsoever* things were written aforetime were written for our learning." (Rom. xv. 4.) Many seem to forget this important statement, at least in so far as the book of Leviticus is concerned. They cannot conceive it possible that they are to learn aught from the rites and ceremonies of a by-gone age, and particularly from such rites and ceremonies as the fifteenth of Leviticus records; but when we remember that God the Holy Ghost has written this very chapter—that every paragraph, every verse, every line of it "is given by inspiration of God, and is profitable," it should lead us to inquire what it means. Surely, what God has writ-

ten His child should read.   No doubt there is need
of spiritual power to know *how*, and spiritual wisdom
to know *when*, to read such a chapter; but the same
holds good with respect to any chapter.   One thing
is certain, if we were sufficiently spiritual, sufficiently heavenly, sufficiently abstracted from nature
and elevated above earth, we should deduce naught
but purely spiritual principles and ideas from this
and kindred chapters. If an angel from heaven were
to read such sections, how should he regard them?
Only in a spiritual and heavenly light, only as the
depositories of the purest and highest morality. And
why should not we do the same?   I believe we are
not aware of what positive contempt we pour upon
the sacred Volume by suffering any portion of it to
be so grossly neglected as the book of Leviticus has
been.   If this book ought not to be read, surely it
ought not to have been written. If it be not "profitable," surely it ought not to have had a place
assigned it in the canon of divine inspiration; but
inasmuch as it hath pleased "the only wise God"
to write this book, it surely ought to please His
children to read it.

No doubt, spiritual wisdom, holy discernment,
and that refined moral sense which only communion
with God can impart—all these things would be
needed in order to form a judgment as to when such
scripture ought to be read. We should feel strongly
disposed to question the sound judgment and refined
taste of a man who could stand up and read the
fifteenth of Leviticus in the midst of an ordinary

congregation. But why? Is it because it is not
"divinely inspired," and as such, "profitable"? By
no means; but because the generality of persons are
not sufficiently spiritual to enter into its pure and
holy lessons.

What, then, are we to learn from the chapter before us? In the first place, we learn to watch, with
holy jealousy, every thing that emanates from nature.
Every movement of, and every emanation from nature
is defiling. Fallen human nature is an impure fountain, and all its streams are polluting. It cannot send
forth aught that is pure, holy, or good. This is a
lesson frequently inculcated in the book of Leviticus, and it is impressively taught in this chapter.

But blessed be the grace that has made such ample provision for nature's defilement! This provision is presented under two distinct forms throughout the entire of the book of God, and throughout
this section of it in particular, namely, "water and
blood." Both these are founded upon the death
of Christ. The blood that expiates and the water
that cleanses flowed from the pierced side of a crucified Christ. (Comp. John xix. 34 with 1 John v. 6.)
"The blood of Jesus Christ His Son cleanseth us
from all sin." (1 John i. 7.) And the Word of
God cleanseth our practical habits and ways. (Ps.
cxix. 9; Eph. v. 26.) Thus we are maintained in
fitness for communion and worship, though passing
through a scene where all is defiling, and carrying
with us a nature every movement of which leaves a
soil behind.

It has been already remarked that our chapter treats of a class of ceremonial defilements less serious than leprosy. This will account for the fact that atonement is here foreshadowed, not by a bullock or a lamb, but by the lowest order of sacrifice, namely, "two turtle-doves." But on the other hand, the cleansing virtue of the Word is continually introduced in the ceremonial actions of "washing," "bathing," and "rinsing." "Wherewithal shall a young man *cleanse* his way? By taking heed thereto according to Thy *Word*." "Husbands, love your wives, even as Christ also loved the Church, and gave Himself for it; that He might *sanctify and cleanse it with the washing of water by the Word*." Water held a most important place in the Levitical system of purification, and as a type of the Word, nothing can be more interesting or instructive.

Thus we can gather up the most valuable points from this fifteenth chapter of Leviticus. We learn, in a very striking manner, the intense holiness of the divine presence. Not a soil, not a stain, not a speck, can be tolerated for a moment in that thrice-hallowed region. "Thus shall ye separate the children of Israel from their uncleanness, that they die not in their uncleanness, when they defile My tabernacle that is among them." (Ver. 31.)

Again, we learn that human nature is the ever-flowing fountain of uncleanness. It is hopelessly defiled; and not only defiled, but defiling. Awake or asleep, sitting, standing, or lying, nature is defiled and defiling: its very touch conveys pollution.

This is a deeply humbling lesson for proud humanity; but thus it is. The book of Leviticus holds up a faithful mirror to nature: it leaves "flesh" nothing to glory in. Men may boast of their refinement, their moral sense, their dignity: let them study the third book of Moses, and there they will see what it is all really worth in God's estimation.

Finally, we learn afresh the expiatory value of the blood of Christ, and the cleansing, purifying, sanctifying virtues of the precious Word of God. When we think of the unsullied purity of the sanctuary, and then reflect upon nature's irremediable defilement, and ask the question, However can *we* enter and dwell *there?* the answer is found in "the blood and water" which flowed from the side of a crucified Christ—a Christ who gave up His life unto death for us, that we might live by Him. "There are three that bear record in earth, the Spirit and the water and the blood; and," blessed be God, "these three agree in one." The Spirit does not convey to our ears a message diverse from that which we find in the Word, and both the Word and the Spirit declare to us the preciousness and efficacy of the blood.

Can we not therefore say that the fifteenth chapter of Leviticus was "written for our learning"? Has it not its own distinct place in the divine canon? Assuredly. There would be a blank were it omitted. We learn in it what we could not learn in the same way any where else. True, all Scripture teaches us the holiness of God, the vileness of nature, the efficacy of the blood, the value of the Word; but the chapter upon which we have been pondering, presents these great truths to our notice, and presses them upon our hearts, in a manner quite peculiar to itself.

May *every section* of our Father's Volume be precious to our hearts. May *every one* of His testimonies be sweeter to us than honey and the honeycomb, and may "*every one* of His righteous judgments" have its due place in our souls.

CHAPTER XVI

THIS chapter unfolds some of the weightiest principles of truth which can possibly engage the renewed mind. It presents the doctrine of atonement with uncommon fullness and power. In short, we must rank the sixteenth chapter of Leviticus amongst the most precious and important sections of inspiration, if indeed it be allowable to make comparisons where all is divine.

Looking at this chapter historically, it furnishes a record of the transactions of the great day of atonement in Israel, whereby Jehovah's relationship with the assembly was established and maintained, and all the sins, failures, and infirmities of the people fully atoned for, so that the Lord God might dwell among them. The blood which was shed upon this solemn day formed the basis of Jehovah's throne in the midst of the congregation. In virtue of it, a holy God could take up His abode in the midst of the people, notwithstanding all their uncleanness.

"The tenth day of the seventh month" was a unique day in Israel: there was no other day in the year like it. The sacrifices of this one day formed the ground of God's dealing in grace, mercy, patience, and forbearance.

Furthermore, we learn from this portion of inspired history, "that the way into the holiest of all was not yet made manifest." God was hidden behind a vail, and man was at a distance. "And the Lord spake unto Moses after the death of the two sons of Aaron, when they offered before the Lord, and died; and the Lord said unto Moses, 'Speak unto Aaron thy brother, that he come not at all times unto the holy place within the vail before the mercy-seat, which is upon the ark, that he die not; for I will appear in the cloud upon the mercy-seat.'"

The way was not open for man to approach at all times into the divine presence, nor was there any provision, in the entire range of the Mosaic ritual, for his abiding there continually. God was shut in from man, and man was shut out from God; nor could "the blood of bulls and goats" open a permanent meeting-place; "a sacrifice of nobler name and richer blood" was needed to accomplish this. "For the law having a shadow of good things to come, and not the very image of the things, can never with those sacrifices which they offered year by year continually make the comers thereunto perfect. For then would they not have ceased to be offered? because that the worshipers once purged should have had no more conscience of sins. But in those sacrifices there is a remembrance again made of sins every year. For it is not possible that the blood of bulls and of goats should take away sins." (Heb. x. 1–4.) Neither the Levitical priesthood nor the Levitical sacrifices could yield perfection. Insufficiency was stamped on the latter, infirmity on the former, imperfection on both. An imperfect man could not be a perfect priest; nor could an imperfect sacrifice give a perfect conscience. Aaron was not competent or entitled to take his seat within the vail, nor could the sacrifices which he offered rend that vail.

Thus much as to our chapter historically: let us now look at it typically.

"Thus shall Aaron come into the holy place: with a young bullock for a *sin*-offering, and a ram for a *burnt*-offering." (Ver. 3.) Here we have the two grand aspects of Christ's atoning work—as that which perfectly maintains the divine glory, and perfectly meets man's deepest need. There is no mention, throughout all the services of this unique and solemn day, of a *meat*-offering or a *peace*-offering. The perfect human life of our blessed Lord is not foreshadowed here, nor is the communion of the soul with God, consequent upon His accomplished work, unfolded. In a word, the one grand subject is "atonement," and that in a double way, namely, first, as meeting all the claims of God—the claims of His nature, the claims of His character, the claims of His throne; and secondly, as perfectly meeting all man's guilt and all his necessities. We

must bear these two points in mind if we would
have a clear understanding of the truth presented
in this chapter, or of the doctrine of the great day
of atonement. "Thus shall Aaron come into the
holy place," with atonement, as securing the glory
of God in every possible way, whether as respects
His counsels of redeeming love toward the Church,
toward Israel, and toward the whole creation, or in
reference to all the claims of His moral administration; and with atonement as fully meeting man's
guilty and needy condition. These two aspects of
the atonement will continually present themselves
to our view as we ponder the precious contents of
our chapter. Their importance cannot possibly be
over-estimated.

"He shall put on the holy linen coat, and he shall
have the linen breeches upon his flesh, and he shall
be girded with a linen girdle, and with the linen
mitre shall he be attired: these are holy garments;
therefore shall he wash his flesh in water, and so put
them on." (Ver. 4.) Aaron's person, washed in
pure water, and robed in the white linen garments,
furnishes a lovely and impressive type of Christ
entering upon the work of atonement. He is seen
to be *personally* and *characteristically* pure and spotless. "For their sakes I sanctify Myself, that they
also might be sanctified through the truth." (John
xvii. 19.) It is peculiarly precious to be called, as
it were, to gaze upon the Person of our divine Priest,
in all His essential holiness. The Holy Ghost delights in every thing that unfolds Christ to the view

of His people; and wherever we behold Him, we see him to be the same spotless, perfect, glorious, precious, peerless Jesus, "the fairest among ten thousand, yea, altogether lovely." He did not need to *do* or to *wear* any thing in order to be pure and spotless; He needed no pure water, no fine linen; He was, intrinsically and practically, "the holy One of God." What Aaron *did*, and what he *wore*—the washing and the robing, are but the faint shadows of what Christ *is*. The law had only a "shadow," and "not the very image of good things to come." Blessed be God, we have not merely the shadow, but the eternal and divine reality—Christ Himself.

"And he shall take of the congregation of the children of Israel two kids of the goats for a sin-offering, and one ram for a burnt-offering. And Aaron shall offer his bullock of the sin-offering, which is for himself, and make atonement for himself and for his house." (Ver. 5, 6.) Aaron and his house represent the Church, not indeed as the "one body," but as a priestly house. It is not the Church as we find it developed in Ephesians and Colossians, but rather as we find it in the first epistle of Peter, in the following well-known passage: "Ye also, as lively stones, are built up a *spiritual house*, a holy priesthood, to offer up spiritual sacrifices, acceptable to God by Jesus Christ." (Chap. ii. 5.) So also in Hebrews—"But Christ as a Son over His own house; *whose house are we*, if we hold fast the confidence and the rejoicing of the hope firm unto the end." (Chap. iii. 6.) We must ever remember that there is no revelation of the mystery of the Church in the Old Testament. Types and shadows there are, but no revelation. That wondrous mystery of Jew and Gentile forming "one body," "one new man," and united to a glorified Christ in heaven, could not, as is obvious, be revealed until Christ had taken His place above. Of this mystery Paul was pre-eminently made a steward and a minister, as he tells us in Ephesians iii. 1–12, a passage which I would commend to the prayerful attention of the Christian reader.

"And he shall take the two goats, and present them before the Lord at the door of the tabernacle of the congregation. And Aaron shall cast lots upon the two goats; one lot for the Lord, and the other lot for the scape-goat. And Aaron shall bring the goat upon which the Lord's lot fell, and offer him for a sin-offering. But the goat on which the lot fell to be the scape-goat, shall be presented alive before the Lord, to make an atonement with him, and to let him go for a scape-goat into the wilderness." (Ver. 7–10.) In these two goats, we have the two aspects of atonement already referred to; "the Lord's lot" fell upon one, and the people's lot fell upon the other. In the case of the former, it was not a question of the persons or the sins which were to be forgiven, nor of God's counsels of grace toward His elect. These things, I need hardly say, are of infinite moment; but they are not involved in the case of "the goat on which the Lord's lot fell." This latter typifies the death of Christ as that wherein God has been perfectly glorified with respect to sin in general. This great truth is fully set forth in the remarkable expression, "the Lord's lot." God has a peculiar portion in the death of Christ—a portion quite distinct—a portion which would hold eternally good even though no sinner were ever to be saved. In order to see the force of this, it is needful to bear in mind how God has been dishonored in this world. His truth has been despised; His authority has been contemned; His majesty has been slighted; His law has been broken; His claims have been disregarded; His name has been blasphemed; His character has been traduced.

Now, the death of Christ has made provision for all this. It has perfectly glorified God in the very place where all these things have been done; it has perfectly vindicated the majesty, the truth, the holiness, the character of God; it has divinely met all the claims of His throne; it has atoned for *sin;* it has furnished a divine remedy for all the mischief which sin introduced into the universe; it affords a ground on which the blessed God can act in grace, mercy, and forbearance toward all; it furnishes a warrant for the eternal expulsion and perdition of the prince of this world; it forms the imperishable foundation of God's moral government. In virtue of the cross, God can act according to His own sovereignty; He can display the matchless glories of His character and the adorable attributes of His nature. He might, in the exercise of inflexible justice, have consigned the human family to the

lake of fire, together with the devil and his angels;
but in that case, where would be His love, His grace,
His mercy, His kindness, His long-suffering, His
compassion, His patience, His perfect goodness?

Then on the other hand, had these precious attributes been exercised in the absence of atonement,
where were the justice, the truth, the majesty, the
holiness, the righteousness, the governmental claims,
yea, the entire moral glory of God? How could
"mercy and truth meet together"? or "righteousness and peace kiss each other"? how could "truth
spring out of the earth"? or "righteousness look
down from heaven"? Impossible. Naught save
the atonement of our Lord Jesus Christ could have
fully glorified God; but that has glorified Him. It
has reflected the full glory of the divine character as
it never could have been reflected amid the brightest
splendors of an unfallen creation. By means of that
atonement, in prospect and retrospect, God has been
exercising forbearance toward this world for well-
nigh six thousand years. In virtue of that atonement, the most wicked, daring, and blasphemous of
the sons of men "live, move, and have their being;"
eat, drink, and sleep. The very morsel which yonder open blaspheming infidel puts into his mouth,
he owes to the atonement, which he knows not,
but impiously ridicules; the sunbeams and showers
which fertilize the fields of the atheist, reach him in
virtue of the atonement of Christ; yea, the very
breath which the infidel and the atheist spend in
blaspheming God's revelation, or denying His exist-

ence, they owe to the atonement of Christ. Were it
not for that precious atonement, instead of blaspheming upon earth, they would be weltering in hell.

Let not my reader misunderstand me, I speak not
here of the forgiveness or salvation of persons.
This is quite another thing, and stands connected,
as every true Christian knows, with the confession
of the name of Jesus and the hearty belief that
God raised Him from the dead. (Rom. x.) This is
plain enough, and fully understood; but it is in no
wise involved in that aspect of the atonement which
we are at present contemplating, and which is so
strikingly foreshadowed by "the goat on which the
Lord's lot fell." God's pardoning and accepting
a sinner is one thing; His bearing with that man,
and showering temporal blessings upon him, is quite
another. Both are in virtue of the cross, but in a
totally different aspect and application thereof.

Nor is this distinction by any means unimportant.
Quite the opposite. Indeed, so important is it that
where it is overlooked, there must be confusion as
to the full doctrine of atonement. Nor is this all.
A clear understanding of God's ways in government, whether in the past, the present, or the future,
will be found involved in this profoundly interesting
point. And finally, in it will be found the key wherewith to expound a number of texts in which many
Christians find considerable difficulty. I shall just
adduce two or three of these passages as examples.

"Behold the Lamb of God, which taketh away
the *sin* of the world." (John i. 29.) With this we

may connect a kindred passage in John's first epistle, in which the Lord Jesus Christ is spoken of as "the propitiation for the whole world."* (Chap. ii. 2.) In both these passages the Lord Jesus is referred to as the One who has perfectly glorified God with respect to "*sin*" and "*the world*," in their broadest acceptation. He is here seen as the great Antitype of "the goat on which the Lord's lot fell." This gives us a most precious view of the atonement of Christ, and one which is too much overlooked, or not clearly apprehended. Whenever the question of *persons* and the forgiveness of *sins* is raised in connection with these and kindred passages of Scripture, the mind is sure to get involved in insuperable difficulties.

So, also, with respect to all those passages in which God's grace to the world at large is presented. They are founded upon that special aspect of the atonement with which we are more immediately occupied. "Go ye into *all the world* and preach the gospel *to every creature*." (Mark. xvi.)—"God so loved *the world*, that He gave His only begotten Son,

---

*The reader will observe, in the above passage, that the words "the sins of" are introduced by the translators, and are not inspired. The divine accuracy of the passage is completely lost by retaining those uninspired words. The doctrine laid down is simply this: In the first clause of the verse, Christ is set forth as the propitiation for His people's actual *sins;* but in the last clause, it is not a question of *sins* or of *persons* at all, but of *sin* and the *world* in general. In fact, the whole verse presents Christ as the Antitype of the two goats, as the One who has borne His people's sins; and also as the One who has perfectly glorified God with respect to sin in general, and made provision for dealing in grace with the world at large, and for the final deliverance and blessing of the whole creation.

that whosoever believeth in Him might not perish, but have everlasting life. For God sent not His Son into the world to condemn *the world*, but that the world through Him might be saved." (John iii. 16, 17.)—"I exhort, therefore, that first of all, supplications, prayers, intercessions, and giving of thanks, be made for *all men;* for kings, and for all that are in authority; that we may lead a quiet and peaceable life in all godliness and honesty. For this is good and acceptable in the sight of God our Saviour; who will have *all men* to be saved, and to come unto the knowledge of the truth. For there is one God, and one Mediator between God and men, the Man Christ Jesus; who gave Himself *a ransom for all*, to be testified in due time." (1 Tim. ii. 1–6.) —"For *the grace of God* that bringeth salvation hath appeared to *all men*." (Titus ii. 11.)—"But we see Jesus, who was made a little lower than the angels, for the suffering of death, crowned with glory and honor; that He by *the grace of God* should taste death *for every man*." (Heb. ii. 9.)—"The Lord is not slack concerning His promise, as some men count slackness; but is long-suffering to usward, not willing that *any* should perish, but that *all* should come to repentance." (2 Peter iii. 9.)

There is no need whatsoever for seeking to avoid the plain sense of the above and similar passages. They bear a clear and unequivocal testimony to divine grace toward all, without the slightest reference to man's responsibility on the one hand, or to God's eternal counsels on the other. These things are just as clearly, just as fully, just as unequivocally, taught in the Word. Man is responsible and God is sovereign. All who bow to Scripture admit these things. But, at the same time, it is of the very last importance to recognize the wide aspect of the grace of God and of the cross of Christ. It glorifies God, and leaves man *wholly* without excuse. Men argue about God's decrees and man's incompetency to believe without divine influence. Their arguments prove that they do not want God; for did they only want Him, He is near enough to be found of them. The grace of God and the atonement of Christ are as wide as they could desire. "*Any*," "*every*," "*whosoever*," and "*all*" are God's own words; and I should like to know who is shut out. If God sends a message of salvation to a man, He surely intends it for him; and what can be more wicked and impious than to reject God's grace, and make Him a liar, and then give His secret decrees as a reason for so doing? It would be, in a certain sense, honest for a man to say at once, The fact is, I do not believe God's Word, and I do not want His grace or His salvation. One could understand this; but for men to cover their hatred of God and His truth with the drapery of a false, because one-sided, theology, is the very highest character of wickedness. It is such as to make us feel, of a truth, that the devil is never more diabolical than when he appears with the Bible in his hand.

If it be true that men are prevented by God's secret decrees and counsels from receiving the gospel, which He has commanded to be preached to them, then on what principle of righteousness will they be "punished with everlasting destruction" for not obeying that gospel? (2 Thess. i. 6–10.) Is there a single soul throughout all the gloomy regions of the lost who blames God's counsels for his being there? Not one. Oh, no; God has made such ample provision in the atonement of Christ, not only for the salvation of those that believe, but also for the aspect of His grace toward those that reject the gospel, that there is no excuse. It is not because a man *cannot*, but because he *will not* believe that he "shall be punished with everlasting destruction." Never was there a more fatal mistake than for a man to ensconce himself behind God's decrees, while deliberately and intelligently refusing God's grace; and this is all the more dangerous because supported by the dogmas of a one-sided theology. God's grace is free to all; and if we ask, How is this? the answer is, "Jehovah's lot" fell upon the true Victim, in order that He might be perfectly glorified as to sin, in its widest aspect, and be free to act in grace toward all, and "preach the gospel to every creature." This grace and this preaching must have a solid basis, and that basis is found in the atonement; and though man should reject, God is glorified in the exercise of grace and in the offer of salvation, because of the basis on which both the one and the other repose. He *is* glorified, and He *shall be* glorified throughout eternity's countless ages.—"Now is My soul troubled; and what shall I say? Father, save Me from this hour: but for this cause came I unto this hour. Father, glorify Thy name. Then came there a voice from heaven, saying, 'I have both glorified it, and will glorify it again.' . . . . Now is the judgment of this world: now shall the prince of this world be cast out. And I, if I be lifted up from the earth, will draw all unto Me." (John xii. 27–32.)

Thus far we have been occupied only with one special point, namely, "the goat on which the Lord's lot fell;" and a cursory reader might suppose that the next thing in order would be the scape-goat, which gives us the other great aspect of the death of Christ, or its application to the sins of the people. But no; ere we come to that, we have the fullest confirmation of that precious line of truth which has been before us, in the fact that the blood of the slain goat, together with the blood of the bullock, was sprinkled upon and before Jehovah's throne, in order to show that all the claims of that throne were answered in the blood of atonement, and full provision made for all the demands of God's moral administration.

"And Aaron shall bring the bullock of the sin-offering which is for himself, and shall make an atonement for himself, and for his house, and shall kill the bullock of the sin-offering which is for himself. And he shall take a censer full of burning coals of fire from off the altar before Lord, and his hands full of sweet incense beaten small, and bring it within the vail. And he shall put the incense upon the fire before the Lord, that the cloud of the incense may cover the mercy-seat that is upon the testimony, that he die not." Here we have a most vivid and striking presentation indeed. The blood of atonement is carried in within the vail, into the holiest of all, and there sprinkled upon the throne of the God of Israel. The cloud of the divine presence was there; and in order that Aaron might appear in the immediate presence of the glory and not die, "the cloud of incense" ascends and "covers the mercy-seat," on which the blood of atonement was to be sprinkled "seven times." The "*sweet* incense beaten *small*" expresses the fragrance of Christ's Person—the sweet odor of His most precious sacrifice.

"And he shall take of the blood of the bullock, and sprinkle it with his finger upon the mercy-seat eastward; and before the mercy-seat shall he sprinkle of the blood with his finger seven times. Then shall he kill the goat of the sin-offering that is for the people, and bring his blood within the vail, and do with that blood as he did with the blood of the bullock, and sprinkle it upon the mercy-seat, and before the mercy-seat." (Ver. 14, 15.) "Seven" is the perfect number; and in the sprinkling of the blood seven times before the mercy-seat, we learn that whatever be the application of the atonement of Christ, whether as to things, to places, or to persons, it is perfectly estimated in the divine presence. The blood which secures the salvation of the Church —the "house" of the true Aaron; the blood which secures the salvation of the "congregation" of Is-

rael; the blood which secures the final restoration
and blessedness of the whole creation—that blood
has been presented before God, sprinkled and accepted according to all the perfectness, fragrance,
and preciousness of Christ. In the power of that
blood God can accomplish all His eternal counsels
of grace. He can save the Church, and raise it into
the very loftiest heights of glory and dignity, despite
of all the power of sin and Satan; He can restore
Israel's scattered tribes; He can unite Judah and
Ephraim; He can accomplish all the promises made
to Abraham, Isaac, and Jacob; He can save and
bless untold millions of the Gentiles; He can restore and bless the wide creation; He can allow the
beams of His glory to lighten up the universe forever; He can display, in the view of angels, men,
and devils, His own eternal glory—the glory of His
character, the glory of His nature, the glory of His
works, the glory of His government,—all this He
can do, and will do; but the one solitary pedestal
upon which the stupendous fabric of glory shall rest
forever, is the blood of the cross—that precious
blood, dear Christian reader, which has spoken
peace—divine and everlasting peace—to your heart
and conscience, in the presence of Infinite Holiness.
The blood which is sprinkled upon the believer's
conscience has been sprinkled "seven times" before
the throne of God. The nearer we get to God, the
more importance and value we find attached to the
blood of Jesus. If we look at the brazen altar, we
find the blood there; if we look at the brazen laver,

we find the blood there; if we look at the golden
altar, we find the blood there; if we look at the vail
of the tabernacle, we find the blood there: but in
no place do we find so much about the blood as
within the vail, before Jehovah's throne, in the immediate presence of the divine glory.

> "In heaven His blood forever speaks,
>   In God the Father's ears."

"And he shall make an atonement for the holy
place, because of the uncleanness of the children of
Israel, and because of their transgressions in all
their sins: and so shall he do for the tabernacle of
the congregation, that remaineth among them in the
midst of their uncleanness." The same truth meets
us all along.   The claims of the sanctuary must
be provided for.   Jehovah's courts, as well as His
throne, must bear witness to the value of the blood.
The tabernacle, in the midst of Israel's uncleanness,
must be fenced round about by the divine provisions
of atonement.   Jehovah provided, in all things, for
His own glory.   The priests and their priestly
service, the place of worship and all therein, must
stand in the power of the blood.   The Holy One
could not have remained for a moment in the midst
of the congregation were it not for the power of the
blood. It was that which left Him free to dwell and
act and rule in the midst of an erring people.

"And there shall be no man in the tabernacle of
the congregation when he goeth in to make an atonement in the holy place, until he come out, and have
made an atonement for himself, and for his house·

hold, and for all the congregation of Israel.'' (Ver.
17.) Aaron needed to offer up sacrifice for his own
sins, as well as for the sins of the people. He could
only enter into the sanctuary in the power of the
blood. We have, in verse 17, a type of the atonement of Christ in its application both to the Church
and to the congregation of Israel. The Church now
enters into the holiest by the blood of Jesus. (Heb.
x.) As to Israel, the vail is still on their hearts.
(2 Cor. iii.) They are still at a distance, although
full provision has been made in the cross for their
forgiveness and restoration when they shall turn to
the Lord. This entire period is, properly speaking,
the day of atonement. The true Aaron is gone in,
with His own blood, into heaven itself, now to appear in the presence of God for us. By and by He
will come forth to lead the congregation of Israel
into the full results of His accomplished work.
Meanwhile, His house—that is to say, all true believers—is associated with Him, having boldness
to enter into the holiest, being brought nigh by the
blood of Jesus.

"And he shall go out unto the altar that is before
the Lord, and make an atonement for it; and shall
take of the blood of the bullock, and of the blood
of the goat, and put it upon the horns of the altar
round about. And he shall sprinkle of the blood
upon it with his finger seven times, and cleanse it,
and hallow it from the uncleanness of the children
of Israel. (Ver. 18, 19.) Thus the atoning blood
was sprinkled every where, from the throne of God

within the vail, to the altar which stood in the court
of the tabernacle of the congregation. "It was
therefore necessary that the patterns of things in
the heavens should be purified with these, but the
heavenly things themselves with better sacrifices
than these. For Christ is not entered into the holy
places made with hands, which are the figures of the
true; but into heaven itself, now to appear in the
presence of God for us: nor yet that He should
offer Himself often, as the high-priest entereth into
the holy place every year with blood of others; for
then must He often have suffered since the foundation of the world; but now *once* in the end of the
world [at the end of every thing earthly, every thing
human] hath He appeared to put away sin by the
sacrifice of Himself. And as it is appointed unto
men once to die, but after this the judgment; so
Christ was once offered to bear the sins of many;
and unto them that look for Him shall He appear
the second time without sin unto salvation." (Heb.
ix. 23–28.)

There is but one way into the holiest of all, and
that is a blood-sprinkled way. It is vain to strive
to enter by any other. Men may attempt to work
themselves in, to pray themselves in, to buy themselves in, to get in by a pathway of ordinances, or
it may be, of half ordinances, half Christ; but it is
of no use. God speaks of *one* way, and but one,
and that way has been thrown open through the rent
vail of the Saviour's flesh. Along that way have the
millions of the saved passed, from age to age; pa-

triarchs, prophets, apostles, martyrs, saints in every
age, from Abel downwards, have trod that blessed
way, and found thereby sure and undisputed access.
The *one* sacrifice of the cross is divinely sufficient
for all.   God asks no more, and He can take no less.
To add aught thereto is to cast dishonor upon that
with which God has declared Himself well pleased,
yea, in which He is infinitely glorified: to diminish
aught therefrom is to deny man's guilt and ruin,
and offer an indignity to the justice and majesty of
the eternal Trinity.

"And when he hath made an end of reconciling
the holy place, and the tabernacle of the congregation, and the altar, he shall bring the live goat.
And Aaron shall lay both his hands upon the head
of the live goat, and confess over him *all* the iniquities of the children of Israel, and *all* their transgressions in *all* their sins, putting them upon the
head of the goat, and shall send him away by the
hand of a fit man into the wilderness.   And the
goat shall bear upon him *all* their iniquities unto a
land not inhabited; and he shall let go the goat in
the wilderness."

Here, then, we have the other grand idea attached
to the death of Christ, namely, the full and final
forgiveness of the people.   If the death of Christ
forms the foundation of the glory of God, it also
forms the foundation of the perfect forgiveness of
sins to all who put their trust in it.   This latter,
blessed be God, is but a secondary—an inferior application of the atonement, though our foolish hearts

would fain regard it as the very highest possible view of the cross to see in it that which puts away all our sins. This is a mistake. God's glory is the first thing, our salvation is the second. To maintain God's glory was the chief—the darling object of the heart of Christ. This object He pursued from first to last, with an undeviating purpose and unflinching fidelity. "Therefore doth My Father love Me, because I lay down My life, that I might take it again." (John x. 17.) "Now is the Son of Man glorified, and God is glorified in Him. If God be glorified in Him, God shall also glorify Him in Himself, and shall straightway glorify Him." (John xiii. 31, 32.) "Listen, O isles, unto Me; and hearken, ye people from far: the Lord hath called Me from the womb; from the bowels of My mother hath He made mention of My name. And He hath made My mouth like a sharp sword; in the shadow of His hand hath He hid Me, and made Me a polished shaft: in His quiver hath He hid Me; and said unto Me, 'Thou art My Servant, O Israel, in whom *I will be glorified.*'" (Isaiah xlix. 1–3.)

Thus the glory of God was the paramount object of the Lord Jesus Christ, in life and in death. He lived and died to glorify His Father's name. Does the Church lose aught by this? Nay. Does Israel? Nay. Do the Gentiles? Nay. In no way could their salvation and blessedness be so perfectly provided for as by being made subsidiary to the glory of God. Hearken to the divine response to Christ, the true Israel, in the sublime passage just quoted.

"It is a light thing that Thou shouldest be My
Servant to raise up the tribes of Jacob, and to restore the preserved of Israel: I will also give Thee
for a light to the Gentiles, that Thou mayest be My
salvation to the ends of the earth."

And is it not a blessed thing to know that God is
glorified in the putting away of our sins? We may
ask, Where are our sins? Put away. By what?
By that act of Christ upon the cross, in which God
has been eternally glorified. Thus it is. The two
goats, on the day of atonement, give the double
aspect of the one act. In the one, we see God's
glory maintained; in the other, sins put away. The
one is as perfect as the other. We are as perfectly
forgiven as God is perfectly glorified, by the death
of Christ. Was there one single point in which God
was not glorified in the cross? Not one. Neither
is there one single point in which we are not perfectly
forgiven. I say "we;" for albeit the congregation
of Israel is the primary object contemplated in the
beautiful and impressive ordinance of the scape-
goat, yet does it hold good, in the fullest way, with
respect to every soul that believes on the Lord Jesus
Christ, that he is as perfectly forgiven as God is
perfectly glorified, by the atonement of the cross.
How many of the sins of Israel did the scape-goat
bear away? "*All*." Precious word! Not one left
behind. And whither did he bear them? "Into a
land not inhabited"—a land where they could never
be found, because there was no one there to look for
them. Could any type be more perfect? could *we*

possibly have a more graphic picture of Christ's accomplished sacrifice, in its primary and secondary aspects? Impossible. We can hang with intense admiration over such a picture, and as we gaze, exclaim, Of a truth, the pencil of the Master is here!

Reader, pause here, and say, do you know that *all* your sins are forgiven, according to the perfection of Christ's sacrifice? If you simply *believe* on His name, they are so,—they are all gone, and gone forever. Say not, as so many anxious souls do, "I fear I do not *realize.*" There is no such word as "realize" in the entire gospel. We are not saved by realization, but by Christ; and the way to get Christ in all His fullness and preciousness is to believe—"*only believe!*" And what will be the result? "The worshipers once purged should have no more conscience of sins." Observe this,—"No more conscience of sins." This must be the result, inasmuch as Christ's sacrifice is perfect—so perfect, that God is glorified therein. Now, it must be obvious to you that Christ's work does not need your realization to be added to it to make it perfect. This could not be. We might as well say that the work of creation was not complete until Adam realized it in the garden of Eden. True, he did realize; but what did he realize? A perfect work. Thus let it be with your precious soul this moment, if it has never been so before. May you now and evermore repose, in artless simplicity, upon the One who has, by one offering, perfected forever them that are

sanctified. And how are they sanctified? **Is it**
by realization? By no means. How then? By **the**
perfect work of Christ.

Having sought (alas! most feebly) to unfold the
doctrine of this marvelous chapter, so far as God
has given me light upon it, there is just one point
further to which I shall merely call my reader's attention ere I close this section. It is contained in
the following quotation: "And this shall be a statute forever unto you, that in the seventh month, on
the tenth day of the month, ye shall afflict your
souls, and do no work at all, whether it be one of
your own country or a stranger that sojourneth
among you. For on that day shall the priest make
an atonement for you, to cleanse you, that ye may
be clean from *all* your sins *before the Lord*. It shall
be *a Sabbath of rest*, and ye shall *afflict your souls*,
by a statute forever." (Ver. 29–31.)

This shall have its full accomplishment in the
saved remnant of Israel by and by, as foretold by
the prophet Zechariah,—"And I will pour upon the
house of David, and upon the inhabitants of Jerusalem, the spirit of grace and of supplications; and
they shall look upon Me whom they have pierced,
and they shall mourn for Him, as one mourneth for
his only son, and shall be in bitterness for Him, as
one that is in bitterness for his first-born. *In that
day* shall there be *a great mourning* in Jerusalem, as
the mourning of Hadadrimmon in the valley of
Megiddon. . . . . *In that day* there shall be *a
fountain opened* to the house of David, and to the

inhabitants of Jerusalem, for sin and for uncleanness. . . . . And it shall come to pass *in that day* that the light shall not be clear [in one place] and dark [in another]; but it shall be one day, [the true and long-expected Sabbath,] which shall be known to the Lord, not day nor night; but it shall come to pass that at evening time it shall be light. And it shall be *in that day* that living waters shall go out from Jerusalem; half of them toward the former sea, and half of them toward the hinder sea: in summer and in winter shall it be. And THE LORD SHALL BE KING OVER ALL THE EARTH: *in that day* shall there be one Lord, and His name one. . . . . *In that day* shall there be upon the bells of the horses, HOLINESS UNTO THE LORD. . . . . And *in that day* there shall be no more the Canaanite in the house of the Lord of hosts." (Zech. xii.–xiv.)

What a day that will be! No marvel that it should be so frequently and so emphatically introduced in the above glowing passage. It will be a bright and blessed "Sabbath of rest" when the mourning remnant shall gather, in the spirit of true penitence, around the open fountain, and enter into the full and final results of the great day of atonement. They shall "afflict their souls," no doubt; for how could they do otherwise, while fixing their repentant gaze "upon Him whom they have pierced"? But, oh, what a Sabbath they will have! Jerusalem will have a brimming cup of salvation, after her long and dreary night of sorrow. Her former desolations shall be forgotten, and her children, restored to their long-lost dwellings, shall take down their harps from the willows, and sing once more the sweet songs of Zion, beneath the peaceful shade of the vine and fig-tree.

Blessed be God, the time is at hand. Every setting sun brings us nearer to that blissful Sabbath. The word is, "Surely, I come quickly;" and all around seems to tell us that "the days are at hand, and the effect of every vision." May we be "sober, and watch unto prayer." May we keep ourselves unspotted from the world; and thus, in the spirit of our minds, the affections of our hearts, and the experience of our souls, be ready to meet the heavenly Bridegroom. Our place for the present is outside the camp. Thank God that it is so! It would be an unspeakable loss to be inside. The same cross which has brought us inside the vail has cast us outside the camp. Christ was cast out thither, and we are with Him there; but He has been received up into heaven, and we are with Him there. Is it not a mercy to be outside of all that which has rejected our blessed Lord and Master? Truly so; and the more we know of Jesus, and the more we know of this present evil world, the more thankful we shall be to find our place outside of it all *with Him*.

CHAPTER XVII

IN this chapter the reader will find two special points, namely, first, that life belongs to Jehovah; and secondly, that the power of atonement is

in the blood. The Lord attached peculiar importance to both these things. He would have them
impressed upon every member of the congregation.

"And the Lord spake unto Moses, saying, 'Speak
unto Aaron, and unto his sons, and unto all the
children of Israel, and say unto them, This is the
thing which the Lord hath commanded, saying,
What man soever there be of the house of Israel,
that killeth an ox, or lamb, or goat, in the camp, or
that killeth it out of the camp, and bringeth it not
unto the door of the tabernacle of the congregation,
to offer an offering unto the Lord, before the tabernacle of the Lord; blood shall be imputed unto that
man; he hath shed blood; and that man shall be
cut off from among his people." This was a most
solemn matter; and we may ask what was involved
in offering a sacrifice otherwise than in the manner
here prescribed. It was nothing less than robbing
Jehovah of His rights, and presenting to Satan that
which was due to God. A man might say, Can I
not offer a sacrifice in one place as well as another?
The answer is, Life belongs to God, and His claim
thereto must be recognized in the place which He
has appointed—before the tabernacle of the Lord.
That was the only meeting-place between God and
man. To offer elsewhere proved that the heart did
not want God.

The moral of this is plain. There is one place
where God has appointed to meet the sinner, and
that is the cross—the antitype of the brazen altar.
There and there alone has God's claims upon the

life been duly recognized. To reject this meeting-place is to bring down judgment upon one's self—it is to trample under foot the just claims of God, and to arrogate to one's self a right to life which all have forfeited. It is important to see this.

"And the priest shall sprinkle the blood upon the altar of the Lord, at the door of the tabernacle of the congregation, and burn the fat for a sweet savor unto the Lord." The blood and the fat belonged to God. The blessed Jesus fully recognized this. He surrendered His life to God, and all His hidden energies were devoted to Him likewise. He voluntarily walked to the altar and there gave up His precious life; and the fragrant odor of His intrinsic excellency ascended to the throne of God. Blessed Jesus! it is sweet, at every step of our way, to be reminded of Thee.

The second point above referred to is clearly stated in verse 11.—"For the life of the flesh is in the blood; and I have given it to you upon the altar, to make an atonement for your souls, for IT IS THE BLOOD THAT MAKETH AN ATONEMENT FOR THE SOUL." The connection between the two points is deeply interesting. When man duly takes his place as one possessing no title whatsoever to life—when he fully recognizes God's claims upon him, then the divine record is, "I have given you the life to make an atonement for your soul." Yes; atonement is God's gift to man; and be it carefully noted that this atonement is in the blood, and *only* in the blood. "It is *the blood* that maketh an atonement for the soul." It is not the blood *and* something else. The word is most explicit. It attributes atonement exclusively to *the blood*. "Without shedding of *blood* is no remission." (Heb. ix. 22.) It was the *death* of Christ that rent the vail. It is "by *the blood* of Jesus" we have "boldness to enter into the holiest." "We have redemption through His *blood*, the forgiveness of sins." (Eph. i. 7; Col. i. 14.) "Having made peace by *the blood* of His cross." "Ye who were afar off are made nigh by *the blood* of His cross." "*The blood* of Jesus Christ His Son cleanseth us from all sin." (1 John i. 7.) "They washed their robes and made them white in *the blood* of the Lamb." (Rev. vii.) "They overcame him by *the blood* of the Lamb." (Rev. xii.)

I would desire to call my reader's earnest attention to the precious and vital doctrine of the blood. I am anxious that he should see its true place. The blood of Christ is the foundation of every thing. It is the ground of God's righteousness in justifying an ungodly sinner that believes on the name of the Son of God; and it is the ground of the sinner's confidence in drawing nigh to a holy God, who is of purer eyes than to behold evil. God would be just in the condemnation of the sinner; but through the death of Christ, He can be just and the justifier of him that believeth—a just God and a Saviour. The righteousness of God is His consistency with Himself—His acting in harmony with His revealed character. Hence, were it not for the cross, His consistency with Himself would, of necessity, demand the death and judgment of the sinner; but in the cross, that death and judgment were borne by the sinner's Surety, so that the same divine consistency is perfectly maintained, while a holy God justifies an ungodly sinner through faith. *It is all through the blood of Jesus*—nothing less, nothing more, nothing different. "It is the blood that maketh an atonement for the soul." This is conclusive. This is God's simple plan of justification. Man's plan is much more cumbrous, much more roundabout. And not only is it cumbrous and roundabout, but it attributes righteousness to something quite different from what I find in the Word. If I look from the third chapter of Genesis down to the close of Revelation, I find the blood of Christ put forward as the alone ground of righteousness. We get pardon, peace, life, righteousness—all by the blood, and nothing but the blood. The entire book of Leviticus, and particularly the chapter upon which we have just been meditating, is a commentary upon the doctrine of the blood. It seems strange to have to insist upon a fact so obvious to every dispassionate, teachable student of holy Scripture; yet so it is. Our minds are prone to slip away from the plain testimony of the Word. We are ready to adopt opinions without ever calmly investigating them in the light of the divine testimonies. In this way we get into confusion, darkness, and error.

May we all learn to give the blood of Christ its due place. It is so precious in God's sight that He will not suffer aught else to be added to or mingled with it. "The life of the flesh is in the blood, and I have given it to you upon the altar, to make an atonement for your souls: for *it is the blood that maketh an atonement for the soul.*"

CHAPTERS XVIII.—XX

THIS section sets before us, in a very remarkable manner, the personal sanctity and moral propriety which Jehovah looked for on the part of those whom He had graciously introduced into relationship with Himself; and, at the same time, it presents a most humiliating picture of the enormities of which human nature is capable.

"And the Lord spake unto Moses, saying, 'Speak unto the children of Israel, and say unto them, *I am the Lord your God.*'" Here we have the foundation of the entire superstructure of moral conduct which these chapters present. Israel's actings were to take their character from the fact that Jehovah was *their* God. They were called to comport themselves in a manner worthy of so high and holy a position. It was God's prerogative to set forth the special character and line of conduct becoming a people with whom He was pleased to associate His name. Hence the frequency of the expressions, "I am the Lord," "I am the Lord your God," "I the Lord your God am holy." Jehovah was their God, and He was holy; hence, therefore, they were called to be holy likewise. His name was involved in their character and acting.

This is the true principle of holiness for the people of God in all ages. They are to be governed and characterized by the revelation which He has made of Himself. Their conduct is to be founded upon what He is, not upon what they are in themselves. This entirely sets aside the principle expressed in the words, "Stand by thyself, I am holier than thou;" a principle so justly repudiated by every sensitive mind. It is not a comparison of one man with another, but a simple statement of the line of conduct which God looks for in those who belong to Him. "After the doings of the land of Egypt, wherein ye dwelt, shall ye not do; and after the doings of the land of Canaan, whither I bring you, shall ye not do; neither shall ye walk in their ordinances." The Egyptians and the Canaanites were all wrong. How was Israel to know this? Who told them? How came they to be right and all besides wrong? These are interesting inquiries; and the answer is as simple as the questions are interesting. Jehovah's Word was the standard by which all questions of right and wrong were to be definitely settled in the judgment of every member of the Israel of God. It was not, by any means, the judgment of an Israelite in opposition to the judgment of an Egyptian or of a Canaanite; but it was the judgment of God above *all*. Egypt might have her practices and her opinions, and so might Canaan; but Israel were to have the opinions and practices laid down in the Word of God. "Ye shall do My judgments, and keep Mine ordinances, to walk therein: I am the Lord your God. Ye shall therefore keep My statutes and My judgments; which, if a man do, he shall live in them: I am the Lord."

It will be well for my reader to get a clear, deep, full, practical sense of this truth. The Word of God must settle every question and govern every conscience: there must be no appeal from its solemn and weighty decision. When God speaks, every heart must bow. Men may form and hold their opinions; they may adopt and defend their practices; but one of the finest traits in the character of "the Israel of God" is, profound reverence for, and implicit subjection to, "every word that proceedeth out of the mouth of the Lord. The exhibition of this valuable feature may perhaps lay them open to the charge of dogmatism, superciliousness, and self-sufficiency, on the part of those who have never duly weighed the matter; but, in truth, nothing can be more unlike dogmatism than simple subjection to the plain truth of God; nothing more unlike superciliousness than reverence for the statements of inspiration; nothing more unlike self-sufficiency than subjection to the divine authority of holy Scripture.

True, there will ever be the need of carefulness as to the tone and manner in which we set forth the authority for our convictions and our conduct. It must be made manifest, so far as it may be, that we are wholly governed, not by our own opinions, but by the Word of God. There is great danger of attaching an importance to an opinion merely because *we* have adopted it. This must be carefully guarded against. *Self* may creep in and display its deformity in the defense of our opinions as much as in any thing else; but we must disallow it in every shape and form, and be governed in all things by "Thus saith the Lord."

But then we are not to expect that every one will be ready to admit the full force of the divine statutes and judgments. It is as persons walk in the integrity and energy of the divine nature that the Word of God will be owned, appreciated, and reverenced. An Egyptian or a Canaanite would have been wholly unable to enter into the meaning or estimate the value of these statutes and judgments, which were to govern the conduct of the circumcised people of God; but that did not in any wise affect the question of Israel's obedience. They were brought into a certain relationship with Jehovah, and that relationship had its distinctive privileges and responsibilities. "I am the Lord *your* God." This was to be the ground of their conduct. They were to act in a way worthy of the One who had become *their* God, and made them *His* people. It was not that they were a whit better than other people. By no means. The Egyptians or Canaanites might have considered that the Israelites were setting themselves up as something superior in refusing to adopt the habits of either nation. But no; the foundation of their peculiar line of conduct and tone of morality was laid in these words: "*I* am the Lord *your God*."

In this great and practically important fact, Jehovah set before His people a ground of conduct which was immovable, and a standard of morality which was as elevated and as enduring as the eternal throne itself.   The moment He entered into a relationship with a people, their ethics were to assume a character and tone worthy of Him.   It was no longer a question as to what they were, either in themselves or in comparison with others ; but of what God was in comparison with all.   This makes a material difference.   To make *self* the ground of action or the standard of ethics is not only presumptuous folly, but it is sure to set one upon a descending scale of action.   If self be my object, I must, of necessity, sink lower and lower every day ; but if, on the other hand, I set the Lord before me, I shall rise higher and higher as, by the power of the Holy Ghost, I grow in conformity to that perfect model which is unfolded to the gaze of faith in the sacred pages of inspiration.   I shall undoubtedly have to prostrate myself in the dust, under a sense of how infinitely short I come of the mark set before me ; but then I can never consent to the setting up of a lower standard, nor can I ever be satisfied until I am conformed in all things to Him who was my substitute on the cross, and is my model in the glory.

Having said thus much on the main principle of the section before us—a principle of unspeakable importance to Christians, in a practical point of view, I feel it needless to enter into any thing like a detailed exposition of statutes which speak for themselves in most obvious terms.   I would merely remark that those statutes range themselves under two distinct heads, namely, first, those which set forth the shameful enormities which the human heart is capable of devising; and secondly, those which exhibit the exquisite tenderness and considerate care of the God of Israel.

As to the first, it is manifest that the Spirit of God could never enact laws for the purpose of preventing evils that have no existence. He does not construct a dam where there is no flood to be resisted: He does not deal with abstract ideas, but with positive realities. Man is, in very deed, capable of perpetrating each and every one of the shameful crimes referred to in this most faithful section of the book of Leviticus. If he were not, why should he be told not to do so. Such a code would be wholly unsuitable for angels, inasmuch as they are incapable of committing the sins referred to; but it suits man, because he has gotten the seeds of those sins in his nature. This is deeply humbling. It is a fresh declaration of the truth that man is a total wreck. From the crown of his head to the sole of his foot, there is not so much as a single speck of moral soundness, as looked at in the light of the divine presence. The being for whom Jehovah thought it needful to write Leviticus xviii.–xx. must be a vile sinner; but that being is *man*—the writer and reader of these lines. How plain it is, therefore, that "they that are in the flesh *cannot* please God." (Rom. viii.) Thank God, the believer is "not in the flesh, but in the Spirit." He has been taken completely out of his old-creation standing, and introduced into the new creation, in which the moral evils aimed at in this our section can have no existence. True, he has gotten the old nature; but it is his happy privilege to "reckon" it as a dead thing, and to walk in the abiding power of the new creation, wherein "all things are of God." This is Christian liberty, even liberty to walk up and down in that fair creation where no trace of evil can ever be found,—hallowed liberty to walk in holiness and purity before God and man,—liberty to tread those lofty walks of personal sanctity whereon the beams of the divine countenance ever pour themselves in living lustre. Reader, this is Christian liberty. It is liberty, not to commit sin, but to taste the celestial sweets of a life of true holiness and moral elevation. May we prize more highly than we have ever done this precious boon of heaven—Christian liberty.

And now, one word as to the second class of statutes contained in our section, namely, those which so touchingly bring out divine tenderness and care. Take the following: "And when ye reap the harvest of your land, thou shalt not wholly reap the corners of thy field, neither shalt thou gather the gleanings of thy harvest. And thou shalt not glean thy vineyard, neither shalt thou gather every grape of thy vineyard; *thou shalt leave them for the poor and stranger:* I am the Lord your God." (Chap. xix. 9, 10.) This ordinance will meet us again in chapter xxiii. but there we shall see it in its dispensational bearing. Here, we contemplate it morally, as unfolding the precious grace of Israel's God. He would think of "the poor and stranger," and He would have His people think of them likewise. When the golden sheaves were being reaped. and the mellow clusters gathered, "the poor and stranger" were to be remembered by the Israel of God, because Jehovah was the God of Israel. The reaper and the grape-gatherer were not to be governed by a spirit of grasping covetousness, which would bare the corners of the field and strip the branches of the vine, but rather by a spirit of large-hearted, genuine benevolence, which would leave a sheaf and a cluster "for the poor and stranger," that they too might rejoice in the unbounded goodness of Him whose paths drop fatness, and on whose open hand all the sons of want may confidently wait.

The book of Ruth furnishes a fine example of one who fully acted out this most benevolent statute. "And Boaz said unto her, [Ruth,] 'At meal-time, come thou hither, and eat of the bread, and dip thy morsel in the vinegar.' And she sat beside the reapers: and he reached her parched corn, and she did eat, and was sufficed, and left. And when she was risen up to glean, Boaz commanded his young men, saying, 'Let her glean even among the sheaves, and reproach her not; *and let fall also some of the handfuls of purpose for her*, and leave them, that she may glean them, and rebuke her not.'" (Ruth ii. 14–16.) Most touching and beautiful grace! Truly, it is good for our poor selfish hearts to be brought in contact with such principles and such practices. Nothing can surpass the exquisite refinement of the words, "let fall also some of the handfuls of purpose for her." It was evidently the desire of this noble Israelite that "the stranger" might have abundance, and have it, too, rather as the fruit of her own gleaning than of his benevolence. This was the very essence of refinement. It was putting her in immediate connection with, and dependence upon, the God of Israel, who had fully recognized and provided for "the gleaner." Boaz was merely acting out that gracious ordinance of which Ruth was reaping the benefit. The same grace that had given him the field gave her the gleanings. They were both debtors to grace. She was the happy recipient of Jehovah's goodness: he was the honored exponent of Jehovah's most gracious institution. All was in most lovely moral order. The creature was blessed and God was glorified. Who would not own that it is good for us to be allowed to breathe such an atmosphere?

Let us now turn to another statute of our section. "Thou shalt not defraud thy neighbor, neither rob him: the wages of him that is hired shall not abide with thee all night until the morning." (Chap. xix. 13.) What tender care is here! The High and Mighty One that inhabiteth eternity can take knowledge of the thoughts and feelings that spring up in the heart of a poor laborer. He knows and takes into account the expectations of such an one in reference to the fruit of his day's toil. The wages

will naturally be looked for.   The laborer's heart
counts upon them: the family meal depends upon
them.   Oh! let them not be held back: send not
the laborer home with a heavy heart, to make the
heart of his wife and family heavy likewise.   By all
means, give him that for which he has wrought, to
which he has a right, and on which his heart is set.
He is a husband, he is a father, and he has borne
the burden and heat of the day that his wife and
children may not go hungry to bed.   Disappoint
him not: give him his due.   Thus does our God
take notice of the very throbbings of the laborer's
heart, and make provision for his rising expectations.   Precious grace !   Most tender, thoughtful,
touching, condescending love !   The bare contemplation of such statutes is sufficient to throw one
into a flood of tenderness.   Could any one read
such passages and not be melted ?   Could any one
read them and thoughtlessly dismiss a poor laborer,
not knowing whether he and his family have wherewithal to meet the cravings of hunger ?

Nothing can be more painful to a tender heart
than the lack of kindly consideration for the poor
so often manifested by the rich.   These latter can
sit down to their sumptuous repast after dismissing
from their door some poor industrious creature who
had come seeking the just reward of his honest labor.
They think not of the aching heart with which that
man returns to his family, to tell them of the dis-
appointment to himself and to them.   Oh, it is terrible!   It is most offensive to God and to all who

have drunk, in any measure, into His grace. If we would know what God thinks of such acting, we have only to hearken to the following accents of holy indignation: "Behold, the hire of the laborers who have reaped down your fields, which is of you kept back by fraud, crieth; and the cries of them that have reaped have entered into the ears of the Lord of Sabaoth." (James v. 4.) "The Lord of Sabaoth" hears the cry of the aggrieved and disappointed laborer. His tender love tells itself forth in the institutions of His moral government; and even though the heart should not be melted by the grace of those institutions, the conduct should, at least, be governed by the righteousness thereof. God will not suffer the claims of the poor to be heartlessly tossed aside by those who are so hardened by the influence of wealth as to be insensible to the appeals of tenderness, and who are so far removed beyond the region of personal need as to be incapable of feeling for those whose lot it is to spend their days amid exhausting toil or pinching poverty. The poor are the special objects of God's care. Again and again He makes provision for them in the statutes of His moral administration; and it is particularly declared of Him who shall ere long assume, in manifested glory, the reins of government, that "He shall deliver the needy when he crieth; the poor also, and him that hath no helper. He shall spare the poor and needy, and shall save the souls of the needy. He shall redeem their souls from deceit and violence; and precious shall their blood be in His sight." (Ps. lxxii. 12–14.)

May we profit by the review of those precious and deeply practical truths. May our hearts be affected, and our conduct influenced by them. We live in a heartless world; and there is a vast amount of self-ishness in our own hearts. We are not sufficiently affected by the thought of the need of others. We are apt to forget the poor in the midst of our abund-ance. We often forget that the very persons whose labor ministers to our personal comfort are living, it may be, in the deepest poverty. Let us think of these things. Let us beware of "grinding the faces of the poor." If the Jews of old were taught, by the statutes and ordinances of the Mosaic economy, to entertain kindly feelings toward the poor, and to deal tenderly and graciously with the sons of toil, how much more ought the higher and more spiritual ethics of the gospel dispensation produce in the hearts and lives of Christians a large-hearted benev-olence toward every form of human need.

True, there is urgent need of prudence and cau-tion, lest we take a man out of the honorable posi-tion in which he was designed and fitted to move, namely, a position of dependence upon the fruits—the precious and fragrant fruits—of honest industry. This would be a grievous injury instead of a benefit. The example of Boaz should instruct in this matter. He allowed Ruth to glean; but he took care to make her gleaning profitable. This is a very safe and a very simple principle. God intends that man should work at something or another, and we run counter to Him when we draw our fellow out of the place of dependence upon the results of patient industry, into that of dependence upon the results of false benevolence. The former is as honorable and elevating as the latter is contemptible and demoralizing. There is no bread so sweet to the taste as that which in nobly earned; but then those who earn their bread should get enough. A man will feed and care for his horses; how much more his fellow, who yields him the labor of his hands from Monday morning till Saturday night.

But some will say, There are two sides to this question. Unquestionably there are; and no doubt one meets with a great deal amongst the poor which is calculated to dry up the springs of benevolence and genuine sympathy. There is much which tends to steel the heart and close the hand; but one thing is certain, it is better to be deceived in ninety-nine cases out of a hundred than to shut up the bowels of compassion against a single worthy object. Our heavenly Father causes His sun to shine upon the evil and on the good; and sendeth rain upon the just and upon the unjust. The same sunbeams that gladden the heart of some devoted servant of Christ are poured upon the path of some ungodly sinner; and the self-same shower that falls upon the tillage of a true believer, enriches also the furrows of some blaspheming infidel. This is to be our model. "Be ye therefore perfect, even as your Father which is in heaven is perfect." (Matt. v. 48.) It is only as we set the Lord before us, and walk in the power of

His grace, that we shall be able to go on from day
to day, meeting, with a tender heart and an open
hand, every possible form of human misery. It is
only as we ourselves are drinking at the exhaustless
fountain of divine love and tenderness, that we shall
be able to go on ministering to human need un-
checked by the oft-repeated manifestation of human
depravity. Our tiny springs would soon be dried up
were they not maintained in unbroken connection
with that ever-gushing source.

The statute which next presents itself for our consideration, exemplifies most touchingly the tender
care of the God of Israel. "Thou shalt not curse
the deaf, nor put a stumbling-block before the blind,
but shalt fear thy God: I am the Lord." (Ver. 14.)
Here a barrier is erected to stem the rising tide of
irritability with which uncontrolled nature would be
almost sure to meet the personal infirmity of deaf-
ness. How well we can understand this! Nature
does not like to be called upon to repeat its words
again and again, in order to meet the deaf man's
infirmity. Jehovah thought of this, and provided
for it. And what is the provision? "Thou shalt
fear thy God." When tried by a deaf person, remember the Lord, and look to Him for grace to
enable you to govern your temper.

The second part of this statute reveals a most
humiliating amount of wickedness in human nature.
The idea of laying a stumbling-block in the way of
the blind is about the most wanton cruelty imagin-
able; and yet man is capable of it. else he would.

not be warned against it. No doubt this, as well as many other statutes, admits of a spiritual application; but that in no wise interferes with the plain literal principle set forth in it. Man is capable of placing a stumbling-block in the way of a fellow-creature afflicted with blindness. Such is man! Truly, the Lord knew what was in man when He wrote the statutes and judgments of the book of Leviticus.

I shall leave my reader to meditate alone upon the remainder of our section. He will find that each statute teaches a double lesson, namely, a lesson with respect to nature's evil tendencies, and also a lesson as to Jehovah's tender care.*

CHAPTERS XXI. & XXII

THESE chapters unfold, with great minuteness of detail, the divine requirements in reference to those who were privileged to draw near as priests to "offer the bread of their God." In this, as in the preceding section, we have conduct as the *result*, not the procuring *cause* of the relationship. This should be carefully borne in mind. The sons of

---

* Verses 16 and 17 demand special attention. "Thou shalt not go up and down as a talebearer among thy people." This is a most seasonable admonition for the people of God in every age. A talebearer is sure to do incalculable mischief. It has been well remarked that a talebearer injures three persons—he injures himself, he injures his hearer, and he injures the subject of his tale. All this he does directly; and as to the indirect consequences, who can recount them? Let us carefully guard against this horrible

Aaron were, in virtue of their birth, priests unto
God.   They all stood in this relationship, one as
well as another.   It was not a matter of attainment,
a question of progress, something which one had
and another had not.   All the sons of Aaron were
priests; they were born into a priestly place.   Their
capacity to understand and enjoy their position and
its attendant privileges was obviously a different
thing altogether.   One might be a babe, and another might have reached the point of mature and
vigorous manhood.   The former would, of necessity,
be unable to eat of the priestly food, being a babe,
for whom "milk," and not "strong meat," was
adapted; but he was as truly a member of the
priestly house as the man who could tread, with
firm step, the courts of the Lord's house, and feed
upon "the wave breast" and "heave shoulder" of
the sacrifice.

This distinction is easily understood in the case
of the sons of Aaron, and hence it will serve to
illustrate, in a very simple manner, the truth as to
the members of the true priestly house, over which
our great High-Priest presides, and to which all true

---

evil.   May we never suffer a tale to pass our lips; and let us never
stand to hearken to a talebearer.   May we always know how to
drive away a backbiting tongue with an angry countenance, as the
north wind driveth away rain.

In verse 17, we learn what ought to take the place of talebearing.
"Thou shalt in any wise rebuke thy neighbor, and not suffer sin
upon him."   In place of carrying to another a tale about my neighbor, I am called upon to go directly to himself and rebuke him, if
there is any thing wrong.   This is the divine method.   Satan's
method is to act the talebearer.

believers belong. (Heb. iii. 6.) Every child of God is a priest. He is enrolled as a member of Christ's priestly house. He may be very ignorant, but his position as a priest is not founded upon knowledge, but upon life; his experience may be very shallow, but his place as a priest does not depend upon experience, but upon life; his capacity may be very limited, but his relationship as a priest does not rest upon an enlarged capacity, but upon life. He was born into the position and relationship of a priest: he did not work himself thereinto. It was not by any efforts of his own that he became a priest: he became a priest by birth. The spiritual priesthood, together with all the spiritual functions attaching thereunto, is the necessary appendage to spiritual birth. The capacity to enjoy the privileges and to discharge the functions of a position must not be confounded with the position itself: they must ever be kept distinct. Relationship is one thing; capacity is quite another.

Furthermore, in looking at the family of Aaron, we see that nothing could break the relationship between him and his sons. There were many things which would interfere with the full enjoyment of the privileges attaching to the relationship. A son of Aaron might "defile himself by the dead;" he might defile himself by forming an unholy alliance; he might have some bodily "blemish;" he might be "blind or lame;" he might be "a dwarf." Any of these things would have interfered very materially with his enjoyment of the privileges and his dis-

charge of the functions pertaining to his relationship, as we read, "No man that hath a blemish of
the seed of Aaron the priest shall come nigh to offer
the offerings of the Lord made by fire: he hath a
blemish: he shall not come nigh to offer the bread
of his God.   He shall eat the bread of his God,
both of the most holy and the holy; only he shall
not go in unto the vail, nor come nigh unto the
altar, because he hath a blemish; that he profane
not my sanctuaries; for I the Lord do sanctify
them." (Chap. xxi. 21–23.)   But none of these
things could possibly touch the fact of a relationship
founded upon the established principles of human
nature.   Though a son of Aaron were a dwarf, that
dwarf was a son of Aaron.   True, he was, as a
dwarf, shorn of many precious privileges and lofty
dignities pertaining to the priesthood, but he was a
son of Aaron all the while.   He could neither enjoy
the same measure or character of communion, nor
yet discharge the same elevated functions of priestly
service, as one who had reached to manhood's appointed stature; but he was a member of the priestly
house, and as such, permitted to "eat the bread of
his God."   The relationship was genuine, though
the development was so defective.

   The spiritual application of all this is as simple as
it is practical.   To be a child of God is one thing;
to be in the enjoyment of priestly communion and
priestly worship is quite another.   The latter is,
alas! interfered with by many things.   Circumstances and associations are allowed to act upon us

by their defiling influence. We are not to suppose
that all Christians enjoy the same elevation of walk,
the same intimacy of fellowship, the same felt nearness to Christ. Alas! alas! they do not. Many
of us have to mourn over our spiritual defects.
There is lameness of walk, defective vision, stunted
growth; or we allow ourselves to be defiled by
contact with evil, and to be weakened and hindered
by unhallowed associations. In a word, as the sons
of Aaron, though being priests by birth, were nevertheless deprived of many privileges through ceremonial defilement and physical defects; so we,
though being priests unto God by spiritual birth,
are deprived of many of the high and holy privileges
of our position by moral defilement and spiritual
defects. We are shorn of many of our dignities
through defective spiritual development. We lack
singleness of eye, spiritual vigor, whole-hearted devotedness. Saved we are, through the free grace
of God, on the ground of Christ's perfect sacrifice.
"We are all the children of God, by faith in Christ
Jesus;" but then, salvation is one thing; communion is quite another: sonship is one thing; obedience is quite another.

These things should be carefully distinguished.
The section before us illustrates the distinction with
great force and clearness. If one of the sons of
Aaron happened to be "broken-footed or broken-
handed," was he deprived of his sonship? Assuredly not. Was he deprived of his priestly position?
By no means. It was distinctly declared, "He shall

eat the bread of his God, both of the most holy and
of the holy." What, then, did he lose by his physical
blemish? He was forbidden to tread some of the
higher walks of priestly service and worship.—"Only
he shall not go in unto the vail, nor come nigh unto
the altar." These were very serious privations;
and though it may be objected that a man could
not help many of these physical defects, that did
not alter the matter. Jehovah could not have a
blemished priest at His altar, or a blemished sacrifice thereon. Both the priest and the sacrifice should
be perfect. "No man that hath a blemish of the
seed of Aaron the priest shall come nigh to offer the
offerings of the Lord made by fire." (Chap. xxi. 22.)
"But whatsoever hath a blemish, that shall ye not
offer; for it shall not be acceptable for you." (Chap.
xxii. 20.)

Now, we have both the perfect priest and the
perfect sacrifice in the Person of our blessed Lord
Jesus Christ. He having "offered Himself without
spot to God," passed into the heavens as our great
High-Priest, where He ever liveth to make interces-
sion for us. The epistle to the Hebrews dwells
elaborately upon these two points. It throws into
vivid contrast the sacrifice and priesthood of the
Mosaic system and the Sacrifice and Priesthood of
Christ. In Him we have divine perfectness, whether
as the Victim or as the Priest. We have all that
God could require, and all that man could need.
His precious blood has put away all our sins, and
His all-prevailing intercession ever maintains us in

all the perfectness of the place into which His blood
has introduced us.   "We are complete in Him"
(Col. ii.); and yet, so feeble and so faltering are
we in ourselves; so full of failure and infirmity; so
prone to err and stumble in our onward way, that
we could not stand for a moment were it not that
"He ever liveth to make intercession for us." These
things have been dwelt upon in the earlier chapters
of this volume, and it is therefore needless to enter
further upon them here.   Those who have any thing
like correct apprehensions of the grand foundation-
truths of Christianity, and any measure of experience in the Christian life, will be able to understand
how it is that though "complete in Him who is the
head of all principality and power," they nevertheless need, while down here amid the infirmities,
conflicts, and buffetings of earth, the powerful advocacy of their adorable and divine High-Priest.
The believer is "washed, sanctified, and justified"
(1 Cor. vi.); he is "accepted in the Beloved"(Eph.
i. 6.); he can never come into judgment, as regards
his person (See John v. 24, where the word is κριθιν
and not κατακριθιν.); death and judgment are behind him, because he is united to Christ, who has
passed through them both on his behalf and in his
stead.   All these things are divinely true of the very
weakest, most unlettered, and inexperienced member of the family of God; but yet, inasmuch as he
carries about with him a nature so incorrigibly bad
and so irremediably ruined that no discipline can
correct it and no medicine cure it, inasmuch as he

is the tenant of a body of sin and death—as he is
surrounded on all sides by hostile influences—as he
is called to cope perpetually with the combined
forces of the world, the flesh, and the devil, he could
never keep his ground, much less make progress,
were he not upheld by the all-prevailing intercession
of his great High-Priest, who bears the names of
His people upon His breast and upon His shoulder.

Some, I am aware, have found great difficulty in
reconciling the idea of the believer's perfect standing in Christ with the need of priesthood. "If," it
is argued, "he is perfect, what need has he of a
priest?" The two things are as distinctly taught in
the Word as they are compatible one with another,
and understood in the experience of every rightly
instructed Christian. It is of the very last importance to apprehend, with clearness and accuracy, the
perfect harmony between these two points. The
believer is perfect in Christ; but in himself, he is a
poor feeble creature, ever liable to fall. Hence the
unspeakable blessedness of having One who can
manage all his affairs for him, at the right hand of
the Majesty in the heavens—One who upholds him
continually by the right hand of His righteousness—
One who will never let him go—One who is able to
save to the uttermost—One who is "the same yesterday, to-day, and forever"—One who will bear
him triumphantly through all the difficulties and
dangers which surround him, and finally "present
him faultless before the presence of His glory with
exceeding joy." Blessed forever be the grace that

has made such ample provision for all our need in the blood of a Spotless Victim and the intercession of a divine High-Priest!

Dear Christian reader, let it be our care so to walk, so to "keep ourselves unspotted from the world, so to stand apart from all unhallowed associations, that we may enjoy the highest privileges and discharge the most elevated functions of our position as members of the priestly house of which Christ is he Head. We have "boldness to enter into the holiest through the blood of Jesus:" "we have a great High-Priest over the house of God." (Heb. x.) Nothing can ever rob us of these privileges. But then our communion may be marred, our worship may be hindered, our holy functions may remain undischarged. Those ceremonial matters against which the sons of Aaron were warned in the section before us, have their antitypes in the Christian economy. Had they to be warned against unholy contact? So have we. Had they to be warned against unholy alliance? So have we. Had they to be warned against all manner of ceremonial uncleanness? So have we to be warned against "all filthiness of the flesh and spirit." (1 Cor. vii.) Were they shorn of many of their loftiest priestly privileges by bodily blemish and imperfect natural growth? So are we by moral blemish and imperfect spiritual growth.

Will any one venture to call in question the practical importance of such principles as these? Is it not obvious that the more highly we estimate the

blessings which attach to that priestly house of
which we have been constituted members, in virtue
of our spiritual birth, the more carefully shall we
guard against every thing which might tend in any
wise to rob us of their enjoyment? Undoubtedly.
And this it is which renders the close study of our
section so pre-eminently practical. May we feel its
power, through the application of God the Holy
Ghost. Then shall we *enjoy* our priestly place; then
shall we faithfully discharge our priestly functions.
We shall be able "to present our bodies a living
sacrifice, holy and acceptable unto God" (Rom.
xii. 1); we shall be able to "offer the sacrifice of
praise to God continually, that is, the fruit of our
lips, giving thanks to His name" (Heb. xiii. 15.); we
shall be able, as members of the "spiritual house"
and the "holy priesthood," to "offer up spiritual
sacrifices, acceptable to God by Jesus Christ"
(1 Pet. ii. 5.); we shall be able, in some small
degree, to anticipate that blissful time when, from
a redeemed creation, the halleluiahs of intelligent
and fervent praise shall ascend to the throne of God
and the Lamb throughout the everlasting ages.

CHAPTER XXIII

ONE of the most profound and comprehensive
chapters in the inspired volume now lies before us, and claims our prayerful study. It contains
the record of the seven great feasts or periodical

solemnities into which Israel's year was divided. In other words, it furnishes us with a perfect view of God's dealings with Israel during the entire period of their most eventful history.

Looking at the feasts separately, we have the Sabbath, the Passover, the feast of unleavened bread, the first-fruits, Pentecost, the feast of trumpets, the day of atonement, and the feast of tabernacles. This would make eight, altogether; but it is very obvious that the Sabbath occupies quite a unique and independent place. It is first presented, and its proper characteristics and attendant circumstances fully set forth; and then we read, "These are the feasts of the Lord, even holy convocations, which ye shall proclaim in their seasons." (Ver. 4.)

So that, strictly speaking, as the attentive reader will observe, Israel's *first* great feast was the Passover, and their *seventh* was the feast of tabernacles. That is to say, divesting them of their typical dress, we have, first, redemption; and last of all, we have the millennial glory. The paschal lamb typified the death of Christ (1 Cor. v. 7.); and the feast of tabernacles typified "the times of the restitution of all things, of which God hath spoken by the mouth of all His holy prophets since the world began." (Acts iii. 21.)

Such was the opening and such the closing feast of the Jewish year. Atonement is the foundation, glory the top-stone; while between these two points we have the resurrection of Christ (ver. 10–14.), the gathering of the Church (ver. 15–21.), the wak-

ing up of Israel to a sense of their long-lost glory
(ver. 24–25.), their repentance and hearty reception
of their Messiah (ver. 27–32.), and, that not one
feature might be lacking in this grand typical repre-
sentation, we have provision made for the Gentiles
to come in at the close of the harvest and glean in
Israel's fields (ver. 22.). All this renders the picture divinely perfect, and evokes from the heart of
every lover of Scripture the most intense admiration.
What could be more complete? The blood of the
Lamb, and practical holiness founded thereon; the
resurrection of Christ from the dead, and His as-
cension into heaven; the descent of the Holy Ghost,
in pentecostal power, to form the Church; the awakening of the remnant; their repentance and restoration; the blessing of "the poor and the stranger;"
the manifestation of the glory; the rest and blessedness of the kingdom,—such are the contents of this
truly marvelous chapter, which we shall now proceed
to examine in detail. May God the Holy Ghost be
our Teacher.

"And the Lord spake unto Moses, saying, 'Speak
unto the children of Israel, and say unto them, Concerning the feasts of the Lord, which ye shall proclaim to be holy convocations, even these are My
feasts. Six days shall work be done; but the seventh day is the Sabbath of rest, a holy convocation;
ye shall do no work therein: it is the Sabbath of the
Lord in all your dwellings.'" The place which the
Sabbath here gets is full of interest. The Lord is
about to furnish a type of all His dealings in grace

with His people; and ere He does so, He sets forth
the Sabbath as the significant expression of that rest
which remaineth for the people of God. It was an
actual solemnity to be observed by Israel, but it
was also a type of what is yet to be when all that
great and glorious work which this chapter foreshadows shall have been accomplished. It is God's
rest, into which all who believe can enter now in
spirit; but which, as to its full and actual accomplishment, yet remains. (Heb. iv.) We work now:
we shall rest by and by. In one sense, the believer
enters into rest; in another sense, he labors to enter
into it. He has found his rest in Christ; he labors
to enter into his rest in glory. He has found his
full mental repose in what Christ has wrought for
him, and his eye rests on that everlasting Sabbath
upon which he shall enter when all his desert toils
and conflicts are over. He cannot rest in the midst
of a scene of sin and wretchedness; "he rests in
Christ, the Son of God, who took the servant's
form;" and while thus resting, he is called to labor
as a worker together with God, in the full assurance
that when all his toil is over, he shall enjoy unbroken, eternal repose in those mansions of unfading light and unalloyed blessedness where labor and
sorrow can never enter. Blessed prospect! May
it brighten more and more each hour in the vision
of faith. May we labor all the more earnestly and
faithfully, as being sure of this most precious rest
at the end. True, there are foretastes of the eternal
Sabbath; but these foretastes only cause us to long

more ardently for the blessed reality—that Sabbath which shall never be broken—that "holy convocation" which shall never be dissolved.

We have already remarked that the Sabbath occupies quite a unique and independent place in this chapter. This is evident from the wording of the fourth verse, where the Lord seems to begin afresh with the expression, "These are the feasts of the Lord," as if to leave the Sabbath quite distinct from the seven feasts which follow, though it be, in reality, the type of that rest to which those feasts so blessedly introduce the soul.

"These are the feasts of the Lord, even holy convocations, which ye shall proclaim in their seasons. In the fourteenth day of the first month at even is the Lord's passover." (Ver. 4, 5.) Here, then, we have the first of the seven periodical solemnities— the offering of that paschal lamb whose blood it was that screened the Israel of God from the sword of the destroying angel on that terrible night when Egypt's first-born were laid low. This is the acknowledged type of the death of Christ, and hence its place in this chapter is divinely appropriate. It forms the foundation of all. We can know nothing of rest, nothing of holiness, nothing of fellowship, save on the ground of the death of Christ. It is peculiarly striking, significant, and beautiful to observe that, directly God's rest is spoken of, the next thing introduced is the blood of the paschal lamb. As much as to say, There is the *rest*, but here is your *title*. No doubt labor will *capacitate* us, but it is the blood that *entitles* us, to enjoy the rest.

"And on the fifteenth day of the same month is the feast of unleavened bread unto the Lord: seven days ye must eat unleavened bread. In the first day ye shall have a holy convocation: ye shall do no servile work therein. But ye shall offer an offering made by fire unto the Lord seven days: in the seventh day is a holy convocation: ye shall do no servile work therein." (Ver. 6–8.)   The people are here assembled around Jehovah in that practical holiness which is founded upon accomplished redemption; and while thus assembled, the fragrant odor of the sacrifice ascends from the altar of Israel to the throne of Israel's God.   This gives us a fine view of that holiness which God looks for in the life of His redeemed.   It is based upon the sacrifice, and it ascends in immediate connection with the acceptable fragrance of the Person of Christ.   "Ye shall do no *servile work* therein; but ye shall offer *an offering made by fire.*"   What a contrast!—the servile work of man's hands, and the sweet savor of Christ's sacrifice!   The practical holiness of God's people is not servile labor; it is the living unfolding of Christ through them, by the power of the Holy Ghost.   "To me to live is Christ."   This is the true idea.   Christ is our life; and every exhibition of that life is, in the divine judgment, redolent with all the fragrance of Christ.   It may be a very trifling matter in man's judgment, but, in so far as it is the outflow of Christ our life, it is unspeakably precious to God.

It ascends to Him and can never be forgotten. "The fruits of righteousness which are by Jesus Christ" are produced in the life of the believer, and no power of earth or hell can prevent their fragrance ascending to the throne of God.

It is needful to ponder deeply the contrast between "servile work" and the outflow of the life of Christ. The type is very vivid. There was a total cessation of manual labor throughout the whole assembly; but the sweet savor of the burnt-offering ascended to God. These were to be the two grand characteristics of the feast of unleavened bread. Man's labor ceased, and the odor of the sacrifice ascended; and this was the type of a believer's life of practical holiness. What a triumphant answer is here to the legalist on the one side, and the antinomian on the other! The former is silenced by the words, "no servile work;" and the latter is confounded by the words, "Ye shall offer an offering made by fire." The most elaborate works of man's hands are "servile;" but the smallest cluster of "the fruits of righteousness" is to the glory and praise of God. Throughout the entire period of the believer's life there must be no servile work —nothing of the hateful and degrading element of legality. There should be only the continual presentation of the life of Christ, wrought out and exhibited by the power of the Holy Ghost. Throughout the "seven days" of Israel's second great periodical solemnity there was to be "no leaven;" but instead thereof, the sweet savor of "an offering made by fire" was to be presented to the Lord. May we fully enter into the practical teaching of this most striking and instructive type.

"And the Lord spake unto Moses, saying, 'Speak unto the children of Israel, and say unto them, When ye be come into the land which I give unto you, and shall reap the harvest thereof, then ye shall bring a sheaf of the first-fruits of your harvest unto the priest; and ye shall wave the sheaf before the Lord, to be accepted for you: on the morrow after the Sabbath the priest shall wave it. And ye shall offer that day when ye wave the sheaf, a he lamb without blemish of the first year, for a burnt-offering unto the Lord. And the meat-offering thereof shall be two tenth deals of fine flour mingled with oil, an offering made by fire unto the Lord for a sweet savor: and the drink-offering thereof shall be of wine, the fourth part of a hin. And ye shall eat neither bread, nor parched corn, nor green ears, until the self-same day that ye have brought an offering unto your God: it shall be a statute forever throughout your generations, in all your dwellings." (Ver. 9–14.)

"But now is Christ risen from the dead, and become the *first-fruits* of them that slept." (1 Cor. xv. 20.) The beautiful ordinance of the presentation of the sheaf of first-fruits typified the resurrection of Christ, who, "at the end of the Sabbath, as it began to dawn toward the first day of the week," rose triumphant from the tomb, having accomplished the glorious work of redemption. His was a "resur-

rection *from among* the dead;" and in it we have
at once the earnest and the type of the resurrection
of His people. "Christ the first-fruits; afterwards
they that are Christ's at His coming." When Christ
comes, His people will be raised "from among the
dead [εκ νεκρων]," that is, those of them that sleep
in Jesus; "but the rest of the dead lived not again
until the thousand years were finished." (Rev. xx.
5.) When, immediately after the transfiguration,
our blessed Lord spoke of His rising "*from among
the dead*," the disciples questioned among themselves what that could mean. (See Mark ix.) Every
orthodox Jew believed in the doctrine of the "resurrection of the dead [αναστασις νεκρων]," but
the idea of a "resurrection from among the dead
[αναστασις εκ νεκρων]" was what the disciples were
unable to grasp; and no doubt many disciples since
then have felt considerable difficulty with respect to
a mystery so profound.

However, if my reader will prayerfully study and
compare 1 Cor. xv. with 1 Thess. iv. 13–18, he will
get much precious instruction upon this most interesting and practical truth. He can also look at
Romans viii. 11 in connection.—"But if the Spirit of
Him that raised up Jesus from the dead [εκ νεκρων]
dwell in you, He that raised up Christ from the dead
shall also quicken your mortal bodies by His Spirit
that dwelleth in you." From all these passages it
will be seen that the resurrection of the Church will
be upon precisely the same principle as the resurrection of Christ. Both the Head and the body are

shown to be raised "from among the dead." The
first sheaf and all the sheaves that follow after are
morally connected.

It must be evident to any one who carefully pon-
ders the subject in the light of Scripture, that there
is a very material difference between the resurrection of the believer and the resurrection of the un-
believer. Both shall be raised; but Revelation xx. 5
proves that there will be a thousand years between
the two, so that they differ both as to the principle
and as to the time. Some have found difficulty in
reference to this subject, from the fact that in John
v. 28 our Lord speaks of "the *hour* in the which *all*
that are in the graves shall hear His voice." How,
it may be asked, can there be a thousand years between the two resurrections, when both are spoken
of as occurring in an "hour"? The answer is very
simple. In verse 28, the quickening of dead souls
is spoken of as occurring in an "hour;" and this
work has been going on for over eighteen hundred
years. Now, if a period of nearly *two* thousand
years can be represented by the word "hour," what
objection can there be to the idea of *one* thousand
years being represented in the same way? Surely,
none whatever, especially when it is expressly stated
that "the rest of the dead lived not again until the
thousand years were finished."

But furthermore, when we find mention made of
"a *first* resurrection," is it not evident that all are
not to be raised together? Why speak of a "first"
if there is but the one? It may be said that "the

first resurrection" refers to the soul; but where is
the Scripture warrant for such a statement? The
solemn fact is this: when the "shout of the arch-
angel and the trump of God" shall be heard, the
redeemed who sleep in Jesus will be raised to meet
Him in the glory; the wicked dead, whoever they
be, from the days of Cain down, will remain in their
graves during the thousand years of millennial blessedness, and at the close of that bright and blissful
period, they shall come forth and stand before "the
great white throne," there to be "judged every
man according to his works," and to pass from the
throne of judgment into the lake of fire. Appalling
thought!

Oh, reader, how is it in reference to your precious
soul? Have you seen, by the eye of faith, the blood
of the paschal Lamb shed to screen you from this
terrible hour? Have you seen the precious Sheaf of
first-fruits reaped and gathered into the heavenly
garner, as the earnest of your being gathered in due
time? These are solemn questions—deeply solemn.
Do not put them aside. See that you are *now* under
the cover of the blood of Jesus. Remember, you
cannot glean so much as a single ear in the fields of
redemption until you have seen the true Sheaf waved
before the Lord. "Ye shall eat neither bread, nor
parched corn, nor green ears, until *the self-same day*
that ye have brought an offering unto your God."
The harvest could not be touched until the sheaf of
first-fruits had been presented, and, with the sheaf,
a burnt-offering and a meat-offering.

"And ye shall count unto you from the morrow after the Sabbath, from the day that ye brought the sheaf of the wave-offering; seven Sabbaths shall be complete: even unto the morrow after the seventh Sabbath shall ye number fifty days; and ye shall offer a new meat-offering unto the Lord. Ye shall bring out of your habitations two wave-loaves of two tenth deals: they shall be of fine flour; they shall be baken with leaven; they are the first-fruits unto the Lord." (Ver. 15–17.) This is the feast of Pentecost—the type of God's people, gathered by the Holy Ghost, and presented before Him, in connection with all the preciousness of Christ. In the passover we have the death of Christ, in the sheaf of first-fruits we have the resurrection of Christ, and in the feast of Pentecost we have the descent of the Holy Ghost to form the Church. All this is divinely perfect. The death and resurrection of Christ had to be accomplished ere the Church could be formed. The sheaf was offered and then the loaves were baked.

And, observe, "they shall be baken *with leaven.*" Why was this? Because they were intended to foreshadow those who, though filled with the Holy Ghost, and adorned with His gifts and graces, had, nevertheless, *evil* dwelling in them. The assembly, on the day of Pentecost, stood in the full value of the blood of Christ, was crowned with the gifts of the Holy Ghost; but there was leaven there also. No power of the Spirit could do away with the fact that there was evil dwelling in the people of God.

It might be suppressed and kept out of view, but it was there. This fact is foreshadowed in the type by the leaven in the two loaves, and it is set forth in the actual history of the Church; for albeit God the Holy Ghost was present in the assembly, the flesh was there likewise to lie unto Him. Flesh is flesh, nor can it ever be made aught else than flesh. The Holy Ghost did not come down on the day of Pentecost to improve nature or do away with the fact of its incurable evil, but to baptize believers into one body, and connect them with their living Head in heaven.

Allusion has already been made, in the chapter on the peace-offering, to the fact that leaven was permitted in connection therewith. It was the divine recognition of the evil in the worshiper. Thus is it also in the ordinance of the "two wave-loaves;" they were to be "baken with *leaven*," because of the *evil* in the antitype.

But, blessed be God, the evil which was divinely recognized was divinely provided for. This gives great rest and comfort to the heart. It is a comfort to be assured that God knows the worst of us; and, moreover, that He has made provision according to *His* knowledge, and not merely according to *ours*. "And ye shall offer *with the bread* seven lambs *without blemish* of the first year, and one young bullock, and two rams; they shall be for a burnt-offering unto the Lord, with their meat-offering and their drink-offerings, even an offering made by fire, of sweet savor unto the Lord." (Ver. 18.) Here, then, we have, in immediate connection with the leavened loaves, the presentation of an unblemished sacrifice, typifying the great and all-important truth that it is Christ's perfectness, and not our sinfulness, that is ever before the view of God. Observe particularly the words, "ye shall offer *with the bread* seven lambs *without blemish*." Precious truth!—deeply precious, though clothed in typic dress! May the reader be enabled to enter into it, to make his own of it, to stay his conscience upon it, to feed and refresh his heart with it, to delight his whole soul in it. Not I, but Christ.

It may, however, be objected that the fact of Christ's being a spotless Lamb is not sufficient to roll the burden of guilt from a sin-stained conscience—a sweet-savor offering would not, of itself, avail for a guilty sinner. This objection might be urged, but our type fully meets and entirely removes it. It is quite true that a burnt-offering would not have been sufficient where "leaven" was in question; and hence we read, "Then ye shall sacrifice one kid of the goats for *a sin-offering*, and two lambs of the first year for a sacrifice of peace-offerings." (Ver. 19.) The "sin-offering" was the answer to the "leaven" in the loaves: "peace" was established, so that communion could be enjoyed, and all went up in immediate connection with the "sweet savor" of the "burnt-offering" unto the Lord.

Thus, on the day of Pentecost, the Church was presented in all the value and excellency of Christ, through the power of the Holy Ghost. Though having in itself the leaven of the old nature, that leaven was not reckoned, because the divine Sin-offering had perfectly answered for it. The power of the Holy Ghost did not remove the leaven, but the blood of the Lamb had atoned for it. This is a most interesting and important distinction. The work of the Spirit in the believer does not remove indwelling evil. It enables him to detect, judge, and subdue the evil; but no amount of spiritual power can do away with the fact that the evil is there—though, blessed be God, the conscience is at perfect ease, inasmuch as the blood of our Sin-offering has eternally settled the whole question; and therefore, instead of our evil being under the eye of God, it has been put out of sight forever, and we are accepted in all the acceptableness of Christ, who offered Himself to God as a sweet-smelling sacrifice, that He might perfectly glorify Him in all things, and be the food of His people forever.

Thus much as to Pentecost—after which a long period is suffered to roll on ere we have any movement amongst the people. There is, however, the notice of "the poor and stranger" in that beautiful ordinance which has already been referred to in its moral aspect. Here we may look at it in a dispensational point of view. "And when ye reap the harvest of your land, thou shalt not make clean riddance of the corners of thy field when thou reapest, neither shalt thou gather any gleaning of thy harvest; thou shalt leave them unto the poor, and to the stranger: I am the Lord your God." (Ver.

22.) Provision is here made for the stranger to glean in Israel's fields. The Gentile is to be brought in to participate in the overflowing goodness of God. When Israel's storehouse and wine-press have been fully furnished, there will be precious sheaves and rich clusters for the Gentile to gather.

We are not, however, to suppose that the spiritual blessings with which the Church is endowed in the heavenlies with Christ are set forth under the figure of a stranger gleaning in Israel's fields. These blessings are as new to the seed of Abraham as they are to the Gentile. They are not the gleanings of Canaan, but the glories of heaven—the glories of Christ. The Church is not merely blessed *by* Christ, but *with* and *in* Christ. The bride of Christ will not be sent forth to gather up, as a stranger, the sheaves and clusters in the corners of Israel's fields and from the branches of Israel's vines. No; she tastes of higher blessings, richer joys, nobler dignities, than aught that Israel ever knew. She is not to glean as a stranger on earth, but to enjoy her own wealthy and happy home in heaven, to which she belongs. This is the "better thing" which God hath, in His manifold wisdom and grace, "reserved" for her. No doubt it will be a gracious privilege for "the stranger" to be permitted to glean after Israel's harvest is reaped; but the Church's portion is incomparably higher, even to be the bride of Israel's King, the partner of His throne, the sharer of His joys, His dignities, and His glories; to be like Him and with Him forever. The eternal man-

sions of the Father's house on high, and not the
ungleaned corners of Israel's fields below, are to be
the Church's portion.   May we ever bear this in
mind, and live, in some small degree, worthy of
such a holy and elevated destination.

"And the Lord spake unto Moses, saying, 'Speak
unto the children of Israel, saying, In the seventh
month, in the first day of the month, shall ye have
a Sabbath, a memorial of blowing of trumpets, a
holy convocation.   Ye shall do no servile work;
but ye shall offer an offering made by fire unto the
Lord.'" (Ver. 23–25.)   A new subject is introduced
here by the words, "the Lord spake unto Moses,"
which, let me remark in passing, affords an interesting help in classifying the subjects of the entire
chapter.   Thus, the Sabbath, the passover, and the
feast of unleavened bread are given under the first
communication; the wave-sheaf, the wave-loaves,
and the ungleaned corners are given under the
second; after which we have a long unnoticed interval; and then comes the soul-stirring feast of
trumpets, on the first day of the seventh month.
This ordinance leads us on to the time, now fast
approaching, when the remnant of Israel shall "blow
the trumpet" for a memorial, calling to remembrance their long-lost glory, and stirring up themselves to seek the Lord.

The feast of trumpets is intimately connected
with another great solemnity, namely, "the day of
atonement."   "*Also* on the tenth day of this seventh
month there shall be a day of atonement: it shall

be a holy convocation unto you; and ye shall afflict your souls, and offer an offering make by fire unto the Lord. And ye shall do no work in that same day; for it is a day of atonement, to make an atonement for you before the Lord your God. . . . It shall be unto you a Sabbath of rest, and ye shall afflict your souls: in the ninth day of the month at even, from even unto even, shall ye celebrate your Sabbath." (Ver. 27–32.) Thus, after the blowing of the trumpets, an interval of eight days elapses, and then we have the day of atonement, with which these things are connected, namely, affliction of soul, atonement for sin, and rest from labor. All these things will find their due place in the experience of the Jewish remnant by and by. "The harvest is past, the summer is ended, and we are not saved." (Jer. viii. 20.) Such will be the pathetic lament of the remnant when the Spirit of God shall have begun to touch their heart and conscience. "And they shall look upon Me whom they have pierced, and they shall mourn for Him, as one mourneth for his only son, and shall be in bitterness for Him, as one that is in bitterness for her first-born. In that day shall there be a great mourning in Jerusalem, as the mourning of Hadadrimmon in the valley of Megiddon. And the land shall mourn, every family apart," etc. (Zech. xii. 10–14.)

What deep mourning, what intense affliction, what genuine penitence, there will be, when, under the mighty action of the Holy Ghost, the conscience of the remnant shall recall the sins of the past—the neglect of the Sabbath, the breach of the law, the stoning of the prophets, the piercing of the Son, the resistance of the Spirit! All these things will come in array on the tablets of an enlightened and exercised conscience, and produce keen affliction of soul.

But the blood of atonement will meet all. "In that day there shall be a fountain opened to the house of David and to the inhabitants of Jerusalem for sin and for uncleanness." (Zech. xiii. 1.) They will be made to feel their guilt and be afflicted, and they will also be led to see the efficacy of the blood, and find perfect peace—a Sabbath of rest unto their souls.

Now, when such results shall have been reached in the experience of Israel in the latter day, for what should we look? Surely, THE GLORY. When the "blindness" is removed and "the vail" taken away, when the heart of the remnant is turned to Jehovah, then shall the bright beams of the "Sun of righteousness" fall, in healing, restoring, and saving power, upon a truly penitent, afflicted, and poor people. To enter elaborately upon this subject would demand a volume in itself. The exercises, the experiences, the conflicts, the trials, the difficulties, and the ultimate blessings of the Jewish remnant are fully detailed throughout the psalms and prophets. The existence of such a body must be clearly seen ere the psalms and prophets can be studied with intelligence and satisfaction. Not but that we may learn much from those portions of inspiration, for "all Scripture is profitable;" but the surest way to make a right use of any portion of the Word of God, is to understand its primary application. If, then, we apply scriptures to the Church, or heavenly body, which belong, strictly speaking, to the Jewish remnant, or earthly body, we must be involved in serious error as to both the one and the other. In point of fact, it happens in many cases that the existence of such a body as the remnant is completely ignored, and the true position and hope of the Church are entirely lost sight of. These are grave errors, which my reader should sedulously seek to avoid. Let him not suppose for a moment that they are mere speculations, fitted only to engage the attention of the curious, and possessing no practical power whatever. There could not be a more erroneous supposition. What! is it of no practical value to us to know whether we belong to earth or heaven? is it of no real moment to us to know whether we shall be at rest in the mansions above or passing through the apocalyptic judgments down here? Who could admit aught so unreasonable? The truth is, it would be difficult to fix on any line of truth more practical than that which unfolds the distinctive destinies of the earthly remnant and the heavenly Church. I shall not pursue the subject further here; but the reader will find it well worthy of his calm and prayerful study. We shall close this section with a view of the feast of tabernacles—the last solemnity of the Jewish year.

"And the Lord spake unto Moses, saying, 'Speak

unto the children of Israel, saying, The fifteenth day of this seventh month shall be the feast of tabernacles for seven days unto the Lord. . . . . Also in the fifteenth day of the seventh month, when ye have gathered in the fruit of the land, ye shall keep a feast unto the Lord seven days: on the first day shall be a Sabbath, and on the eighth shall be a Sabbath. And ye shall take you on the first day the boughs of goodly trees, branches of palm-trees, and boughs of thick trees, and willows of the brook; and ye shall rejoice before the Lord your God seven days. And ye shall keep it a feast unto the Lord seven days in the year: it shall be a statute forever in your generations; ye shall celebrate it in the seventh month. Ye shall dwell in booths seven days: all that are Israelites born shall dwell in booths; that your generations may know that I made the children of Israel to dwell in booths, when I brought them out of the land of Egypt: I am the Lord your God.'" (Ver. 33–43.)

This feast points us forward to the time of Israel's glory in the latter day, and therefore it forms a most lovely and appropriate close to the whole series of feasts. The harvest was gathered in, all was done, the storehouses were amply furnished, and Jehovah would have His people to give expression to their festive joy. But, alas! they seem to have had but little heart to enter into the divine thought in reference to this most delightful ordinance. They lost sight of the fact that they had been strangers and pilgrims, and hence their long neglect of this feast.

From the days of Joshua down to the time of Nehemiah, the feast of tabernacles had never once been celebrated. It was reserved for the feeble remnant that returned from the Babylonish captivity to do what had not been done even in the bright days of Solomon. "And all the congregation of them that were come again out of the captivity made booths, and sat under the booths: for since the days of Joshua the son of Nun, unto that day, had not the children of Israel done so. And there was very great gladness." (Neh. viii. 17.) How refreshing it must have been to those who had hung their harps on the willows of Babylon, to find themselves beneath the shade of the willows of Canaan! It was a sweet foretaste of that time of which the feast of tabernacles was the type, when Israel's restored tribes shall repose within those millennial bowers which the faithful hand of Jehovah will erect for them in the land which He sware to give unto Abraham and to his seed forever. Thrice-happy moment when the heavenly and the earthly shall meet as intimated in "the first day" and "the eighth day" of the feast of tabernacles! "The heavens shall hear the earth, and the earth shall hear the corn and the wine and the oil, and they shall hear Jezreel."

There is a fine passage in the last chapter of Zechariah which goes to prove very distinctly that the true celebration of the feast of tabernacles belongs to the glory of the latter day.—"And it shall come to pass that every one that is left of all the nations which came against Jerusalem, shall even go

352

LEVITICUS

up from year to year to worship the King, the Lord
of hosts, and to keep the feast of tabernacles.''
(Chap. xiv. 16.) What a scene! Who would seek
to rob it of its characteristic beauty by a vague
system of interpretation falsely called spiritualizing?
Surely, Jerusalem means Jerusalem, nations mean
nations, and the feast of tabernacles means the
feast of tabernacles. Is there any thing incredible
in this? Surely, nothing, save to man's reason,
which rejects all that lies beyond its narrow range.
The feast of tabernacles shall yet be celebrated in
the land of Canaan, and the nations of the saved
shall go up thither to participate in its glorious and
hallowed festivities. Jerusalem's warfare shall then
be accomplished; the roar of battle shall cease; the
sword and the spear shall be transformed into the
implements of peaceful agriculture; Israel shall
repose beneath the refreshing shade of their vines
and fig-trees; and all the earth shall rejoice in
the government of ''the Prince of Peace.'' Such
is the prospect presented in the unerring pages
of inspiration. The types foreshadow it, the
prophets prophesy of it, faith believes it, and hope
anticipates it.

NOTE.—At the close of our chapter we read,
''And Moses declared unto the children of Israel
the feasts of the Lord.'' This was their true character, their original title; but in the gospel of John
they are called ''*feasts of the Jews.*'' They had long
ceased to be Jehovah's feasts. He was shut out

They did not want Him; and hence, in John vii, when Jesus was asked to go up to "*the Jews' feast of tabernacles,*" He answered, "My time is not yet come;" and when He did go up, it was "privately," to take His place outside of the whole thing, and to call upon every thirsty soul to come unto Him and drink. There is a solemn lesson in this. Divine institutions are speedily marred in the hands of man; but, oh! how deeply blessed to know that the thirsty soul that feels the barrenness and drought connected with a scene of empty religious formality, has only to flee to Jesus and drink freely of His exhaustless springs, and so become a channel of blessing to others.

CHAPTER XXIV.

THERE is very much to interest the spiritual mind in this brief section. We have seen in chapter xxiii. the history of the dealings of God with Israel, from the offering up of the true paschal Lamb, until the rest and glory of the millennial kingdom. In the chapter now before us, we have two grand ideas, namely, first, the unfailing record and memorial of the twelve tribes, maintained before God by the power of the Spirit and the efficacy of Christ's priesthood; and secondly, the apostacy of Israel after the flesh, and divine judgment executed thereon. It is the clear apprehension of the former that will enable us to contemplate the latter.

"And the Lord spake unto Moses, saying, 'Command the children of Israel, that they bring unto thee *pure* oil olive, *beaten* for the light, to cause the lamps to burn *continually*. Without the vail of the testimony, in the tabernacle of the congregation, shall Aaron order it *from the evening unto the morning*, before the Lord *continually;* it shall be a statute forever in your generations. He shall order the lamps upon the *pure* candlestick before the Lord *continually.*'" (Ver. 1–4.) The "pure oil" represents the grace of the Holy Spirit, founded upon the work of Christ, as exhibited by the candlestick of "beaten gold." The "olive" was *pressed* to yield the "oil," and the gold was "*beaten*" to form the candlestick. In other words, the grace and light of the Spirit are founded upon the death of Christ, and maintained in clearness and power by the priesthood of Christ. The golden lamp diffused its light throughout the precincts of the sanctuary during the dreary hours of night, when darkness brooded over the nation and all were wrapped in slumber. In all this we have a vivid presentation of God's faithfulness to His people whatever might be their outward condition. Darkness and slumber might settle down upon them, but the lamp was to burn "continually." The high-priest was responsible to keep the steady light of testimony burning during the tedious hours of the night. "Without the vail of the testimony, in the tabernacle of the congregation, shall Aaron order it from the evening unto the morning, before the Lord continually." The maintenance of this light was not left dependent upon

Israel: God had provided one whose office it was to look after it and order it continually.

But further, we read, "And thou shalt take fine flour, and bake twelve cakes thereof: two tenth deals shall be in one cake. And thou shalt set them in two rows, six in a row, upon the *pure* table before the Lord. And thou shalt put *pure* frankincense upon each row, that it may be on the bread for a memorial, even an offering made by fire unto the Lord. Every Sabbath he shall set it in order before the Lord *continually*, being taken from the children of Israel by an everlasting covenant. And it shall be Aaron's and his sons'; and they shall eat it in the holy place: for it is most holy unto him of the offerings of the Lord made by fire, by a perpetual statute." (Ver. 5–9.) There is no mention of leaven in these loaves. They represent, I doubt not, Christ in immediate connection with "the twelve tribes of Israel." They were laid up in the sanctuary before the Lord, on the pure table, for seven days, after which they became the food of Aaron and his sons, furnishing another striking figure of Israel's condition in the view of Jehovah, whatever might be their outward aspect. The twelve tribes are ever before Him. Their memorial can never perish. They are ranged in divine order in the sanctuary, covered with the fragrant incense of Christ, and reflected from the pure table whereon they rest beneath the bright beams of that golden lamp which shines with undimmed lustre through the darkest hour of the nation's moral night.

Now, it is well to see that we are not sacrificing sound judgment or divine truth on the altar of fancy, when we venture to interpret, after such a fashion, the mystic furniture of the sanctuary. We are taught in Hebrews ix. that all these things were "the patterns of things in the heavens;" and again, in Hebrews x. 1, that they were "a shadow of good things to come." We are therefore warranted in believing that there are "things in the heavens" answering to the "patterns"—that there is a substance answering to the "shadow." In a word, we are warranted in believing that there is that "in the heavens" which answers to "the seven lamps," "the pure table," and the "twelve loaves." This is not human imagination, but divine truth, on which faith has fed in all ages. What was the meaning of Elijah's altar of "twelve stones" on the top of Carmel? It was nothing else than the expression of his faith in that truth of which the "twelve loaves" were "the pattern" or "the shadow." He believed in the unbroken unity of the nation, maintained before God in the eternal stability of the promise made to Abraham, Isaac, and Jacob, whatever might be the external condition of the nation. Man might look in vain for the manifested unity of the twelve tribes; but faith could always look within the hallowed inclosure of the sanctuary, and there see the twelve loaves, covered with pure frankincense, ranged in divine order on the pure table; and even though all without were wrapped in midnight's gloomy shades, yet could faith discern, by the light of the *seven* golden lamps, the same grand truth foreshadowed, namely, the indissoluble unity of Israel's twelve tribes.

Thus it was then, and thus it is now. The night is dark and gloomy. There is not, in all this lower world, so much as a single ray by which the human eye can trace the unity of Israel's tribes. They are scattered among the nations, and lost to man's vision; but their memorial is before the Lord. Faith owns this, because it knows that "all the promises of God are yea and amen in Christ Jesus." It sees in the upper sanctuary, by the Spirit's perfect light, the twelve tribes faithfully memorialized. Hearken to the following noble accents of faith: "And now I stand and am judged for the hope of the promise made of God unto our fathers: unto which promise *our twelve tribes*, instantly serving God night and day [νυκτα και ημεραν], hope to come." (Acts xxvi. 6, 7.) Now, if King Agrippa had asked Paul, Where are the twelve tribes? could he have shown them to him? No. But why not? Was it because they were not to be seen? No; but because Agrippa had not eyes to see them. The twelve tribes lay far beyond the range of Agrippa's vision. It needed the eye of faith and the gracious light of the Spirit of God to be able to discern the twelve loaves, ordered upon the pure table in the sanctuary of God. There they were, and Paul saw them there, though the moment in which he gave utterance to his sublime conviction was as dark as it well could be. Faith is not governed by appear-

ances.   It takes its stand upon the lofty rock of
God's eternal Word, and, in all the calmness and
certainty of that holy elevation, feeds upon the immutable word of Him who cannot lie. Unbelief may
stupidly stare about and ask, Where are the twelve
tribes ? or how can they be found and restored ?
It is impossible to give an answer.   Not because
there is no answer to be given, but because unbelief
is utterly incapable of rising to the elevated point
from which the answer can be seen.   Faith is as
sure that the memorial of the twelve tribes of Israel
is before the eye of Israel's God, as it is that the
twelve loaves were laid on the golden table every
Sabbath day.   But who can convince the skeptic or
the infidel of this ? who can secure credence for
such a truth from those who are governed, in all
things, by reason or sense, and know nothing of
what it is to hope against hope ?   Faith finds divine
certainties and eternal realities in the midst of a
scene where reason and sense can find nothing.
Oh for a more profound faith !   May we grasp, with
more intense earnestness, every word that proceedeth out of the mouth of the Lord, and feed upon it
in all the artless simplicity of a little child.

We shall now turn to the second point in our
chapter, namely, the apostacy of Israel after the
flesh, and the divine judgment thereon.

"And the son of an Israelitish woman, whose
father was an Egyptian, went out among the children of Israel : and this son of an Israelitish woman
and a man of Israel strove together in the camp :

and the Israelitish woman's son blasphemed the
name of the LORD, and cursed. And they brought
him unto Moses; . . . . . and they put him in
ward, that the mind of the Lord might be showed
them.   And the Lord spake unto Moses, saying,
'Bring forth him that hath cursed without the camp;
and let all that heard him lay their hands upon his
head, and let all the congregation stone him.' . . .
. . . And Moses spake to the children of Israel,
that they should bring forth him that had cursed
out of the camp, and stone him with stones.   And
the children of Israel did as the Lord commanded
Moses." (Ver. 10–23.)

The peculiar place assigned by the inspired pen-
man to this narrative is striking and interesting.   I
have no doubt whatever but that it is designed to
give us the opposite side of the picture presented in
the opening verses of the chapter.   Israel after the
flesh has grievously failed, and sinned against Jehovah; the name of the Lord has been blasphemed
amongst the Gentiles; wrath has come upon the
nation; the judgments of an offended God have
fallen upon them; but the day is coming when the
dark and heavy cloud of judgment shall roll away,
and then shall the twelve tribes, in their unbroken
unity, stand forth before all the nations as the
amazing monument of Jehovah's faithfulness and
loving-kindness.   "And in that day thou shalt say,
O Lord, I will praise Thee; though Thou wast angry
with me, Thine anger is turned away, and Thou
comfortedst me.   Behold, God is my salvation; I

will trust, and not be afraid: for the Lord JEHO-
VAH is my strength and my song, He also is become my salvation. Therefore with joy shall ye
draw water out of the wells of salvation. And in
that day shall ye say, Praise the Lord, call upon His
name, declare His doings among the people, make
mention that His name is exalted. Sing unto the
Lord; for he hath done excellent things: this is
known in all the earth. Cry out and shout, thou
inhabitant of Zion; for great is the Holy One of
Israel in the midst of thee." (Isa. xii.) "For I
would not, brethren, that ye should be ignorant of
this mystery, lest ye should be wise in your own
conceits, that blindness in part is happened to Israel,
until the fullness of the Gentiles be come in. And
so all Israel shall be saved: as it is written, 'There
shall come out of Sion the Deliverer, and shall turn
away ungodliness from Jacob. For this is My covenant unto them, when I shall take away their sins.'
As concerning the gospel, they are enemies for your
sakes; but as touching the election, they are beloved
for the fathers' sakes. For the gifts and calling of
God are without repentance. For as ye in times
past have not believed God, yet have now obtained
mercy through their unbelief; even so have these
also now not believed in your mercy, that they also
may obtain mercy. For God hath concluded them
all in unbelief, that He might have mercy upon all.
O the depth of the riches both of the wisdom and
knowledge of God! how unsearchable are His judgments, and His ways past finding out! For who

hath known the mind of the Lord? or who hath been His counselor? or who hath first given to Him, and it shall be recompensed to him again? For of Him and through Him and to Him are all things; to whom be glory forever. Amen." (Rom. xi. 25–36.)

Passages might be multiplied to prove that though Israel is suffering the divine judgment because of sin, yet "the gifts and calling of God are without repentance"—that though the blasphemer is being stoned without the camp, the twelve loaves are undisturbed within the sanctuary. "The voices of the prophets" declare, and the voices of apostles re-echo the glorious truth that "all Israel shall be saved;" not because they have not sinned, but because "the gifts and calling of God are without repentance." Let Christians beware how they tamper with "the promises made unto the fathers." If these promises be explained away or misapplied, it must necessarily weaken our moral sense of the divine integrity and accuracy of Scripture as a whole. If one part may be explained away, so may another; if one passage may be vaguely interpreted, so may another; and thus it would come to pass that we should be deprived of all that blessed certainty which constitutes the foundation of our repose in reference to all that the Lord hath spoken. But more of this as we dwell upon the remaining chapters of our book.

THE intelligent reader will discern a strong moral link between this and the preceding chapter. In chapter xxiv, we learn that the house of Israel is preserved for the land of Canaan; in chapter xxv, we learn that the land of Canaan is preserved for the house of Israel. Taking both together, we have the record of a truth which no power of earth or hell can obliterate—"All Israel shall be saved," and "the land shall not be sold forever." The former of these statements enunciates a principle which has stood like a rock amid the ocean of conflicting interpretations, while the latter declares a fact which many nations of the uncircumcised have sought in vain to ignore.

The reader will, I doubt not, observe the peculiar way in which our chapter opens.—"And the Lord spake unto Moses *in Mount Sinai.*" The principal part of the communications contained in the book of Leviticus is characterized by the fact of its emanating "from the tabernacle of the congregation." This is easily accounted for. Those communications have special reference to the service, communion, and worship of the priests, or to the moral condition of the people, and hence they are issued, as might be expected, from "the tabernacle of the congregation," that grand centre of all that appertained in any way to priestly service. Here, however, the communication is made from quite a different point. "The Lord spake unto Moses *in Mount Sinai*." Now, we know that every expression in Scripture has its own special meaning, and we are justified in expecting a different line of communication from "Mount Sinai" from that which reaches us from "the tabernacle of the congregation." And so it is. The chapter at which we have now arrived treats of Jehovah's claims as Lord of all the earth. It is not the worship and communion of a priestly house, or the internal ordering of the nation; but the claims of God in government, His right to give a certain portion of the earth to a certain people to hold as tenants under Him. In a word, it is not to Jehovah in "the tabernacle"—the place of *worship;* but Jehovah in "Mount Sinai"—the place of *government.*

"And the Lord spake unto Moses in Mount Sinai, saying, 'Speak unto the children of Israel, and say unto them, When ye come into the land which I give you, then shall the land keep a Sabbath unto the Lord. Six years thou shalt sow thy field, and six years thou shalt prune thy vineyard. That which groweth of its own accord of thy harvest thou shalt not reap, neither gather the grapes of thy vine undressed; for it is a year of rest unto the land. And the Sabbath of the land shall be meat for you; for thee, and for thy servant, and for thy maid, and for thy hired servant, and for thy stranger that sojourneth with thee, and for thy cattle, and for the beast that are in thy land, shall all the increase thereof be meat.'" (Ver. 1–7.)

Here, then, we have the special feature of the
Lord's land.   He would have it to enjoy a sabbatic
year, and in that year there was to be the evidence
of the rich profusion with which He would bless
those who held as tenants under Him.   Happy,
highly privileged tenantry!   What an honor to hold
immediately under Jehovah!   No rent! no taxes!
no burdens!   Well might it be said, "Happy is the
people that is in such a case ; yea, happy is the nation whose God is Jehovah."   We know, alas! that
Israel failed to take full possession of that wealthy
land of which Jehovah made them a present.   He
had given it *all;* He had given it *forever.*   They
took but *a part,* and that *for a time.*   Still, there it
is.   The property is there, though the tenants are
ejected for the present.   "The land shall not be sold
forever : for *the land is Mine;* for ye are strangers
and sojourners *with Me."*   What does this mean,
but that Canaan belongs specially to Jehovah, and
that He will hold it through the tribes of Israel ?
True, "the earth is the Lord's," but that is quite
another thing.   It is plain that He has been pleased,
for His own unsearchable purposes, to take special
possession of the land of Canaan, and to submit
that land to a peculiar line of treatment, to mark it
off from all other lands, by calling it His own, and
to distinguish it by judgments and ordinances and
periodical solemnities, the mere contemplation of
which enlightens the understanding and affects the
heart.   Where, throughout all the earth, do we read
of a land enjoying a year of unbroken repose—a

year of richest abundance ?   The rationalist may ask, How can these things be ? the skeptic may doubt if they could be; but faith finds a satisfying answer from the lips of Jehovah—"And if ye shall say, What shall we eat the seventh year? behold, we shall not sow, nor gather in our increase: then I will command My blessing upon you in the sixth year, and it shall bring forth fruit for three years.   And ye shall sow the eighth year, and eat yet of old fruit until the ninth year; until her fruits come in ye shall eat of the old store." (Ver. 20–22.)   Nature might say, What shall we do for *our sowing?*   God's answer is, "I will command *My blessing.*"   God's "blessing" is better far than man's "sowing."   He was not going to let them starve in His sabbatic year.   They were to feed upon the fruits of His blessing, while they celebrated His year of rest—a year which pointed forward to that eternal Sabbath that remains for the people of God.

"And thou shalt number seven Sabbaths of years unto thee, seven times seven years; and the space of the seven Sabbaths of years shall be unto thee forty and nine years.   Then shalt thou cause the trumpet of the jubilee to sound on the tenth day of the seventh month; in the day of atonement shall ye make the trumpet sound throughout all your land." (Ver. 8, 9.)   It is peculiarly interesting to note the various methods in which the millennial rest was held up to view in the Jewish economy.   Every seventh day was a sabbatic day; every seventh year was a sabbatic year; and every seven times seven

years there was a jubilee. Each and all of these
typical solemnities held up to the vision of faith the
blessed prospect of a time when labor and sorrow
should cease ; when "the sweat of the brow" would
no longer be needed to satisfy the cravings of hunger ; but when a millennial earth, enriched by the
copious showers of divine grace, and fertilized by
the bright beams of the Sun of righteousness, should
pour its abundance into the storehouse and wine-
press of the people of God. Happy time! happy
people! How blessed to be assured that these things
are not the pencilings of imagination or the flights of
fancy, but the substantial verities of divine revelation, to be enjoyed by faith, which is "the substance of things hoped for, the conviction of things
not seen."

Of all the Jewish solemnities the jubilee would
seem to have been the most soul-stirring and en-
rapturing.   It stood immediately connected with
the great day of atonement. It was when the blood
of the victim was shed that the emancipating sound
of the jubilee trump was heard through the hills and
valleys of the land of Canaan. That longed-for note
was designed to wake up the nation from the very
centre of its moral being—to stir the deepest depths
of the soul, and to send a shining river of divine
and ineffable joy through the length and breadth of
the land.   "In the day of atonement shall ye make
the trumpet sound throughout *all* your land."   Not
a corner was to remain unvisited by "the joyful
sound."   The aspect of the jubilee was as wide as

the aspect of the atonement on which the jubilee was based.

"And ye shall hallow the fiftieth year, and proclaim liberty throughout all the land unto all the inhabitants thereof: it shall be a jubilee unto you; and ye shall return every man unto his possession, and ye shall return every man unto his family. A jubilee shall that fiftieth year be unto you: ye shall not sow, neither reap that which groweth of itself in it, nor gather the grapes in it of thy vine undressed. For it is the jubilee; it shall be holy unto you: ye shall eat the increase thereof out of the field. In the year of this jubilee ye shall return every man unto his possession." (Ver. 8–13.) All estates and conditions of the people were permitted to feel the hallowed and refreshing influence of this most noble institution. The exile returned; the captive was emancipated; the debtor set free; each family opened its bosom to receive once more its long-lost members; each inheritance received back its exiled owner. The sound of the trumpet was the welcome and soul-stirring signal for the captive to escape, for the slave to cast aside the chains of his bondage, for the man-slayer to return to his home, for the ruined and poverty-stricken to rise to the possession of their forfeited inheritance. No sooner had the trumpet's thrice-welcome sound fallen upon the ear than the mighty tide of blessing rose majestically and sent its refreshing undulations into the most remote corners of Jehovah's highly favored land.

"And if thou sell aught unto thy neighbor, or buyest aught of thy neighbor's hand, ye shall not oppress one another: according to the number of years after the jubilee thou shalt buy of thy neighbor, and according unto the number of years of the fruits he shall sell unto thee. According to the multitude of years thou shalt increase the price thereof, and according to the fewness of years thou shalt diminish the price of it; for according to the number of the years of the fruits doth he sell unto thee. Ye shall not therefore oppress one another; but thou shalt fear thy God: for I am the Lord your God." (Ver. 14–17.) The year of jubilee reminded both buyer and seller that the land belonged to Jehovah and was not to be sold. "The fruits" might be sold, but that was all: Jehovah could never give up the land to any one. It is important to get this point well fixed in the mind; it may open up a very extensive line of truth. If the land of Canaan is not to be sold—if Jehovah declares it to be His forever, then for whom does He want it? who is to hold under Him? Those to whom He gave it by an everlasting covenant, that they might have it in possession as long as the moon endureth—even to all generations.

There is no spot in all the earth like unto the land of Canaan in the divine estimation. There Jehovah set up His throne and His sanctuary; there His priests stood to minister continually before Him; there the voices of His prophets were heard testifying of present ruin and future restoration and glory;

there the Baptist began, continued, and ended his career as the forerunner of the Messiah; there the blessed One was born of a woman; there He was baptized; there He preached and taught; there He labored and died; form thence He ascended in triumph to the right hand of God; thither God the Holy Ghost descended, in Pentecostal power; from thence the overflowing tide of gospel testimony emanated to the ends of the earth; thither the Lord of glory will descend ere long, and plant His foot "on the Mount of Olives;" there His throne will be reestablished and His worship restored. In a word, His eyes and His heart are there continually; its dust is precious in His sight; it is the centre of all His thoughts and operations as touching this earth; and it is His purpose to make it an eternal excellency, the joy of many generations.

It is, then, I repeat, immensely important to get a firm hold of this interesting line of truth with respect to the land of Canaan. Of that land Jehovah hath said, "IT IS MINE." Who shall take it from Him? Where is the king or the emperor—where the power, human or diabolical, that can wrest "the pleasant land" out of Jehovah's omnipotent grasp? True, it has been a bone of contention, an apple of discord, to the nations. It has been, and it will yet be, the scene and centre of cruel war and bloodshed. But far above all the din of battle and the strife of nations, these words fall with divine clearness, fullness, and power upon the ear of faith: *"The land is Mine!"* Jehovah can never give up that land, nor

those "twelve tribes" through whom He is to in-
herit it forever. Let my reader think of this; let
him ponder it deeply; let him guard against all
looseness of thought and vagueness of interpretation
as to this subject. God hath not cast away His people, or the land which He sware to give unto them
for an everlasting possession. "The twelve loaves"
of Leviticus xxiv. bear witness to the former, and
"the jubilee" of Leviticus xxv. bears witness to the
latter. The memorial of the "twelve tribes of Israel" is ever before the Lord, and the moment is
rapidly approaching when the trump of jubilee shall
be heard upon the mountains of Palestine. Then,
in reality, the captive shall cast off the ignominious
chain which for ages has bound him; then shall the
exile return to that happy home from which he has
so long been banished; then shall every debt be
canceled, every burden removed, and every tear
wiped away. "For thus saith the Lord, 'Behold, I
will extend peace to her [Jerusalem] like a river,
and the glory of the Gentiles like a flowing stream:
then shall ye suck, ye shall be borne upon her sides,
and be dandled upon her knees. As one whom his
mother comforteth, so will I comfort you; and ye
shall be comforted in Jerusalem. And when ye see
this, your heart shall rejoice, and your bones shall
flourish like an herb; and the hand of the Lord
shall be known toward His servants, and His indignation toward His enemies. For, behold, the Lord
will come with fire, and with His chariots like a
whirlwind, to render His anger with fury, and His

rebuke with flames of fire. For by fire and by His
sword will the Lord plead with all flesh: and the
slain of the Lord shall be many. . . . . For I
know their works and their thoughts; it shall come
that I will gather all nations and tongues; and they
shall come and see My glory. And I will set a sign
among them, and I will send those that escape of
them unto the nations, to Tarshish, Pul, and Lud,
that draw the bow, to Tubal and Javan, to the isles
afar off, that have not heard My fame, neither have
seen My glory; and they shall declare My glory
among the Gentiles. And they shall bring all your
brethren for an offering unto the Lord, out of all
nations, upon horses, and in chariots, and in litters,
and upon mules, and upon swift beasts, to My holy
mountain Jerusalem, saith the Lord, as the children
of Israel bring an offering in a clean vessel into the
house of the Lord. And I will also take of them
for priests and for Levites, saith the Lord. For as
the new heavens and the new earth, which I will
make, shall remain before Me, saith the Lord, so
shall your seed and your name remain. And it shall
come to pass, that from one new moon to another,
and from one Sabbath to another, shall all flesh come
to worship before Me, saith the Lord.'" (Isaiah
lxvi. 12--23.)

And now let us look for a moment at the practical
effect of the jubilee—its influence upon the transactions between man and man.—"And if thou sell
aught unto thy neighbor, or buyest aught of thy
neighbor's hand, ye shall not oppress one another.

According to the number of years after the jubilee thou shalt buy of thy neighbor, and according to the number of years of the fruits he shall sell unto thee." The scale of prices was to be regulated by the jubilee. If that glorious event were at hand, the price was low; if far off, the price was high. All human compacts as to land were broken up the moment the trump of jubilee was heard, for the land was Jehovah's; and the jubilee brought all back to its normal condition.

This teaches us a fine lesson. If our hearts are cherishing the abiding hope of the Lord's return, we shall set light by all earthly things. It is morally impossible that we can be in the attitude of waiting for the Son from heaven, and not be detached from this present world. "Let your moderation be known unto all men: the Lord is at hand." (Phil. iv.) A person may hold "the doctrine of the millennium," as it is called, or the doctrine of "the second advent," and be a thorough man of the world; but one who lives in the habitual expectation of Christ's appearing must be separated from that which will be judged and broken up when He comes. It is not a question of the shortness and uncertainty of human life, which is quite true; or of the transitory and unsatisfying character of the things of time, which is equally true. It is far more potent and influential than either or both of these,—it is this: *"The Lord is at hand."* May our hearts be affected and our conduct in all things influenced by this most precious and sanctifying truth.

CHAPTER XXVI

THIS chapter requires little in the way of note or exposition. It contains a most solemn and affecting record of the blessings of obedience on the one hand, and the terrible consequences of disobedience on the other. Had Israel walked in obedience, they would have been invincible. "I will give peace in the land, and ye shall lie down, and none shall make you afraid; and I will rid evil beasts out of the land, neither shall the sword go through your land. And ye shall chase your enemies, and they shall fall before you by the sword. And five of you shall chase a hundred, and a hundred of you shall put ten thousand to flight; and your enemies shall fall before you by the sword. For I will have respect unto you, and make you fruitful, and multiply you, and establish My covenant with you. And ye shall eat old store, and bring forth the old because of the new. And I will set My tabernacle among you; and My soul shall not abhor you. And I will walk among you, and will be your God, and ye shall be My people. I am the Lord your God, which brought you forth out of the land of Egypt, that ye should not be their bondsmen; and I have broken the bands of your yoke, and made you go upright." (Ver. 6–13.)

The presence of God should ever have been their shield and buckler. No weapon formed against them could prosper. But then the divine presence was only to be enjoyed by an obedient people. Jehovah could not sanction by His presence disobedience or wickedness. The uncircumcised nations around might depend upon their prowess and their military resources: Israel had only the arm of Jehovah to depend upon, and that arm could never be stretched forth to shield unholiness or disobedience. Their strength was, to walk with God in a spirit of dependence and obedience. So long as they walked thus, there was a wall of fire round about them, to protect them from every enemy and every evil.

But, alas! Israel failed altogether. Notwithstanding the solemn and appalling picture placed before their eyes, in verses 14–33 of this chapter, they forsook the Lord and served other gods, and thus brought upon themselves the sore judgments threatened in this section, the bare record of which is sufficient to make the ears tingle. Under the heavy weight of these judgments they are suffering at this very hour. Scattered and peeled, wasted and outcast, they are the monuments of Jehovah's inflexible truth and justice. They read aloud, to all the nations of the earth, a most impressive lesson on the subject of the moral government of God— a lesson which it would be profitable for these nations to study deeply—yea, and a lesson which it would be salutary for our own hearts to ponder likewise.

We are very prone to confound two things which are clearly distinguished in the Word, namely;

God's *government* and God's *grace*. The evils which result from this confusion are various. It is sure to lead to an enfeebled sense of the dignity and solemnity of government, and of the purity, fullness, and elevation of grace. It is quite true that God in government reserves to Himself the sovereign right to act in patience, long-suffering, and mercy; but the exercise of these attributes, in connection with His throne of government, must never be confounded with the unconditional actings of pure and absolute grace.

The chapter before us is a record of divine government, and yet, in it we find such clauses as the following: "If they shall confess their iniquity, and the iniquity of their fathers, with their trespass which they trespassed against Me; and that also they have walked contrary unto Me, and that I also have walked contrary unto them, and have brought them into the land of their enemies; if then their uncircumcised hearts be humbled, and they then accept of the punishment of their iniquity: then will I remember My covenant with Jacob, and also My covenant with Isaac, and also My covenant with Abraham will I remember; and I will remember the land. The land also shall be left of them, and shall enjoy her Sabbaths, while she lieth desolate without them; and they shall accept of the punishment of their iniquity: because, even because they despised My judgments, and because their soul abhorred My statutes. And yet, for all that, when they be in the land of their enemies, I will not cast them away,

neither will I abhor them, to destroy them utterly,
and to break My covenant with them; for I am the
Lord their God.   But I will for their sakes remember the covenant of their ancestors, whom I brought
forth out of the land of Egypt in the sight of the
heathen, that I might be their God: I am the
Lord.'' (Ver. 40–45.)

Here we find God in government, meeting, in
long-suffering mercy, the very earliest and faintest
breathings of a broken and penitent spirit.   The
history of the judges and of the kings presents
many instances of the exercise of this blessed attribute of the divine government.   Again and again
the soul of Jehovah was grieved for Israel (Judges
x. 16.), and He sent them one deliverer after another, until at length there remained no hope, and
the righteous claims of His throne demanded their
expulsion from that land which they were wholly
incompetent to keep.

All this is *government*.   But by and by, Israel will
be brought into possession of the land of Canaan
on the ground of unqualified and unchangeable
grace — grace exercised in divine righteousness,
through the blood of the cross.   It will not be by
works of law, nor yet by the institutions of an
evanescent economy, but by that grace which
''reigns through righteousness, by Jesus Christ
our Lord.''   Wherefore, they shall never again be
driven forth from their possession.   No enemy shall
ever molest them.   They shall enjoy undisturbed
repose behind the shield of Jehovah's favor.   Their

tenure of the land will be according to the eternal
stability of divine grace and the efficacy of the
blood of the everlasting covenant. ''They shall be
saved in the Lord with an everlasting salvation.''

May the Spirit of God lead us into more enlarged
apprehensions of divine truth, and endow us with a
greater capacity to try the things that differ, and
rightly to divide the word of truth.

CHAPTER XXVII

THIS closing section of our book treats of the
''singular vow,'' or the voluntary act whereby
a person devoted himself or his property unto the
Lord. ''And the Lord spake unto Moses, saying,
'Speak unto the children of Israel, and say unto
them, When a man shall make a singular vow, the
persons shall be for the Lord by thy estimation.
And thy estimation shall be . . . . after the shekel
of the sanctuary.'''

Now, in the case of a person devoting himself or
his beast, his house or his field, unto the Lord, it
was obviously a question of capacity or worth; and
hence there was a certain scale of valuation, according to age. Moses, as the representative of the
claims of God, was called upon to estimate, in each
case, according to the standard of the sanctuary.
If a man undertakes to make a vow, he must be
tried by the standard of righteousness; and, moreover, in all cases, we are called upon to recognize

the difference between *capacity* and *title*. In Exodus
xxx. 15, we read, in reference to the atonement
money, "The rich shall not give more, and the poor
shall not give less, than half a shekel, when they
give an offering unto the Lord, to make an atonement for your souls." In the matter of atonement,
all stood upon one common level. Thus it must
ever be. High and low, rich and poor, learned and
ignorant, old and young—all have one common title.
"There is no difference." All stand alike on the
ground of the infinite preciousness of the blood of
Christ. There may be a vast difference as to capacity; as to title, there is none: there may be a
vast difference as to experience; as to title, there is
none: there may be a vast difference as to knowledge, gift, and fruitfulness; as to title, there is
none. The sapling and the tree, the babe and the
father, the convert of yesterday and the matured believer, are all on the same ground. "The rich shall
not give more, and the poor shall not give less."
Nothing more could be given; nothing less could be
taken. "We have boldness to enter into the holiest by the blood of Jesus." This is our title to
enter. Our capacity to worship, when we have entered, will depend upon our spiritual energy. Christ
is our title: the Holy Ghost is our capacity. Self
has nothing to do with either the one or the other.
What a mercy! We get in by the blood of Jesus;
we enjoy what we find there by the Holy Ghost.
The blood of Jesus opens the door; the Holy Ghost
conducts us through the house: the blood of Jesus

opens the casket; the Holy Ghost unfolds the precious contents: the blood of Jesus makes the casket ours; the Holy Ghost enables us to appreciate its rare and costly gems.

But in Leviticus xxvii, it is entirely a question of ability, capacity, or worth. Moses had a certain standard, from which he could not possibly descend; he had a certain rule, from which he could not possibly swerve. If any one could come up to that, well; if not, he had to take his place accordingly.

What, then, was to be done in reference to the person who was unable to rise to the height of the claims set forth by the representative of divine righteousness? Hear the consolatory answer—"But if he be *poorer* than thy estimation, then he shall present himself before *the priest*, and the priest shall value him; *according to his ability* that vowed shall the priest value him." (Ver. 8.) In other words, if it be a question of man's undertaking to meet the claims of *righteousness*, then he must meet them; but if, on the other hand, a man feels himself wholly unable to meet those claims, he has only to fall back upon *grace*, which will take him up just as he is. Moses is the representative of the claims of divine righteousness: the priest is the exponent of the provisions of divine grace. The poor man who was unable to stand before Moses, fell back into the arms of the priest. Thus it is ever. If we cannot "*dig*," we can "*beg*;" and directly we take the place of a beggar, it is no longer a question of what we are able to *earn*, but of what God is pleased to *give*.

> "Grace all the work shall crown
> Through everlasting days."

How happy it is to be debtors to grace! how happy
to take, when God is glorified in giving! When
man is in question, it is infinitely better to dig than
to beg; but when God is in question, the case is the
very reverse.

I would just add that I believe this entire chapter
bears, in an especial manner, upon the nation of
Israel. It is intimately connected with the two preceding chapters. Israel made "a singular vow"
at the foot of Mount Horeb; but they were quite
unable to meet the claims of law—they were far
"poorer than Moses' estimation." But, blessed be
God, they will come in under the rich provisions
of divine grace. Having learnt their total inability
"to dig," they will not be "ashamed to beg;" and
hence they shall experience the deep blessedness of
being cast upon the sovereign mercy of Jehovah,
which stretches, like a golden chain, "from everlasting to everlasting." It is well to be poor, when
the knowledge of our poverty serves but to unfold
to us the exhaustless riches of divine grace. That
grace can never suffer any one to go empty away.
It can never tell any one that he is too poor. It can
meet the very deepest human need; and not only
so, but it is glorified in meeting it. This holds
good in every case. It is true of any individual
sinner, and it is true with respect to Israel, who,
having been valued by the lawgiver, have proved

"poorer than his estimation." Grace is the grand and only resource for all. It is the basis of our salvation, the basis of a life of practical godliness, and the basis of those imperishable hopes which animate us amid the trials and conflicts of this sin-stricken world. May we cherish a deeper sense of grace, and more ardent desire for the glory.

We shall here close our meditations upon this most profound and precious book. If the foregoing pages should be used of God to awaken an interest in a section of inspiration which has been so much neglected by the Church in all ages, they shall not have been written in vain.

C. H. M.